BRIEF CANDLE
STONEY BOWES
DA PONTE'S LAST STAND
CONFESSIONS OF ZENO

For Thetis Blacker
with warm good wishes
from
Carlo Ardito

2006.

By the same author:

Waiting for the Barbarians

A Bed for the Knight

Eduardo de Filippo: Four Plays

CARLO ARDITO

---

# BRIEF CANDLE
# STONEY BOWES
# DA PONTE'S LAST STAND
# CONFESSIONS OF ZENO

AMBER LANE PRESS

All rights whatsoever in these plays are strictly reserved and application for professional performance should be made before rehearsals begin to:
Brendan Davis, Film Rights Ltd,
483 Southbank House, Black Prince Road,
Albert Embankment, London SE1 7SJ

Application for amateur performance should be made before rehearsals begin to:
Brendan Davis, Film Rights Ltd,
483 Southbank House, Black Prince Road,
Albert Embankment, London SE1 7SJ

No performance may be given unless a licence has been obtained.

First published in 1998 by
Amber Lane Press Ltd,
Church Street, Charlbury, Oxford OX7 3PR
Telephone and fax: 01608 810024

Printed and bound by The Guernsey Press Co. Ltd, Guernsey, C.I.

Copyright © Carlo Ardito, 1998

ISBN 1 872868 23 1

The cover illustration 'Mozart at the Billiard Table' by Batt is reprinted from the *Oxford Companion to Music* (tenth edition) edited by Scholes by permission of Oxford University Press.

CONDITIONS OF SALE
This book is sold subject to the condition that it shall not, by way of trade or otherwise, be lent, re-sold, hired out or otherwise circulated without the publisher's prior consent in any form of binding or cover other than that in which it is published and without a similar condition including this condition being imposed on the subsequent purchaser.

## CONTENTS

| | |
|---|---|
| Introduction | 7 |
| Brief Candle | 13 |
| Stoney Bowes | 73 |
| Da Ponte's Last Stand | 135 |
| Confessions of Zeno | 185 |

*For Christa*

## INTRODUCTION

THE PROTAGONISTS of the first three pieces in this volume are historical characters, and one of the problems this raises is that audiences often expect such plays to be accurate biographical representations of the lives of each character. To some extent I have probably fulfilled these expectations, since the lives of Marie Bashkirtseff, Stoney Bowes and Lorenzo da Ponte respectively were so remarkable and rich in incident that little if any invention is demanded of the dramatist. I must, however, declare that these are plays and not documentaries, and that consequently I have felt free to resort to imagination as well as fact to flesh out my characters.

MARIE BASHKIRTSEFF would have needed no introduction three generations ago, when her fame spread throughout the world immediately after the publication of her journals. The daughter of Russian aristocrats who had settled on the French Riviera, from her earliest years she displayed a feverish ambition to succeed in the arts, and resolutely refused to accept half-truths or second best. At the age of thirteen she set herself to study English, Italian, German, Latin, Greek, drawing and music. She dreamed of becoming a great singer, fell in love with a Scottish duke, and insisted on owning a racehorse. At sixteen, on a journey to Russia, she took with her, as well as thirty dresses, works by Plato, Ariosto, Shakespeare, Plutarch, and some English novels. She captivated her father's family with her wit and chic, and disconcerted young men with her scholarship. At seventeen, having decided to devote herself to the study of painting, she joined one of the few studios which at that time accepted women, and less than three years later, in 1880, her first painting was exhibited at the Paris Salon. In 1884 her dreams began to be realised. Her picture *Le Meeting* attracted public attention. It was enthusiastically reviewed, and was reproduced in the illustrated magazines in France, Germany and Russia. Art dealers began to search out the rising artist, and society journals commented on her beauty. In 1884 she began a correspondence with Guy de Maupassant. She approached him under an assumed name and he was intrigued by the mysterious stranger. Everything was pointing to continuing triumphs, but in October 1884 Marie Bashkirtseff died of tuberculosis. She was twenty-four.

ANDREW ROBINSON STONEY, an Irishman, otherwise known as Stoney Bowes, was the original of Thackeray's infamous character, Barry Lyndon. He was born in 1747 and began his career as a lieutenant in the 30th Regiment of Foot. While stationed in Newcastle he married a local heiress, Hannah Newton of Burnopfield, Co. Durham, who brought him a fortune of £30,000. He treated her as he treated all his women — abominably. He beat her (he once dislocated her jaw), locked her up in confined spaces, all but starved her, and not surprisingly she soon died in suspicious circumstances, just as the rascally Stoney was becoming interested in the person and immense wealth of the recently widowed Mary Eleanor Bowes, Countess of Strathmore, one of the richest heiresses in Europe. A practised ladies' man, Stoney pursued the Countess and resorted to various stratagems to impress her. His master-stroke was to get himself wounded in a duel he brought about supposedly to defend the lady's honour. Four days after the duel the couple were married. Under the terms of Mary Eleanor Bowes' father's will, and as a condition of her marriage settlement, her first husband, the 9th Earl of Strathmore had agreed to "use the surname of Bowes in addition to any title of honour to which he might have right, an arrangement further covenanted to any issue of the marriage". The 9th Earl duly substituted the surname of Bowes for that of Lyon, and Stoney adopted the name of Bowes himself on marrying Mary Eleanor. A later Earl, however, resurrected the discarded surname and recast the family names as Bowes Lyon, which survives to this day. Stoney Bowes, henceforth nicknamed 'the fortune hunter', proceeded to spend the rest of his life in attempting to appropriate the Countess's fortune, and indeed made several inroads into her assets — he virtually denuded the richly forested Gibside estate of trees in order to pay for election expenses. True to form, Stoney beat his wife, was openly unfaithful to her, encouraged her to take laudanum, seized as much of her fortune as he could lay his hands on, and even abducted her and imprisoned her in Streatlam Castle, one of her properties, in a desperate attempt to force her to sign over her wealth to him. She finally outwitted him and Stoney Bowes ended his days in the King's Bench Prison. He died in 1810, to the very last embarking on lawsuits to grab some or all of his wife's money. In this melodrama I have attempted to represent in dramatic terms and with some licence a character in all his unvarnished unpleasantness and amorality — a theatrical treatment, as it were, of the psychopathology of greed. I have also tried to provide an excursion into the perennial sport of marrying heiresses, a game where the result did not always turn out to the advantage of those whose hopes were inflamed by the prospect of great wealth. I am indebted to Roger C. Norris, M.A., of Durham University Library for providing me with precious information on Andrew Robinson Stoney, to Miss Camilla Cameron of Burke's Peerage for information on the Earls of Strathmore and Kinghorne, and to Mr Howard Coutts of the Bowes Museum for his courtesy and advice during a recent visit to Barnard Castle. To my friend the novelist Julian Fane my gratitude is due for helping me to solve (not for the first time) a tricky theatrical problem. Since money plays such an important part in my story, it is as well to be aware of the value of the sums dealt with in present day terms. I am advised by experts in this most uncertain of fields that the multiplier to be applied in this case is 100. Thus £10,000 in the 1770s would be worth £1,000,000 in the 1990s. An audience would benefit from a short programme note outlining these calculations. The lyrics of the songs are from contemporary broadsheets, and with minimal emendations I have set them to traditional airs.

LORENZO DA PONTE's real name was Emanuele Conegliano, and he was born in 1749 at Ceneda, in northern Italy. His father, a Jew, was left a widower, and when Emanuele was fourteen had himself and his three sons baptised so that he could marry a young Catholic girl. In accordance with the custom of the time, the eldest son took the name of the sponsor, Monsignor Lorenzo da Ponte, bishop of

Ceneda. Young Lorenzo studied in the seminary of the town, and by the time he was twenty-two he was giving lessons in rhetoric and in Italian and had taken minor orders for the priesthood. He went on to Venice, where he eked out a precarious living by teaching and writing poetry and by less legitimate activities, plunging zestfully into the dissolute life of the Venetian Republic. He got into, and out of, one scrape after another until, in 1779, the patience of even the lenient authorities of Venice was overtaxed, and they banished da Ponte from all Venetian territories. He made his way to Vienna, via Dresden, armed with a letter of introduction to Antonio Salieri, court composer to Joseph II. There Salieri (who was later rumoured to have poisoned Mozart) helped to get da Ponte appointed Poet to the Imperial Theatres, and he enjoyed some years of success, writing many libretti (including *The Marriage of Figaro, Don Giovanni* and *Cosi Fan Tutte* for Mozart) as well as poems for special occasions. He met and corresponded with Casanova. After the death of Joseph II (1790) da Ponte left Vienna. Most of the next thirteen years (1792–1805) were spent in London, where he was for part of the time librettist of the King's Theatre and a bookseller. In 1805 da Ponte, as a result of one of his frequent financial crises, sailed to the United States. After spells of varying duration in New York, Elizabethtown and Sunbury, he eventually settled in New York where he taught Italian. In 1825 he was appointed Professor of Italian Literature at Columbia College, a post which gave him prestige but no salary. In the 1820s da Ponte wrote his memoirs, which still make lively reading today. He died in New York in 1838, at the age of eighty-nine. In *Da Ponte's Last Stand* I deal with the last year of da Ponte's life in New York. In his none-too-reliable memoirs he tells us little about his thirty-three years in America, other than give us dispiriting accounts of a harsh struggle for existence and of a variety of commercial ventures mostly doomed to failure. It is happily a matter of recorded fact that he was able to hear his *Don Giovanni* again in America when Manuel Garcia and his famous daughter Maria Malibran went over from Europe and mounted the first production of that opera at the Park Theatre, New York. It is possibly at some such event that Lorenzo da Ponte met my fictional journalist, who after a series of exhaustive interviews brought his life to an unseemly though deeply satisfying conclusion.

CONFESSIONS OF ZENO, by Italo Svevo, is one of the first major European novels to make extensive use of Freudian techniques and theories for the purposes of narrative strategy. It was published in 1923 with the encouragement and support of James Joyce, who championed Svevo's work from the outset. I was originally commissioned by BBC Radio to dramatise this novel as part of a festival planned to mark the fiftieth anniversary of Svevo's death — a festival which owing to economies imposed by higher assessors in the end consisted solely of my play and an excellent talk by Professor Brian Moloney of Hull University. The play, directed by Glyn Dearman, was warmly received and subsequently repeated, and encouraged me to embark on the stage version which forms part of this volume. Zeno Cosini is a middle-aged businessman who has himself psychoanalysed in the hope of finding a cure for his various complexes and psychosomatic disorders. He considers himself a failure at all things most men would achieve as a matter of course: at his studies, in his relationship with his father, his wife and his mistress, and in his business career. He also hopes psychoanalysis will cure him of his addiction to smoking, although through self-deception he fails to see that he is in reality addicted to giving up smoking. Set in Trieste when that city was still part of Austria-Hungary, the story follows our anti-hero through his painful and comic transformation from comparative failure to success, achieved in spite of the ministrations of his Freudian analyst, whom Zeno in the end comes to regard as a failure along with all the characters he had hitherto regarded as successful. Paradoxically and comically Zeno achieves his recovery through a flexible concept of truth and a thoroughly amoral view of life. I am grateful to Stella Quilley for her skilful and sensitive staging of the play in 1995.

Carlo Ardito<br>
London, 1998

# BRIEF CANDLE

---

from the life and journals of
Marie Bashkirtseff (1860-1884)

## Characters

Marie Bashkirtseff
Mme Bashkirtseff, Marie's mother
Mme Romanoff, Marie's aunt
Dina, Marie's cousin
Misha, a manservant
Narrator *

* who will double as the Duke of Hamilton, Pietro, Alexis, Pius IX, Wartel, Victor Emmanuel II, Marie's father, Julien Bastien-Lepage, Guy de Maupassant

The action of the play takes place between 1873 and 1884 in Nice, Paris, Rome, Naples, St Petersburg, Moscow and Gavrontsy. These places may be suggested if necessary by slide projections, and each scene should be sparingly depicted by a simple arrangement of tables, chairs and sofas. A clothes-rack on castors of the type used in department stores will be somewhere on the set throughout, and will carry the NARRATOR's various disguises consisting mostly of coats, tunics, hats, etcetera, to be used as required by the action.

The play is structured as a series of episodes and may benefit from fairly stylised direction, taken at a brisk pace verging at times on the flickering brittleness of silent movies.

A recording of Tosti's 'April' required for Scene Eight should be easily obtainable, and a French, Italian or English version would be equally acceptable; a mezzo soprano rendering would be preferable. The discerning director's obvious choice for the 'Radetzky March' will be the Berlin Philharmonic orchestra's recording conducted by von Karajan.

I am indebted to Denis Quilley for suggesting a delightful piece of business which I have gratefully incorporated in Scene Seventeen as an accompaniment to Guy de Maupassant's third letter.

*Brief Candle* was first performed in Great Britain
at the Lyric Theatre Hammersmith Studio
on 9 September 1990 with the following cast:

Marie Bashkirtseff ... Sue Broomfield
Mme Bashkirtseff, Marie's mother ... Eve Schickle
Mme Romanoff, Marie's aunt ... Wendy Macadam
Dina, Marie's cousin ... Camilla Evans
Misha, a manservant ... Reg Jessup
Narrator ... Tom Knight

Directed by Peter Leslie Wild

## ONE

*A table piled high with notebooks bound in black, most of them of the thick exercise-book variety. The* NARRATOR *is dipping into them at random. Upstage seated in a semicircle are the rest of the cast,* MARIE, DINA, MME BASHKIRTSEFF, MME ROMANOFF *and* MISHA.

NARRATOR [*shuts one of the notebooks, turns to the audience and points at the pile of books on the table*] Marie Bashkirtseff's journals. The Bibliothèque Nationale in Paris where this lot eventually fetched up counted one hundred and three volumes, and one was missing. Not a bad output for a busy practising painter who travelled a great deal, led a frantically active social life and died at the age of ... t—

MARIE    Twenty-three.

MME BASHKIRTSEFF    [*firmly*] Twenty-four, dear.

NARRATOR    Twenty-four ... or thereabouts. Let's try to find out why someone with such colossal ambition, talent and desire to succeed should have failed so dismally in her lifetime — for in her lifetime, according to her own exacting standards, fail she most resoundingly did.

MME ROMANOFF    She didn't fail! What nonsense he's talking! Marie was a very gifted girl.

MME BASHKIRTSEFF    Thank you, Sophie. My Masha was so clever! Everybody said so. She even got a prize at the Paris Salon.

NARRATOR    [*turning to look at the two women with some impatience*] Indeed seldom has a creative artist been born into a family of mental stature so startlingly inferior to her own. You have just had proof of this from her mother [*points at her, and* MME BASHKIRTSEFF *smiles and nods*] and from her aunt Madame Romanoff. [MME ROMANOFF *nods also*] and there's her daughter Dina, who was Marie's constant companion throughout her life ...

DINA    [*cutting in*] But Marie was clever! I'm older but she always

|          | did better than me at her lessons, and painted like an old master ... and was very beautiful, and all the young men ... |
|----------|---|
| MARIE    | [*curt*] Do be quiet, Dina. Let him get on with it. |
| NARRATOR | Thank you. And next to her is Misha, one of the many faithful retainers who travelled with them from Russia. [MISHA *touches an imaginary forelock.*] Er ... Misha [*points at the notebooks*] ... clear them away, there's a good chap. They've seen them now... |

> [MISHA *rises and with a groan begins to clear the books from the table, and as the* NARRATOR *continues* MISHA *will complete his task in two or three trips by stacking a large pile of the notebooks on his arms each time; he will then resume his seat, resentfully brushing the dust off his sleeves.*]

|          | Let me see ... She was ... Where was I ...? |
|----------|---|
| MARIE    | [*laughs and nudges* DINA] What do you know ... I do believe he's stuck! [*She picks a paper from a folder on her knees and hands it to* DINA.] Go and give him this. |

> [*Giggling,* DINA *takes the paper, rises and awkwardly walks up to the* NARRATOR *and hands him the sheet. He takes it superciliously.*]

|          | |
|----------|---|
| NARRATOR | Ah, yes. Thank you. This appears to be an extract from the Encyclopaedia Britannica, early 1900s ... [*He reads.*] Maria Bashkirtseff, 1860-1884. Russian artist and writer, born at Gavrontsy in Russia on 11th November 1860. Her parents lived apart and Marie spent her childhood in various health resorts in Germany and the Riviera, as she was always sickly. She received a good education and began to study singing. Her voice failed her and she began the serious study of painting in Tony Robert-Fleury's studio in Paris in 1877 at the age of 17. She corresponded under an assumed name with Guy de Maupassant. The diaries she kept from childhood constitute a record of extraordinary interest and were published posthumously in an edited version. Although it is as a diarist and not as a painter that she is remembered, in 1884, the year of her death, one of her paintings now in the Paris Museum of Modern Art gained her an honourable |

mention at the Paris Salon. Her health, always delicate, failed her, and she died of tuberculosis that autumn. There follows a bibliography ... [*He folds up the sheet.*]

MME BASHKIRTSEFF  A paragraph in a reference book. Is that all there was to Marie's life? Nothing about us, about our family?

MME ROMANOFF  I was going to say! There's no mention even that our father, General Babanine, was of noble Tartar origin.

MME BASHKIRTSEFF  Of the first invasion. Or that my estranged husband, bless him, was a Marshal of the Nobility.

MISHA  [*with a wink*] What about your great uncle the Grand Duke Alexei, eh?

MME ROMANOFF  Shush, Misha. We never talk of him. He lost his wife at cards. Remember?

NARRATOR  Do you mind? [*He resumes.*] Like all wealthy Russian families they travelled with a large retinue: the family doctor, governesses, nurses, dogs of various descriptions ... [*as an afterthought*] ... and servants, of course. They were part of that floating Russian population which drank the waters at Baden Baden, gambled its thousands at Monte Carlo and looked on Paris as its earthly paradise. Marie kept her journals from a very early age ... since the age of four to be precise and even then visions of future greatness haunted her.

MARIE  I know that one day I shall marry the Czar, save his throne by introducing social reforms and be remembered as a great queen by my people.

NARRATOR  See what I mean? And as she grew older she hankered after everything at once — whatever success was to be obtained: the glamour of youth and beauty, rank and even greater wealth with their glittering gifts ... an artist's fame, the power of a queen of society — all, all — or nothing. She was a bundle of contradictions. Take her religion. Now her religion —

MME BASHKIRTSEFF  [*interrupting*] Marie was very religious, don't you go saying anything else!

NARRATOR  ... her religion was an odd compound of idolatry and cold reasoning. The nature of her prayers — she was constantly praying — is essentially similar to a savage's worship of his totem pole: inclined to be extremely devout if his requests were granted, but apt to smash it up if they were not. [*He clears his throat.*] Which, er ...

MARIE  [*to* DINA] He's getting off the point ...

MME ROMANOFF  He's not doing very well, is he ...

MME BASHKIRTSEFF  Who gave him the job?

DINA  [*trying to attract the* NARRATOR*'s attention*] Sir! Sir!

> [*The* NARRATOR *turns crossly as he is struggling with his memory to remember his lines.*]

DINA  Can we get started? Please.

THE OTHERS
( Hear hear!
( Get on with it!
( What a funny sort of fellow...
( Shouldn't be allowed!

NARRATOR  All right. All right. Ladies and gentlemen: we give you the story of an ambitious girl who wanted fame. She got it. At a price. She had to be young and dead. [*He turns to the others.*] Satisfied?

> [*Fadeout.*]


## TWO

*Nice, 1873.* MARIE *and* DINA *on a park bench.* MARIE *is looking at passers-by on the promenade.* DINA *is reading.*

MARIE  There she goes. Did you see her, Dina?

DINA  [*looking up from her book*] I wasn't looking. Who was it?

MARIE  His mistress. In her landau. She's just driven past.

DINA  [*puts her book away*] Whose mistress?

MARIE  My duke's mistress.

DINA  Your duke's? Marie, is this another of your daydreams?

| MARIE | This is no daydream. I've discussed it with my mama and yours. And if you weren't such a goose with your head in the clouds most of the time you'd know about him too. He's a most desirable match for me. |
|---|---|
| DINA | He is, is he? Yes, of course, your duke ... What sort of duke is he? French? Italian? |
| MARIE | Certainly not! He's a real duke. A Scottish duke. The Duke of Hamilton. |
| DINA | Now you mention the name I seem to remember mama spoke of him. He's staying for the season. His yacht's in the harbour. |
| MARIE | The very largest yacht. And he's rented two of the most luxurious villas in Nice. One for himself, the other for his mistress. And he brought the yacht along just in case ... Dukes of the blood royal know how to do things in style. |
| DINA | Of the blood royal? |
| MARIE | Well, he's bound to be a royal duke at least ... [*suddenly torn by doubt*] ... don't you think? |
| DINA | Darling, I don't want to spoil your fun, but what about Monsieur Borreel? I thought you were in love with him. |
| MARIE | Him! I've done with him! Off with the old and on with the new! I've decided he's not my type. I simply hate the moustache he's trying to grow. More like a smudge than a moustache. No. You have him, Dina. He'll suit you. You're not so particular, are you? You're more easily satisfied. |
| DINA | Thank you very much. That's very big-hearted of you. But even if I were interested, how am I to make Monsieur Borreel's acquaintance? I don't think you've ever met him. |
| MARIE | I'm sure aunt Sophie can arrange an introduction. Aunt Sophie can arrange anything. |
| DINA | And this ... Duke of Hamilton. Have you met him? |
| MARIE | I have not. How could you even imagine such a thing! It'd be most improper. Especially while he's still keeping a mistress. |
| DINA | Quite. |

| | |
|---|---|
| MARIE | He'll have to give her up. Then, after a decent interval I'll agree to make his acquaintance. Mind you, by that time he'll have quite possibly noticed me ... or heard of me. I shall make sure he does, now that I think of it. And someone ought to tell him that my grandpapa Babanine is of noble Tartar origin ... of the ... |
| DINA | ... first Tartar invasion. |
| MARIE | Precisely. [*Pause.*] His mistress ... Oh, but she's so beautiful, so exquisitely elegant! It isn't fair. I'm sure she gets her clothes from Worth. How I envy her! |
| DINA | You sound as if you approved of her. |
| MARIE | I most decidedly do not approve of her. But I like her. And she's so daring! |
| DINA | Is she? |
| MARIE | Why, think: she rode past just now in her landau — with her top down! |

> [*They both giggle, as* MISHA *approaches and addresses them from a respectful distance.*]

| | |
|---|---|
| MISHA | [*roughly, but with obvious affection*] Hey, there! You're to come home at once, Miss Marie! |
| MARIE | Misha! What are you doing on the Promenade des Anglais? You don't fit in the landscape, somehow. |
| MISHA | Your mother says to tell you your drawing master's just arrived. She didn't know where you'd disappeared to. |
| MARIE | Well, here I am. You've found me. |
| MISHA | I've been looking all over for you. It's not seemly for two young turtle doves to be out on their own in this sinful town. |
| DINA | Come, Misha, don't be so old-fashioned. |
| MISHA | Are you coming? |
| MARIE | In a moment. Tell me, what's the drawing master like? |
| MISHA | A pale young man reeking of tobacco. What'll he teach you, I wonder ... |
| MARIE | Now, Misha, you know I love drawing. And I need lessons. |
| MISHA | You once drew a beautiful Russian church. And a head of |

| | Our Lord. In my opinion that's all the drawing you'll ever need to learn. |
|---|---|
| MARIE | That's enough, Misha. We'll come home in a few minutes. You go on before us. |

[MISHA *leaves muttering under his breath.*]

| | Where was I? Oh yes, his mistress. You've seen her go past just now. The duke usually follows either in his own carriage or on foot a few minutes later. He won't be long now. I know his movements. You'll be able to see him. |
|---|---|
| DINA | How very strange. Don't they go about together? |
| MARIE | You don't understand, do you, darling? As well as being the handsomest duke in Christendom and the richest and the most talented, he's also the soul of discretion. Discretion — now there's a word of paramount importance in affairs of the heart! |
| DINA | You're so clever, Marie. But why should he bother to be so discreet? |
| MARIE | Because a man in his position, bachelor though he is, shouldn't be seen in public with a [*lowers her voice*] cocotte, even a grande cocotte. Moreover, whatever her ... her calling, he's such a great gentleman he wouldn't dream of compromising her. |
| DINA | I see. |
| MARIE | Thank heaven she's old. |
| DINA | How old? |
| MARIE | Very, very old. Thirty at the very least. Imagine, more than twice my age! She may be beautiful and dress in the height of fashion, but she's old — so there! Wouldn't you agree that between the two he's simply bound to pick a ... mature girl of thirteen? |
| DINA | Not unless he wants a brush with the law, darling. You're under age ... |
| MARIE | Oh, I've no intention of marrying him yet. But I have youth on my side and men rather like that. I can wait, say ... about three years. I'll be sixteen then, like you, and ready for marriage. |

| DINA | I don't think I feel particularly ready for marriage ... |
|---|---|
| MARIE | [*dismissively*] I'm precocious and you're not, everybody says so. But still, do be careful, I'd hate to have a spinster for a cousin ... Spinsters smell of mothballs. Oh look, look! There he is! Isn't he handsome? |

> [*The* DUKE OF HAMILTON, *not the most handsome of men, walks past along the promenade across the stage, a vacant, rather foppish look on his face. He is a little overweight.*]

| DINA | Well ... |
|---|---|
| MARIE | [*impatiently*] Isn't he though? |
| DINA | I wouldn't call him a Greek god exactly... I think even Michelangelo would have found him a trifle stout. |
| MARIE | How little you know about beauty! Don't you see ... he's the ideal weight for a duke. Dukes should be well covered ... it goes with their position. And dukes should be as cuddly as baby Siberian bears ... |
| DINA | [*stroking* MARIE's *cheek*] You're so full of energy, Marie, so full of enthusiasm. What a wonderful life you're going to have! |
| MARIE | I am, I am! Oh yes I am! Shall I tell you what I want to do? I want to go into the world, I want to shine in it, I want to occupy a supreme position ... I want to be rich — I want to have pictures, palaces, jewels, I want to be the centre of a circle that shall be political, brilliant, literary, scientific, er ... philanthropic and ... and ... frivolous. I want all that and my duke: d'you think God will give it all to me? |

> [DINA *impulsively embraces* MARIE.]

Look at the sea, Dina. Look at it. Can you see how vast it is?

> [DINA *nods.*]

Do you know what I want to do with it?

> [DINA *shakes her head.*]

I want to drink it all!

> [*Fadeout.*]

## THREE

*Rome, 1876. A drawing room.* MARIE *is sitting on a sofa reading. The* NARRATOR *enters and walks up to the clothes trolley. He begins to change into* PIETRO ANTONELLI's *clothes.*

NARRATOR  She wanted to drink up the whole sea ... but in the event only a few pitiful spoonfuls were doled out to her. Although she saw him perhaps half a dozen times on the promenade at Nice, she never once got to meet her duke.

MARIE  [*raises her head disdainfully from her book*] It was my choice not to meet him. He wasn't ready for me. More to the point, I wasn't ready for him.

NARRATOR  A likely story!

MARIE  I chose instead to concentrate on my studies, which included English, French, Italian, Latin, German, the piano, singing, drawing ... all the sciences such as geography, cosmography, arithmetic, grammar, literature, history, natural history, rhetoric, mythology and physics. [*She calmly resumes reading.*]

NARRATOR  Well, let us say she put a brave face on disappointment. And now, three years later and as she would put it in the middle age of her youth — at seventeen that is — was she ready for love once again? Was she? The Bashkirtseffs and their suite were in Rome for a few months, and one Pietro Antonelli, Cardinal Antonelli's nephew, was a frequent caller. [*He has now finished dressing as* PIETRO.]

[DINA *enters, takes* PIETRO *by the hand and leads him towards* MARIE.]

DINA  Marie! Marie! Look who's here ... [*with a look of complicity at* PIETRO] Such a surprise!

MARIE  Such a punctual surprise, Pietro. We're just about to go in to tea. Won't you join us?

[PIETRO *mumbles shyly and kisses her outstretched hand.*]

| | |
|---|---|
| DINA | Of course he'll stay to tea. |
| PIETRO | [*only has eyes for* MARIE *and stares wild-eyed at her*] You wore an enchanting hat yesterday. Enchanting. |
| MARIE | I'm so glad you liked it. I've discovered that the clothes we wear can alter the course of the seasons, consequently I decided that yesterday was to be the last day of winter, and I wore a felt hat. This morning I put on a straw hat and it was spring. |
| PIETRO | Enchanting! |
| DINA | Pietro has a surprise for you ... |
| MARIE | Another surprise? |
| PIETRO | The hunter you liked so much when we went riding yesterday ... |
| MARIE | [*with joyful anticipation*] Yes ...? |
| PIETRO | My father says you can have him for the season. |
| DINA | Isn't that simply marvellous, Masha? |
| MARIE | I am most grateful to the Count. Of course mama will insist on a fee ... |
| PIETRO | Don't you dare! He'd be mortally offended. [*Pause.*] You're really pleased? |
| MARIE | I'm ecstatic! I adore that horse. And oh we'll be able to go riding every day in the Bois ... what am I saying ... in the Borghese Gardens I mean. I'm so excited I can't think. Yes. I'll write to Monsieur Worth, my dressmaker, immediately. Tonight. Remind me, Dinochka. I shall ask him to design me a riding habit which will include your father's riding colours! |
| DINA | [*glancing at* PIETRO] She thinks of everything! |
| MARIE | Pietro ... You will come riding with me? |
| PIETRO | Well ... as ... as often as I can. |
| MARIE | Oh ...? |
| PIETRO | There may be difficulties. |
| MARIE | A Papal interdict on riding with me perhaps? I hear His Holiness takes a fatherly interest in you. |

| | |
|---|---|
| PIETRO | [*downcast*] Do be serious, please. |
| MARIE | Didn't you tell me your uncle the Cardinal objects to my not being a Roman Catholic? |
| PIETRO | Cardinals tend to be biased when it comes to religion. |
| MARIE | And he probably also objects to my being a woman. |
| PIETRO | Of course not. Some of his best friends are nuns. |
| MARIE | Precisely. They'll try to stop you seeing me. |
| PIETRO | I shan't listen to them. I promise. I'll go riding with you every day. |
| DINA | [*to* MARIE] What did I tell you? |
| MARIE | Are you quite sure you will, Pietro? Those priests are devilish. They'll stop you seeing me. |
| PIETRO | Never. Never! I am ... wholly committed to you. You don't believe me? [*turns to* DINA] You believe me Dina, don't you? |
| DINA | Yes, yes. Only please don't spend too much time doubting one another. Can't you enjoy being together and leave it at that? [*She begins to leave.*] I'm going in to tea ... come soon ... |

[DINA *goes and the two spend some time looking at each other.*]

| | |
|---|---|
| PIETRO | Marie. Marie. I love you. |
| MARIE | How many women have you said that to? |
| PIETRO | Not one. Ever. I have never loved. I hate women. I've only ever had ... flings with ... mercenary women. |
| MARIE | So. You hate women. |
| PIETRO | Yes. But to me you are not a woman. You're a goddess. |
| MARIE | Hypocrite! |
| PIETRO | Are you such a bad judge of character you can't see I'm telling you the truth? But ... you ... have you ... how often have you been in love? |
| MARIE | Twice. |
| PIETRO | Oh. |
| MARIE | Maybe ... maybe more. |
| PIETRO | How I'd like to be the more! |

| | |
|---|---|
| MARIE | Silly boy! I don't think you can possibly be in love with me. You look too much like a priest to be in love with me ... or anybody. It obviously runs in the family. |
| PIETRO | You can be very cruel, Marie. Besides, I loathe priests. |
| MARIE | Yet I hear you may be one soon? |
| PIETRO | Never! I'd rather be a soldier! |
| MARIE | You ... a soldier? All those years you spent in the seminary hardly count as military training. |
| PIETRO | Damn the seminary! Damn the Jesuits! I hate them. That's why I'm always on bad terms with my family. |
| MARIE | Listen to me. You're ambitious and — |
| PIETRO | [*cutting in*] No I'm not ... |
| MARIE | You are ambitious. Nothing wrong with that. Every wellborn man ought to be. Or woman. You are ambitious and would like nothing better than to be a bishop or a cardinal and have your slipper kissed! |
| PIETRO | [*grabs her hand and proceeds to smother it with kisses*] What an adorable little hand ... |
| MARIE | I think we'd better go in to tea. |
| PIETRO | [*still holding her hand, and sitting at her feet*] I see you are wholly indifferent to me. |
| MARIE | [*pensively*] I am not indifferent to you, Pietro. |
| PIETRO | It's even possible you find me ... repulsive. That's it. You did say I looked like a priest. |
| MARIE | [*not without affection*] Pietro! Let me look at you. As a matter of fact I think you're remarkably handsome. I can tell. I'm an artist. I think I'll sketch your head and shoulders before we go back to France. You have a pale clear complexion, beautiful brown eyes, a long straight nose ... pretty ears, a little mouth, very passable teeth and [*She pulls his moustache playfully.*] a very manly moustache for a boy of twenty-three. |
| PIETRO | Now I know you're making fun of me. I suppose you're comparing me with your English duke. Unfavourably. I bet you never pulled his leg ... or his moustache. |
| MARIE | [*with a start*] How do you know about him? |

PIETRO    Dina told me.

MARIE    She talks too much! I never even met him, so you see you can hardly regard him as a rival. Besides, he wasn't English. He was Scottish. But ...

PIETRO    Yes?

MARIE    I admit I was in love with him. Very much. You see, you don't have to know people ... to be on speaking terms with them ... to love them, or be in love with them. I love God and I love the Czar, but I don't know them personally.

PIETRO    Your duke. Was he rich? Good-looking?

MARIE    [*dreamily*] Oh yes! Fabulously rich. Richer than your family, if that is possible. And very handsome. When he winters on the Riviera he rents at least two villas and has his yacht moored nearby for guests. He has a London house, a palace in Scotland and countless country houses that stand in thousands of acres ... Married to him I would have been the most highly placed, the most honoured woman in Britain.

PIETRO    No you wouldn't. Here in Italy, or in France or any country which calls itself civilised the most honoured of living creatures is woman. In Britain it is the horse.

DINA    [*off*] Are you coming you two?

MARIE    In a moment! [*Pause.*] I could get to love you Pietro, but it wouldn't be any good.

PIETRO    Not even if we were married?

MARIE    Especially if we were married. I'd make a very poor wife.

PIETRO    I don't understand. Why?

MARIE    Because I've too many things to do, and too little time to do them in. Life is so short. Too short even if I live to be a hundred. I have too much of some things and too little of others, and a character not made to last. And I seem to have the self-absorption, the vanity, the corrosive ambition of an actress, a painter and a politician rolled into one. I can't help it. I'm made that way. How I wish sometimes that your kind of love were enough ...

PIETRO    But ...

| | |
|---|---|
| MARIE | No. Please don't interrupt. There was a time when I thought that love ... love between a man and a woman that is, would be enough. But now I know it won't. It can't. In the order of my priorities what you call love takes bottom place. No — don't be sad. You'll marry a beautiful, rich principessa and live happily ever after. I know. |
| PIETRO | I shall never love another woman. |
| MARIE | In that case you'll become a bishop or a cardinal and when you die you'll go straight to heaven and be a darling saint! |
| PIETRO | Marie. It's you I love. |
| MARIE | A temporary aberration, I assure you. Even mama and aunt Romanoff seek my advice in these matters. It's all in the novels of Monsieur Stendhal. |
| PIETRO | I love you, Marie. |
| MARIE | I believe you do. And I'm very grateful. |

> [*She runs her hand through* PIETRO's *hair affectionately. She is obviously moved and quite close to embracing him, but checks herself not so much out of moral restraint as because she has been telling* PIETRO *the truth: she feels she has outgrown this kind of passion.*]

| | |
|---|---|
| PIETRO | Marie ... |
| DINA | [*off*] Marie! Are you coming? [*She enters.*] Oh, you're impossible! |
| MARIE | [*holding* PIETRO's *face in her hands and looking at him fondly*] I think she's right, don't you? |

> [*Fadeout.*]

## FOUR

*Rome, 1876.* MME ROMANOFF *at her needlework. She will continue to be so engaged throughout the scene.* MARIE *is shuffling some papers she has been busy with.*

MARIE   There. That should do.

MME ROMANOFF   Don't tire your poor eyes with all that scribbling. What have you been writing today?

MARIE   I've prepared a French history lesson for the servants.

MME ROMANOFF   For the servants? Whatever for?

MARIE   Darling aunt, they're so hopelessly ignorant. They're Russian, but we live in France and they should know something of the history of their adoptive country.

MME ROMANOFF   I don't see why they should. It'll only weigh them down with unnecessary information. It might even give them subversive ideas. Besides, they wouldn't want to know. It's all much too complicated for them.

MARIE   Not if they're given the facts simply and plainly. Here is my history of modern France for them. Listen. The last king was Louis XVI. He was very good, but the Republicans cut off his head. The Republicans are the people who only want to get money and honours. They also beheaded his wife, Marie Antoinette, and made a Republic instead. Then France was very wretched, and there was a man born in Corsica called Napoleon Bonaparte. He was so clever and brave that they made him a colonel and then a general. Then he conquered the whole world, and the French liked him very much. But when he went to Russia he forgot to take the soldiers' greatcoats, and they were wretched because of the cold; and the Russians burned Moscow. Then Napoleon, who was already Emperor, went back to France; but because he was unlucky, the French didn't like him any more, because they only like those who are lucky. And all the other kings wanted to be revenged, so they said he must abdicate. Then he went to the island of Elba, then he came back to Paris for a hundred days. After that they chased him all over the place. Then he saw an English ship and asked them to save him. They took him on board and made him prisoner, and took him to St Helena, where he died.

MME ROMANOFF   [*matter-of-fact*] Well, well. Is that what happened? Fancy that.

MARIE   Didn't you know?

MME ROMANOFF   I did vaguely hear that something of the kind did occur. But Madame de Beaumarchais told me we're not to believe everything we're taught in the schoolroom.

MARIE   It's all true, I tell you. The gist of it.

MME ROMANOFF   It must be if you say so. You're so knowledgeable.

MARIE   Am I, I wonder? I'm quite at home with facts, I know. But not with feelings. Not yet. How I wish I could be clear about my own feelings. [*Pause.*] About love.

MME ROMANOFF   Ah yes, love. That's all in store for you, my child.

MARIE   What about Pietro?

MME ROMANOFF   He would be a good match for you. The family is good. Well-connected. And rich.

MARIE   You think wealth is important?

MME ROMANOFF   Very important. I have known devoted couples suffer agonies of doubt and estrangement — all on account of money. You may despise money, but it's necessary.

MARIE   In that case I should like to be rich, so I won't have to think about money at all.

MME ROMANOFF   Now that's what I call a sensible aspiration. And you could do worse than Pietro.

MARIE   But do I love him?

MME ROMANOFF   Well — do you?

MARIE   I do when I miss him. When I allow myself to miss him. Which isn't often, especially when I'm drawing or singing. Oh dear, I can't make myself out. I love and yet I don't.

MME ROMANOFF   That is a most unsatisfactory state of mind.

MARIE   Besides, once we go back to France he'll think no more of me than of last winter's snow. I shan't exist for him.

MME ROMANOFF   I doubt that. But it's true that his family are set against the match.

MARIE   Tell me, aunt Sophie. Why am I sometimes tortured by visions of unsatisfied love when art should engage all my faculties?

MME ROMANOFF   I can't help you with the second part of your question. As for the first, just ask yourself: do I love him?

MARIE   Then my answer must be no. I've said as much to him.

MME ROMANOFF   You're young enough to change your mind. When you get to my age you begin to look at things from a different point of view, and realise that nothing much in this world is worth worrying about.

> [*Fadeout.*]

## FIVE

*Rome, 1876. The darkened consulting room of* ALEXIS, *a famous clairvoyant. The* NARRATOR *is standing by the clothes trolley, putting on the dressing gown* ALEXIS *wears when receiving clients.*

NARRATOR   She didn't love Pietro and yet was fascinated by the power game that was being played against her by his family. She had renounced him but not the politics of the intrigue. Marie prevailed on her Aunt Romanoff — a dedicated patron of fortune tellers and clairvoyants — to take her to see the famous Alexis, who might impart interesting news on Pietro's family.

> [*He walks up to a sofa centre stage and lies down on it as* MME ROMANOFF *and* MARIE *enter.*]

MME ROMANOFF   Good afternoon, Alexis.

ALEXIS   Good afternoon. Who is the person with you?

MME ROMANOFF   A young woman who needs your help. Not a medical consultation.

> [*She places* MARIE'S *hand into* ALEXIS', *whose eyes will remain half-closed throughout the interview.* MARIE *sits on the sofa.*]

ALEXIS   Ah, but all the same I may tell you your young friend is about to become very ill.

MARIE   Oh.

ALEXIS   You must take good care of yourself, young woman. What have you come to see me about?

| | |
|---|---|
| MARIE | I've come to consult you about this person. [*She hands over a sealed envelope to* ALEXIS.] |
| ALEXIS | What's in this envelope? |
| MARIE | The photograph of the uncle of someone who may be very close to me. |
| ALEXIS | [*feeling the envelope with both his hands*] I can see him. Yes. |
| MARIE | Where is he? |
| ALEXIS | Here. In Rome. In a palace, surrounded by important people. He is young ... no! He is grey-haired. In a uniform of sorts. He's over sixty. |
| MARIE | What kind of uniform? |
| ALEXIS | A strange one. It isn't an army uniform. |
| MARIE | You're quite right. |
| ALEXIS | It's ... an ecclesiastical vestment. Wait a moment ... he enjoys high office. In the church. That's it. He is a bishop. No: a cardinal. |
| MARIE | Yes. Yes. That's him. What's he thinking about? |
| ALEXIS | Something very serious. To do with a member of his family. And you. |
| MARIE | Tell me more. More. |
| ALEXIS | He has written a letter to a young man. |
| MARIE | [*begins to walk up and down the room in her excitement*] What does the letter say? |
| ALEXIS | Don't be so restless. You tire me. Think quietly. I can't keep up with you. He is telling the young man that he must stop seeing you. The young man is unhappy. Unhappy and ambitious. |
| MARIE | Ambitious? Then he can't possibly love me. |
| ALEXIS | But he does. He does. With him love and ambition go together. |
| MARIE | How strange! Tell me more about his character. |
| ALEXIS | He's just the opposite of you. |
| MARIE | Does he often see the cardinal his uncle? |

| | |
|---|---|
| ALEXIS | No. They've been estranged for some time. They correspond, though. The young man is very confused. Both the cardinal and his mother are against any further contact between you and the young man. He would like to marry you, but there are other considerations. |
| MARIE | He evidently doesn't care about me. |
| ALEXIS | He does. He does, I tell you. If you were with him permanently, you and his ambition would march in step. |
| MARIE | You really think he loves me? |
| ALEXIS | Yes. Very much. |
| MARIE | Since when? |
| ALEXIS | You ask too many questions. You tire me. I can't concentrate any more ... |
| MARIE | Please! Do try, do ... |
| ALEXIS | I can't. I'm too tired. You must go now. But first tell me ... do you love him? |
| MARIE | Love him? Love him? Certainly not! |

[*Fadeout.*]


## SIX

*Rome, 1876.* MARIE *is sitting at a small writing desk upstage left, writing and reading from her journal. A papal chair and a footstool centre stage.*

MARIE  No. I couldn't possibly fulfil myself through Pietro. Or any other man. They tell me that when Pietro was at death's door six years ago, his mother made him eat slips of paper on which the word Maria was written over and over again. Maria Maria Maria. She did this in the hope that the Virgin might cure him. Could that be the reason why he fell in love with me? I'm tempted to call that superstition, but then, what about me? Only last evening I counted the beads of my rosary. There are sixty. I prostrated myself sixty times, each time hitting the floor with my forehead. I was bruised and quite out of breath, but somehow secure in the knowledge that I had done something pleasing in the sight of God.

MME BASHKIRTSEFF  [*enters hurriedly while dressing*] Darling, you still haven't dressed. We're expected at the Vatican shortly.

MARIE  You're not dressed either. I shan't be long, mama. Just a few more lines, then I'll dress. I'll be very quick.

MME BASHKIRTSEFF  I do so hope you will be. It's a private audience. We can't possibly be late. And your aunt as usual is ready and waiting. [*She dashes out again.*]

MARIE  [*resuming journal*] His Holiness has granted us a private audience. I suspect that Cardinal Antonelli, Pietro's uncle, has asked the Pope to warn me off the young man. If so it will be a quite unnecessary ploy, since I really have no time for Pietro. Really, those Cardinals! At a party at the Antonellis the other night there were three or four of them who looked at me greedily just as if they were coming out of the opera at Nice. Will the Pope bring up the subject of religion with me? I hope not, because I am beginning to doubt the existence of the soul. If it is the soul which animates the body and is the thinking essence, why should it be annihilated by ... say a mere pistol shot in the head or ... indigestion caused by a tainted lobster? If one concludes that the soul is a mere invention, then all our most intimate and cherished beliefs begin to collapse one after another, like falling scenery when a theatre is on fire.

MME BASHKIRTSEFF  [*off*] Marie! Marie! Are you coming?

MME ROMANOFF  [*off*] We're going to be late!

MARIE  Coming! Coming! [*resumes journal*] I can't really decide. And it's important that I should, especially today if only for social reasons. I ask myself: Is the Pope God's representative on earth or just an elderly gentleman in fancy dress? [*She snaps the journal shut and goes out quickly.*]

> [*The lights fade on the empty stage for a few seconds and fade up again to denote the passage of time.* MARIE, *her mother and aunt, now in a Vatican audience room,*

*enter slowly.* POPE PIUS IX, *dressed in white with a red cloak and leaning on an ivory-headed stick, enters from the opposite side, followed by* MISHA *in the full canonicals of a cardinal in attendance. The* POPE *lowers himself slowly onto the papal chair and the cardinal whispers in the* POPE's *ear. The* POPE *nods and smiles at the three women, who come forward. They each kneel and kiss his ring. He nods benevolently.*]

PIUS IX   Russians, then ... from St Petersburg?

MME BASHKIRTSEFF   No, Holy Father. From Little Russia. This is my sister ... [*The* POPE *smiles at* MME ROMANOFF.] My daughter Marie.

PIUS IX   [*looks long and intently at* MARIE] She is very young. And very beautiful. I can see why she has turned young Antonelli's head.

MME BASHKIRTSEFF   Marie may be a little headstrong, Holiness, but she is also a dutiful and religious girl.

PIUS IX   Naturally. All the most troublesome of our Lord's children are dutiful and religious. [*He raises a hand with open palm and the cardinal hands the* POPE *two rosaries, which he presents to the two women.*] Remember me in your prayers. And now we would like to be left alone with the child. We have special blessings for the young. And special warnings.

> [*The two women begin to leave. The* POPE *raises his hand again in a single sweeping gesture which begins as a sign of benediction on the two women as they exit and ends as a startlingly informal crooked forefinger inviting* MARIE *to come closer. He points to the footstool, which he delicately kicks in her direction with a slippered foot.*]

Come closer. Sit there, child. I'm a little deaf, you see.

[MARIE *is suddenly seized by a fit of coughing.*]

MARIE   I am so sorry, Holy Father.

PIUS IX   On the contrary, let me apologise. Our corridors are cold and draughty ... and as interminable as eternity. Have you caught a chill?

| | |
|---|---|
| MARIE | A chill? No. They tell me I am seriously ill. The doctors say there's something wrong with my lungs. |
| PIUS IX | I shall pray for you. And the good God will heal you and you will live a long and useful life in his service. Have you a vocation? |
| MARIE | I don't think so, Holy Father. |
| PIUS IX | No. I was afraid of that. Well, even a secular life can be spent in his service. Now look, child: I hear unbecoming reports of Pietro Antonelli's ... er... infatuation for you. His family suspect you may be encouraging him. Is this true? You see ... before meeting you ... he had a vocation. His uncle had great hopes of him. He is meant for the priesthood. The Church runs in the family, as it were. |
| MARIE | So I was right. He is to be a priest. |
| PIUS IX | [*genially*] Oh yes. Without a doubt. That is, given a clear run, clear especially of the kind of obstacle course presented by you and other worldly temptations ... |
| MARIE | [*contemptuously*] A priest! |
| PIUS IX | He's bound to go far in the Church. I said a priest in a manner of speaking ... the highest offices would be open to him. Certainly a cardinal's hat wouldn't be beyond his reach ... the Antonellis have managed it with unfailing regularity for centuries ... And who knows, he might even ... [*He pats the arm of the papal chair in some disquiet, then shakes his head as if to clear it of unwelcome thoughts and addresses* MARIE *in earnest.*] The boy must be left alone, young lady. |
| MARIE | Holy Father, I have never regarded Pietro as other than a ... young comrade. |
| PIUS IX | [*considerably relieved*] But then I have been misinformed. You have no ... designs on him? |
| MARIE | Shall I be brutally frank with you, Holiness? |
| PIUS IX | The chair of St Peter expects no less. |
| MARIE | The young man in question leaves me absolutely cold. |
| PIUS IX | Splendid! |
| MARIE | In fact, I find him quite ... repulsive. I find most men repulsive. |

PIUS IX   Better still! Are you sure you haven't a vocation? Women who detest men as much as you seem to, tend to make the most admirable nuns.

MARIE   Have no fear, Holy Father. We shall be leaving for Nice the day after tomorrow. So you see another temptation will be removed from Pietro's path. Please reassure the cardinal his uncle.

PIUS IX   [*nodding pensively*] You strike me as remarkably mature for a girl of sixteeen. I want you to know that today you have made an old man very happy. Believe me, there are enough complications in a Pope's life without all this nonsense about young Antonelli. [*Suddenly formal, he begins to rise.*] You say you will be leaving for Nice the day after tomorrow — but remember that your destination is not Nice, Paris or St Petersburg. It is the Kingdom of Heaven. And in order to get there safely, my dear, take my advice: don't wait till the last day of your life to make the necessary preparations. Start now. [*He begins to go and turns before leaving the stage, flanked by the cardinal at whom he points a finger, smiling at* MARIE *with pontifical kindliness.*] Start immediately. Even my friend the cardinal knows this.

[*They sweep out.*]

[*The lights fade and* MARIE *goes up to the writing desk and begins to write in her journal.*]

MARIE   It seems that I am seriously ill. The Italian doctor hardly knows me and has no interest in deceiving me. My right side is injured and the lung is damaged. Provided I take care of myself it will not get worse, though it will never be completely cured. He recommends violent methods such as cauterisation or a mustard plaster. A mustard plaster! That means a yellow stain for a year. When I go out I shall have to wear a bunch of flowers on my right collar bone to conceal the horrible stain. I think I'll wait a week first. Then if I'm still not better I'll submit to this infamy. God is wicked.

[*Fadeout.*]

## SEVEN

*Paris 1876.* MME BASHKIRTSEFF *and* MARIE. MISHA *is mending a chair in a corner.*

MME BASHKIRTSEFF   The doctor said you should rest. And not strain your voice.

MARIE   Singing lessons wouldn't exhaust me. Most exercises are quite gentle.

MME BASHKIRTSEFF   Isn't your drawing enough to keep you occupied?

MARIE   Mama, you don't understand. Music and art are not pastimes. They're a way of life. A discipline.

MME BASHKIRTSEFF   More like a scourge than a discipline if it makes you ill. Marie, darling, we're in Paris. It's spring. Lots of young men are making eyes at you. Pietro has written to you. Isn't that enough?

MARIE   No, mama. But don't let's go into that again. I know it upsets you.

MME BASHKIRTSEFF   Your head should be full of the sweetest romantic notions.

MARIE   Well it isn't, mother.

MME BASHKIRTSEFF   [*dreamily*] When I was your age, all I thought about was ball gowns. And dances. I can still see the Venetian chandeliers in the Galitzines' ballroom.

MARIE   [*more gently, falling in with her mother's memories*] Did you dance a great deal?

MME BASHKIRTSEFF   Oh yes I did. They had to tear me away from the dance floor and send me to bed. In my day we weren't allowed to stay up late. Times have changed. And then ...

MARIE   Yes ...?

MME BASHKIRTSEFF   And then I met your father.

MARIE   [*with a hint of sadness*] Yes.

MME BASHKIRTSEFF   He was so handsome. So vital. I fell in love head over heels with him. He was my whole world. [*Pause.*] And I was so happy for a time.

MARIE   Mama, what has happened? Why isn't papa here with us?

MME BASHKIRTSEFF   He has duties in Russia. Don't forget he is a Marshal of the Nobility.

MARIE   [*dismissive*] Of the provincial nobility.

MME BASHKIRTSEFF   Be that as it may, he wouldn't have the time to travel round Europe with us.

MARIE   Don't you miss him?

MME BASHKIRTSEFF   Of course I do, child.

MARIE   Doesn't he love us ... I mean you ... any more?

MME BASHKIRTSEFF   He does. Of course he does. He writes to us regularly. I read out all his letters to you. He's a most devoted husband and father.

MARIE   [*darkly*] I've heard stories. Ugly stories. About other women.

MME BASHKIRTSEFF   [*with some bitterness*] Gossip. Malicious gossip. That's all. I forbid you even to entertain such thoughts. [*less severely*] Families have their ups and downs. But on the whole we're a happy lot. Even if my Babanine relations don't approve of the Bashkirtseffs. My parents had ambitious plans for me. As you know.

MARIE   I do I do, mama. Oh, just think: if you'd married you-know-who I'd be a princess!

MISHA   [*has finished mending the chair which he plants firmly by* MARIE's *side*] A princess? Yes, and I'd be the Czar of all Russia. [*He turns to* MME BASHKIRTSEFF.] You're putting too many fancy ideas in your daughter's head. Listen to me — take her to the Russian church and teach her to pray. She'd be much better employed that way.

MME BASHKIRTSEFF   [*mildly reproachful*] Misha, how dare you speak to us like that. You're not supposed to listen. Why, you're a servant. You're meant to merge with the furniture. [*in an undertone*] Go away.

## EIGHT

*Paris, 1876.* MARIE, MME BASHKIRTSEFF *and* MME ROMANOFF.

MARIE ... but don't you see, it's the best way to find out whether my voice is any good or not! Aunt Sophie, please convince mama ...

MME ROMANOFF It's not such a bad idea, you know ...

MME BASHKIRTSEFF [*to* MARIE] I'm not sure I quite understand what you want to do.

MARIE Listen carefully then. Perhaps you'll understand this time. Monsieur Wartel is the best singing teacher in Paris, isn't he? To make absolutely sure he won't take me on as a pupil simply because I'm a rich gentlewoman, I'll disguise myself as a poor girl, and you and aunt Sophie'll take me along to him. You'll tell him I'm a poor little waif you're trying to help. Whose singing shows promise. That you'd like a professional opinion.

MME BASHKIRTSEFF Dear me. Are you sure it'll work?

MARIE It's the only way I'll be able to learn the truth about my voice. And I have last year's frock which will do beautifully for my Cinderella act.

MME ROMANOFF It should be fun ...

MME BASHKIRTSEFF Oh ... very well. If you're sure it won't lead to a muddle ... Monsieur Wartel you say ...

MME ROMANOFF Leave it to me. I'll make the appointment.

MARIE Bless you! [*She coughs repeatedly.*] Bless you both. I'll practise Tosti's 'April' as an audition piece.

[*The lights fade and come up again as* MME BASHKIRTSEFF *and* MME ROMANOFF *sit on two chairs outside* WARTEL's *studio.* MARIE *can be heard singing with striking professionalism the last few bars of Tosti's 'April' to a piano accompaniment.*]

MME ROMANOFF  She sings like an angel.

MME BASHKIRTSEFF  Yes ... but I'm worried, Sophie. I don't like that chesty cough.

MME ROMANOFF  Just a chill, my dear.

MME BASHKIRTSEFF  In July? A chill? She spat blood last week.

MME ROMANOFF  Dr Walitzky says she'll be all right. And the trip to Russia will do her good. He says a change of climate works wonders. [*Pause.*] Is that why we're always on the move, I wonder?

[*The music swells and the song comes to an end on a high note expertly sustained by the singer. The two women look apprehensively at the studio door, which presently opens.* MARIE, *flushed, is led in with some ceremony by* WARTEL.]

MARIE  Was I right, sir? Am I a contralto?

WARTEL  I'd say more of a mezzo soprano. The voice is young. Its pitch will rise. [*He grins.*] You sang charmingly.

MME BASHKIRTSEFF  What is your opinion?

WARTEL  She has a good voice, a good voice, but you understand she'll have to work very hard. Good but as yet undeveloped ... unfermented, like young wine. There's good material there, quite a good range. But she must work.

MME BASHKIRTSEFF  Then you think her voice is worth cultivating?

WARTEL  Unquestionably. Provided she's dedicated.

MARIE  I sang badly, I know. [*She coughs.*] I was nervous.

WARTEL  Ah well, my dear, you must get accustomed to control that nervousness. It would be entirely out of place on the stage. [*He smiles.*] I take it you have been having lessons.

MARIE  No. At least, never from a singing teacher.

WARTEL  Remarkable. Quite remarkable.

MME BASHKIRTSEFF   Maestro ... would you consider taking her on as a pupil?

WARTEL   Most certainly. [*with a savage grin at* MARIE] I shall work you very hard. I shall work you into the ground.

>[MARIE *throws herself into* MME ROMANOFF's *open arms and the two hug each other delightedly.* WARTEL, *no longer smiling, turns to* MME BASHKIRTSEFF.]

The girl's got a nasty cough. She'd better do something about it.

>[*Fadeout.*]


## NINE

*Naples, 1876.* MMES BASHKIRTSEFF *and* ROMANOFF *at opposite ends of the stage, bent on needlework throughout the scene.*

*The* NARRATOR *enters.*

NARRATOR   One fine April morning in 1876 while on holiday at Naples she met the King.

MME BASHKIRTSEFF   [*in some alarm*] The King?

MME ROMANOFF   [*with a delighted smile*] The King!

NARRATOR   None other than Victor Emmanuel II, while he was paying a call on the Prince of Prussia at the hotel where the Bashkirtseffs were staying. With her customary boldness Marie barred his way across a corridor.

MME BASHKIRTSEFF   [*raising her head from her needlework reproachfully*] The cheek!

MME ROMANOFF   [*nodding enthusiastically*] What splendid initiative!

>[*The* NARRATOR *goes up to the clothes trolley and begins to change into the* KING's *tunic, beard and moustache.*]

NARRATOR   It was just as well that Victor Emmanuel II had an eye for a pretty girl. While wary, like most monarchs, of attempts on his life he usually welcomed those on his virtue ...

[*He strides purposefully across the stage as* VICTOR EMMANUEL II, *followed by* MISHA, *who enters fully dressed as an aide-de-camp.* MARIE *dashes in from the right and bars his way, breaking into a coquettish curtsey from which she will not rise until forced to by the* KING.]

MARIE    May I crave a word with you, sir ...?

THE KING [*stops abruptly, looks at* MARIE *and twirls his moustache*] Oh ... hm ... yes?

MARIE    Oh ... Your Majesty!

THE KING Get up, get up child. No need to be shy. Hm ... Is there anything I can do for you? [*He helps her up.*]

MARIE    Absolutely nothing, sir. Or rather, nothing that you haven't already done. You've just made it possible for me to boast for the rest of my life that I have actually spoken to the kindest and best of kings.

THE KING Nicely put. Very nicely put. And what is your name?

MARIE    Marie Bashkirtseff, sir.

THE KING Russian?

MARIE    Yes, sir.

THE KING You are in Naples with the ballet?

MARIE    No, sir. I am touring Europe with my family. With my mama, that is, our physician Dr Walitzky, my cousin Dina and my aunt Romanoff ...

THE KING [*cutting in*] Romanoff? Are you by any chance related to ...

MARIE    [*quickly*] Very distantly ... if at all, sir. But naturally I simply worship our great royal family.

THE KING Good. Very good. It does you credit. And your father?

MARIE    He's a Marshal of the Nobility in Poltava ... and his presence is sometimes required at Court, as you'll appreciate ... My grandpapa Babanine, on my mother's side ... was of noble Tartar origin ...

THE KING Indeed ...?

MARIE    [*pointedly*] Of the first Tartar invasion, of course.

| THE KING | Of course. Will you do me the honour of escorting me to my carriage, Mademoiselle Bashkirtseff? |
|---|---|
| MARIE | [*curtseying*] Your wish is my command, Majesty ... |

> [*The KING offers MARIE his arm, on which she places a gloved left hand which the KING will pat now and then with his free hand to emphasise a point. They begin to walk across the stage to the initially muted strains of the 'Radetzky March', followed at a respectful distance by the aide-de-camp. They turn to walk across the stage again at approximately the spot where MME BASHKIRTSEFF and MME ROMANOFF respectively are sitting, thus giving a triumphant MARIE the opportunity to address either her mother or her aunt by leaning slightly away from the KING, with whom from now on she will be seen conversing soundlessly as they step across the stage a few times, possibly in time to the music. The ensuing dumb conversation between the KING and MARIE offers the director a number of opportunities for stylised mime.*]

[*to* MME BASHKIRTSEFF] He has squeezed my hand twice, mama. Twice! I shall wear my gloves for at least a week!

> [MME BASHKIRTSEFF *shakes her head in silent disapproval.*]

> [*The* KING *and* MARIE *turn and cross the stage again.*]

[*to* MME ROMANOFF] Isn't he the most perfect of kings? Apart from our beloved Czar, naturally ...

> [MME ROMANOFF *nods, beaming approval.*]

> [*The* KING *and* MARIE *turn and cross the stage again.*]

[*to* MME BASHKIRTSEFF] So much more suitable than the Duke of Hamilton, don't you think, mama ...?

> [*The* KING *and* MARIE *turn for the last time, cross the stage as the music swells and exit.*]
>
> [*Slow fadeout.*]

## [INTERVAL]

## TEN

*St Petersburg, 1876. The* NARRATOR, *at the trolley, is putting on the tunic of a Marshal of the Nobility which he will wear now and in a subsequent scene as* MARIE's *father.* MARIE *is sitting on a sofa with her journal, having just arrived. There are trunks and suitcases in the room.*

MARIE  A few more minutes and my father will be here. I haven't seen him or Russia since I was a little girl. How I wish I could bring about a reconciliation between him and mama! Since we arrived in St Petersburg I have been troubled by a strange whistling in my chest. My nails are red. I cough, and my voice has quite gone. When I woke up this morning I asked myself what I really wanted. To go into society? To paint a superb picture and win the Prix de Rome under a man's name? To recover my voice? To marry Napoleon IV? — I want my voice to come back at once.

[BASHKIRTSEFF *walks slowly towards her and when he is quite close to her he claps his hands with delight.*]

BASHKIRTSEFF  Is it really my little Marie?

MARIE  [*throws the journal aside and leaps from the sofa joyfully*] Papa! My own papa!

BASHKIRTSEFF  My beautiful Masha ...

MARIE  Papa! Oh papa!

BASHKIRTSEFF  You really promise ... I have your word of honour you really are my little daughter?

MARIE  Yes! Yes!

[*More endearments in the Russian manner.*]

BASHKIRTSEFF  Let me look at you. How you've grown! And the latest Paris fashions, I see ...

MARIE  Can you tell?

BASHKIRTSEFF  Just about. What very pretty gloves ... I can read gloves as some people can read hands. And I can see you're going to be quite a flirt...

MARIE  I'm so happy to be here. To see you again...

BASHKIRTSEFF  [*sits her down beside him*] And I can also see that underneath all this French finery there's wild Cossack blood in your veins, eh? Where's Dina?

MARIE  Out shopping. Misha's taken her. They'll be back soon.

BASHKIRTSEFF  Misha, that bigoted old son of a serf — how is he? I hope he's looking after you well. I haven't kicked him in the behind for years! How does he like living in Europe?

MARIE  He grumbles all the time. But he's so happy now he's back in Russia, if only for the summer. In all these years he hasn't learnt a word of French. Or hardly ...

BASHKIRTSEFF  What about you, Marie? Your mother writes that you've forgotten all your Russian, that you speak it like a foreigner these days. I haven't noticed. It isn't true, is it?

MARIE  No, not entirely, but I do have to make a little effort. I'll be able to practise it the whole summer through ...

BASHKIRTSEFF  Good. It's the only language worth knowing. I'm off to Gavrontsy later today to make arrangements for your arrival. You'll love Gavrontsy. I don't expect you can remember it. You were born there. The best countryside in the whole of Russia. You're stopping at Moscow on your way I hear ...

MARIE  If it's all right with you. Dina and I have never been to Moscow.

BASHKIRTSEFF  Don't stay too long. One or two days at the most, do you hear? Then join me in Gavrontsy. [*looks at his watch*] But today before I go I'm taking you to lunch. I hope Dinoschka'll be back soon.

MARIE  Papa ...

BASHKIRTSEFF  Yes?

MARIE  Don't you miss ... us?

BASHKIRTSEFF  Naturally I miss you. Constantly. What kind of a father would I be if I didn't?

MARIE  I didn't just mean me. I meant us. Mama too.

BASHKIRTSEFF  Your mother is a most difficult woman.

MARIE  My mother is a saint.

BASHKIRTSEFF  The two often go together. Let's talk about you. I'm dying to hear all your news.

MARIE  Promise first you'll let me have a good long talk with you about mother some time.

BASHKIRTSEFF  All right. When we're in the country. Things are quieter, easier there. Tell me about yourself. I know you read a great deal. Have you brought many books with you?

MARIE  A few ... a volume each of Plato, Dante, Ariosto and Shakespeare. A few French novels, and some English ones by Bulwer-Lytton, Collins and Dickens.

BASHKIRTSEFF  Stop! Stop! I am impressed! Do you really think you'll profit by all this reading?

MARIE  I don't know. I get very cross sometimes if I'm at a loss for a word or phrase and then find my thoughts gracefully expressed by some well-known writer. It's annoying beyond measure.

BASHKIRTSEFF  You want to be a writer?

MARIE  Not really. I wanted to be a singer but my voice has gone. Something to do with my chest. Don't ask me what it is. Mama and Dr Walitzky say the air at Gavrontsy will be good for me. [*Pause.*] I think I'm going to be a painter.

BASHKIRTSEFF  Good. A wholesome pastime for well brought up girls. I approve.

MARIE  I mean I'm going to choose painting as a profession.

BASHKIRTSEFF  As a prof ...? But Marie, only men ... depraved men with beards, soiled clothes and ghastly diseases become professional painters. It's hardly a fit occupation for a gentlewoman. Or for a woman of any description.

MARIE  That's partly why I want to be a painter. I see no reason why a woman shouldn't be one. But mostly because I'm good at it.

BASHKIRTSEFF  You'll soon grow out of it.

MARIE  I doubt it. When I get back to Paris I shall try to get accepted

|                 | by Rodolphe Julian: he's a famous artist who's opened a school of painting for women. |
| --- | --- |
| BASHKIRTSEFF | Trust the French to do a disgusting thing like that! |
| MARIE | What's disgusting about it? |
| BASHKIRTSEFF | School of painting ... simply an excuse to make you girls take your clothes off ... |
| MARIE | But don't you see ... It's us who'll be doing the sketching or painting. Of course there will be studies from the nude. If anything it'll be men who'll have to pose in the nude for us. |
| BASHKIRTSEFF | Even worse. I forbid it, do you hear? I absolutely — |

[MISHA *and* DINA *enter.*]

| MISHA | Master! |
| --- | --- |
| BASHKIRTSEFF | Misha, you old good-for-nothing! |
| DINA | Uncle! |

[DINA *and* BASHKIRTSEFF *embrace.*]

| BASHKIRTSEFF | Dina, my little niece... |
| --- | --- |
| MISHA | You look older, Konstantin Pavlovich. |
| BASHKIRTSEFF | And you Misha look as scruffy and villainous as ever. |
| MISHA | Thank you, master. One could always rely on you for a kind word. |
| BASHKIRTSEFF | I hope you're looking after my two young ladies properly. I'll skin you alive if you're not. |
| MISHA | I treat them like the pieces of Dresden china they are, don't worry. [*He begins to shift and tidy some trunks and suitcases.*] But you ... shame on you. You should see more of your daughter. Why don't you take them both to Kiev. It would be good for their souls and they'd enjoy it. |
| MARIE | Would we, Misha? |
| DINA | Kiev? |
| BASHKIRTSEFF | [*dismissively*] It's his birthplace ... |
| MISHA | Oh not just because it's my home town, but because Kiev is the mother of all Russian towns, and the holiest: that's what St Vladimir said. His very words. And he was baptised in the Dnieper, a mighty river ... |

BASHKIRTSEFF  Once he starts on the Dnieper he'll never finish. Tell us later, Misha; we're off to lunch now. We're in a hurry. Come girls ...

[*He begins to leave with* DINA *and* MARIE.]

MISHA  That's right, master. Run, run whenever you hear the word of the righteous. Run! Just when you should be thinking of your immortal soul. You'll regret it one day, but it'll be too late. Were you not baptised in the Dnieper yourself, Constantin Pavlovich?

BASHKIRTSEFF  Certainly not.

MISHA  So much the worse for you. St Vladimir baptised all his people in the Dnieper, winter or summer. It was good for their souls, he said. Many of them drowned. In their thousands some say. But their sins were washed away. That's the way with us Russians.

[*Fadeout.*]


ELEVEN


*Moscow, 1876.* DINA *is sitting at a table with a vacant chair opposite her.* MARIE *is standing at the other end of the stage.*

MARIE  About an hour before the train was due in the station I threw my book aside so as to get a good view of Moscow, our real capital, the city which is really and truly a Russian one. Petersburg is a German copy; still, as the Russians have made the copy it beats the Germans hollow. The very mud in the road is Russian. Everything is open-hearted, simple, pious and loyal. The churches with their domes shaped and coloured like green figs upside down are a magic sight. The people here are equally free from French impudence or the stupid, heavy German gravity.

DINA  Marie thinks we came to Moscow to do the sights. The real reason is that the family wanted a celebrated chest specialist to examine her.

| | |
|---|---|
| MARIE | In between looking at churches we called on a Russian doctor my Aunt Romanoff had arranged for me to see. He prodded me all over and prescribed asses' milk and gelatine. My ears are beginning to hurt. |
| DINA | While Marie was dressing in the consulting room the doctor came out to speak to me. He shook his head and said both her lungs were affected. |
| MARIE | I have such a pain between my neck and my left ear, right inside. It's driving me mad. I can't hear all that well. I saw the doctor again today. He has added cod liver oil to the list of delicacies I'm to take for my health. He wants me to rest. How can I rest? |
| DINA | The doctor doesn't hold out much hope. He says that rest and possibly country air would help — a little. We leave for Gavrontsy tomorrow. |
| MARIE | Look on the bright side: I don't need my voice or my hearing to be a painter. And there's no need for me to display my collar bone, which the doctor painted with iodine this morning. |

> [MARIE *joins* DINA *at the table and sits on the vacant armchair.*]

| | |
|---|---|
| DINA | I thought you were in bed. It's where you ought to be. |
| MARIE | I'm too restless to lie down. |
| DINA | The doctor said you should rest, especially before the journey. It's a long way to Gavrontsy. |
| MARIE | How I wish I could unpack my sketching things! I'd like to do a study of the church opposite. |
| DINA | You'll have plenty of opportunities for that in the country. [*calls out*] Misha! |
| MISHA | [*enters*] Yes? |
| DINA | Have you finished packing? |
| MISHA | Not yet. And I won't finish either if you keep calling me while I'm in the middle of it. |
| MARIE | Don't be cross, Misha. You've been cross ever since we've been in Russia. |

| | |
|---|---|
| MISHA | Who wouldn't be, I ask you ... You haven't been out much, have you, miss? Things have changed too much for my liking. You were too young when we left to notice the difference. But I can tell. Our people are not the same. The streets are riddled with spies. |
| MARIE | Is it the government? Or the anarchists? Or the new sect they call communists? |
| MISHA | The lot of them. The masters and the people. They're all getting ready for something nasty. Very nasty. It'll happen pretty soon. I can smell it in the air. |
| DINA | There's a great deal of godlessness. I noticed that many of the churches in Petersburg and even here in Moscow are quite empty. |
| MISHA | You've taken the words right out of my mouth. Our people have lost their faith. Consequently they've lost their way. They're a lost people. |
| DINA | Then we must pray for them, Misha. |
| MISHA | I know what I'd do if I were in charge. |
| DINA | What would you do? |
| MISHA | I'd force every man jack of them, from every corner of Russia without exception to walk barefoot on a pilgrimage to Kiev. Once they got there I'd make them wash in the Dnieper and cleanse their souls. |

[*Fadeout.*]


## TWELVE

*Gavrontsy, 1876.*

MARIE  The view from the balcony is delightful. Scattered about opposite are the red house and summer houses; the mountain to the right with the church half way up quite hidden in the trees, and the family vault a little further on. To the left of the river, the trees, the fields, the horizon. And to think that it all belongs to us, that we are the sovereign lords of all this

— that all the houses, the church, the great square which is like a small town, everything, everything belongs to us, as far as the eye can see, and the servants, nearly sixty in number, and all ...

[BASHKIRTSEFF *enters.*]

BASHKIRTSEFF  What did I tell you? I said the country air would do you a world of good. Bring the colour back to your cheeks. You look the picture of health, little Masha.

MARIE  I'm feeling much better. You've been very kind. I'm happy here.

BASHKIRTSEFF  Of course you are. It's your home. Your roots are here.

MARIE  They are. Here in Gavrontsy I am Russian. Intensely Russian. For whatever I am, I am intensely.

BASHKIRTSEFF  Won't you stay another month?

MARIE  I can't. You know mama and aunt Sophie are expecting us. And I'll have to be in Paris in time to enrol at art school.

BASHKIRTSEFF  Stay a little longer and let me find a husband for you from these parts. Someone who'll make you forget all this art nonsense.

MARIE  Not that again. Please, papa. I'm not ready to get married.

BASHKIRTSEFF  Yes you are. You're sixteen. Bashkirtseff women marry young. Another three or four years and you'll be too old.

MARIE  Too old at twenty? Perhaps. Perhaps I'm too old now. Papa, if ever I want a husband I'll come and let you find me one here. I promise. There are few rich husbands to be found in Paris, and not at all in Italy.

[MISHA *enters.*]

MISHA  Dinner is served, master. And Prince Victor is here again.

BASHKIRTSEFF  Good. [*He winks at* MISHA.] Did you hear that, Marie? Victor is here again.

MARIE  How very nice.

BASHKIRTSEFF  I'm sure he keeps calling because you're here.

MARIE  Not because of Dina?

BASHKIRTSEFF  No. Count Vassily calls because of Dina. Now ... Victor.

|   |   |
|---|---|
| | There's a good match for you. What about him, would you consider ...? |
| MARIE | No, papa. Not him. Especially not him. He's gross and crude and drinks too much and beats his servants. |
| MISHA | Hear that, master? A perfect description of our Russian nobility! |
| BASHKIRTSEFF | Quiet, you dog! Get out! We'll be in to dine presently. |

[MISHA *goes out, grumbling.*]

|   |   |
|---|---|
| MARIE | If you're so keen on marriage as an institution, why don't you do something about yours? I've told you how happy it would make me to see you together with mama again. |
| BASHKIRTSEFF | I cannot, child. There are too many reasons that would make it impossible. |
| MARIE | Such as your mistress and your two children by her? |
| BASHKIRTSEFF | You know about her too? You shouldn't stand in judgment of your father. I knew that woman before I even met your mother. |
| MARIE | I know. And you went back to her two weeks after your marriage. |
| BASHKIRTSEFF | Who told you that? |
| MARIE | It's one of the most popular anecdotes on the Riviera. It has been for years. |
| BASHKIRTSEFF | No! |
| MARIE | You can imagine mama's feelings. |
| BASHKIRTSEFF | Oh dear. It's too embarrassing to hear this sort of thing from one's own daughter. You're so worldly. At your age you should be thinking of pretty things ... flowers ... lace bonnets and twinkling stars. Not about broken marriages and ... |
| MARIE | Adultery? |

[BASHKIRTSEFF *raises his hands in horror.*]

My dear papa, more often than not adultery should be put down to tight lacing and pinching shoes. And to lack of a wholesome occupation. Not to immoral leanings.

BASHKIRTSEFF  But Masha ...

MARIE   Really, it's time you stopped treating me as a child, don't you think? [*She gives him her arm.*] Shall we go in to dinner?

[*Fadeout.*]


## THIRTEEN

*Paris, 1877.* MMES BASHKIRTSEFF *and* ROMANOFF *with* MARIE.

MME BASHKIRTSEFF   This studio where you've enrolled ... Will you be there every day?

MARIE   Yes. I don't have to, but I have so much catching up to do. The classes are at specific times, but we're allowed to work there and practise on our own whenever we like.

MME ROMANOFF   You'll need a chaperone, of course.

MARIE   A chaperone? Don't be ridiculous! I'd die of embarrassment.

MME ROMANOFF   Nevertheless I think — and I'm sure your mother agrees —

MARIE   [*cutting in*] But I don't need a chaperone at school. It's absurd. The studio is a school.

MME ROMANOFF   A school? What kind of a school, I'd like to know, with ... undraped men and women lying around.

MARIE   What a thing to say! Models are there for life studies. Besides, they stand or lie perfectly still.

MME ROMANOFF   In the most improper poses, I shouldn't wonder. I really do think you should have an escort. Your mother and I will think of one.

MARIE   [*to her mother*] Please, mama. Don't listen to her. I'm grown up. I can't have a chaperone at art school. I doubt they'd allow it.

MME BASHKIRTSEFF   You're only seventeen, and your aunt has your best interests at heart. [*She turns to* MME ROMANOFF.] But I have heard that it's a reputable establishment, and that perfectly respectable girls attend the classes. And the teachers are quite eminent and respected painters.

MME ROMANOFF  Painters: you've made my point exactly. Eminent, respected you say — and quite likely licentious to a man. I know about painters. I could tell you a story or two. [*affecting lofty impartiality*] Still, she's your daughter.

MME BASHKIRTSEFF  I don't think Marie'll come to much harm. [*to* MARIE] What sort of pictures will you paint?

MARIE  I won't be doing any painting to start with. [*earnestly*] You see, I have an awful lot to learn. And because of my lack of formal tuition I have a great many gaps to fill. I'll have to wait some time before I can actually paint.

MME BASHKIRTSEFF  [*good-naturedly attempting to show serious interest*] Tell me more, dear.

MARIE  You see, I think we have reached the time when painting has very nearly achieved perfection. The old painters began by hard lines and colours that were too violent. They achieved feebleness bordering on confusion. They never achieved a faithful copy of nature, whatever they may say and write to the contrary.

MME BASHKIRTSEFF  [*the subject clearly beyond her, but pretending to follow*] Is that so?

MARIE  [*in full flow*] Let us ignore all art between the early masters and modern art ...

MME BASHKIRTSEFF  Let us by all means ...

MARIE  ... and by modern I mean here Raphael, Titian and their contemporaries ... harshness, colours that dazzle you, primitively drawn lines are the hallmarks of the first. But — softened tints, shades so harmonised as to lose much of their relief are typical of the second ...

MME BASHKIRTSEFF  [*wholly at sea, but unwilling to admit it*] You don't say!

MARIE  ... and of course what we want now is to take up, with the end of the brush so to speak, the excessively striking colours from the pictures of the early masters and with them some of the blandness of the moderns. [*triumphantly*] Then you will have perfection.

MME BASHKIRTSEFF  [*nonplussed, turns to* MME ROMANOFF] I'm inclined to agree with her!

MARIE  There's also that latest style of painting which seems to consist of painting by patches — in my opinion a grave mistake, although by means of it one may produce some striking effects. In this new style, objects, houses, churches are not clearly defined, and are lacking in precision of form. [*sententiously*] That's a tendency to be avoided.

MME ROMANOFF  Let me get this clear, Marie: at this studio, will they be teaching you or will you be teaching them?

MARIE  [*deflated but good-humouredly childlike*] You're making fun of me. It's not fair.

MME ROMANOFF  I suppose you'll come home smelling of turpentine every day.

MARIE  Yes! Isn't it exciting?

MME BASHKIRTSEFF  [*gathers up her shawl and begins to leave*] Be considerate, Marie. You know your aunt gets headaches if she smells solvents. In future you'd better make sure you have yourself rubbed down with eau-de-cologne before you join us for tea.

[*Fadeout.*]


FOURTEEN

*Paris, 1877.* RODOLPHE JULIAN's *school.* MARIE *is working at the easel. Two other unattended easels and stools will suggest she is alone in the studio.* JULIEN BASTIEN-LEPAGE *enters and walks up to* MARIE, *who will not be aware of his approach until he is immediately behind her.*

MARIE  [*starting*] Oh —

BASTIEN-LEPAGE  I am sorry. Have I frightened you?

MARIE  Yes. I didn't hear you coming. [*She coughs.*]

BASTIEN-LEPAGE  Do you know what day it is today?

MARIE  Saturday?

BASTIEN-LEPAGE  Saturday. Saturday evening. No one works on a Saturday evening.

MARIE  I have to make up for lost time.

BASTIEN-LEPAGE  May I have a look at what you've been doing?

MARIE  I only started here ten days ago. The others are very much better than me. You must make allowances.

BASTIEN-LEPAGE  So the others are better than you, you say.

[*He takes a drawing from a stool beside* MARIE.]

MARIE  Yes. I'm so pleased Monsieur Julian accepted me at all. I don't mind working all hours. I've a lot of catching up to do.

BASTIEN-LEPAGE  Where did you work before?

MARIE  Nowhere.

BASTIEN-LEPAGE  Nowhere? I meant which studio did you work in?

MARIE  I didn't. I took thirty-two private lessons in sketching to amuse myself. A long time ago.

BASTIEN-LEPAGE  That isn't working.

MARIE  I never said it was. You are Monsieur ...

BASTIEN-LEPAGE  Bastien-Lepage. How do you do.

MARIE  Bastien-Lepage the painter? How exciting ... I'm delighted to make your acquaintance ...

BASTIEN-LEPAGE  And I yours. Mlle ...?

MARIE  Marie Bashkirtseff.

BASTIEN-LEPAGE  You never drew from life before you came here?

MARIE  Never.

BASTIEN-LEPAGE  Impossible.

MARIE  Nevertheless it's the truth.

BASTIEN-LEPAGE  You are telling me you've never had professional tuition?

MARIE  I was made to copy engravings when I was a little girl. Does that count?

BASTIEN-LEPAGE  Hardly. That's not at all what I meant. [*Pause.*] You're telling me the truth?

MARIE  Will my word of honour do?

BASTIEN-LEPAGE  Well then, you show quite outstanding promise. That's all I can say. You're really gifted. I must urge you to work.

MARIE  I have done nothing else for ten days.

BASTIEN-LEPAGE  Show me some more of your work.

[MARIE *produces more drawings.*]

BASTIEN-LEPAGE  [*singling one out and examining it*] Did you do this study unaided?

MARIE  That one? Yes. It's a head of my mother. A sort of study. She doesn't believe I'll ever be good enough to paint her portrait in oils.

BASTIEN-LEPAGE  You can tell her from me, my dear, that if in three months you can't do her portrait, full face, three quarters or profile, just as she likes and professional in every detail ... I'll ... I'll ...

MARIE  Yes?

BASTIEN-LEPAGE  I'll eat my hat!

[*Fadeout.*]


## FIFTEEN

*Paris, 1880.* MARIE *at her writing desk in the small hours. A cheval mirror in a corner.*

MARIE  Bastien-Lepage came today and took particular notice of me. My study of the nude pleased him so much that he showed it to the others as an example. Just look at it, he said, there is depth in it, the tone is not bad and the proportions very good. All the students stood up and came to see my drawing. I just stood there, blushing. [*Pause.*] The past three years have flown, and they tell me the work I've done equals six years. I get to the studio at nine, take half an hour for lunch, stay till five and go back from eight till ten, which makes nine and a half hours. This doesn't leave much time for me to go to the theatre and see people, but I manage somehow. [*She coughs.*]

DINA [*off*] Put your light out, Marie. It's late. Go to bed!

MARIE In a moment! [*Pause.*] I can barely hear. I am definitely going deaf. As if it was not bad enough to lose my voice ... to be ill ... why add this too? Is it God who punishes? The God of forgiveness, of goodness, of mercy? The most determined enemy would be less inexorable. I don't always hear what people say, and I tremble in front of them. I can't bring myself to say to everyone: Speak a little louder ... I can't hear all that well! Why must I be so cruelly separated from the rest of the world?

[DINA *enters.*]

DINA Marie, it's two in the morning. Dr Walitzky says you'll get worse again unless you rest.

MARIE Let me be, Dinochka. I'm too restless to go to sleep. I've been working well at the studio and I'm busy planning tomorrow's work.

DINA You won't be able to go to the studio at all if you have a relapse. I'm not sure we should allow you to go anyway. Why don't you take a break?

MARIE I couldn't just now. Last week I painted a bad picture. This week a much better one. It seems to me that one failure is not a proof that we have no talent, while one successful piece of work is proof positive that we have. I'm obviously talented, don't you think?

DINA It's too late for me even to understand what you're saying. I don't think you do, either. You've probably got a temperature and you're delirious. Go to bed. Please.

MARIE In a moment.

DINA Goodnight. [*She goes.*]

MARIE Goodnight.

> [MARIE *goes up to the mirror, looks at herself and slowly takes off her robe. She is naked and will stand for some time as if fascinated by her own reflection. She wraps the robe about her, returns to the writing desk and resumes her journal.*]

I sometimes enjoy looking at my face in the mirror at

twilight, with candles behind me, so as to have a blue reflection on my face and my ears transparent red. But most of all, if I had the time, I would stand for hours quite naked in front of the mirror. Never have I seen such white, fine, elegant skin. Having stared at myself I feel sorry for all those not lucky enough to have seen me. [*Pause.*] A naked woman is the most beautiful object in creation. A woman like me.

[*Fadeout.*]


## SIXTEEN

*Paris, 1883.* MARIE *in her room. There is a knock at the door.*

DINA    [*off*] Are you still awake?

MARIE    Yes. Come in.

       [DINA *enters.*]

DINA    How did the exhibition go?

MARIE    [*shows her a boxed medal*] Here. Pin it on your blouse.

DINA    [*with a cry of delight*] Oh darling — you got it! You got the award!

MARIE    After six years' hard work. [*She coughs.*] Was it worth it do you think?

DINA    Of course it was. And you'll get the Prix de Rome one day. So I've heard.

MARIE    Oh ... says who?

DINA    Me for a start. And someone else. Someone whose opinion you value.

MARIE    May I know who that is?

DINA    Bastien-Lepage.

MARIE    Bast — No! You're making it up!

DINA    Cross my heart. He told me the day before you came back from your cure at Soden.

MARIE    The Prix de Rome. If only I could believe it was within my reach ...

| | |
|---|---|
| DINA | He also said he didn't think you could go on working quite so hard at the studio unless your health improved. |
| MARIE | He's a great one to talk! Dr Walitzky says he's far more consumptive than I am. Positively galloping. |
| DINA | How can you joke about things like that! |
| MARIE | Anyway, I am looking after myself. At Soden I did all the doctors asked me to do. I didn't do any painting. I slept and took the waters and went for long walks and even took to knitting. But no painting. |
| DINA | Knitting? You? |
| MARIE | Yes. I felt the urge to draw coming on so strongly that I snatched her knitting from my chambermaid ... just for the sake of keeping my hands occupied and not reaching for my charcoal and pencils. The poor girl was quite put out, and left the room in tears. It was a stocking. I remember now I went on knitting all day and never really got anywhere. The stocking got longer and longer because I didn't know how to do the heel. I was still knitting at midnight. It was the longest stocking in the world. But I didn't do any sketching that day or the day after. |
| DINA | Do you feel any better now? |
| MARIE | I don't know. The doctors don't even bother to lie to me any more. Not even dear Walitzky. My lungs will never heal properly. |
| DINA | They would at least stand a chance in a dry climate. But you won't leave France. What's the point of driving yourself into ... |
| MARIE | ... the grave? Is that what you were going to say? Come to that, what's the good of anything? To have spent six years working ten hours a day ... for that medal? Is that what I did it for? Or the Prix de Rome? What have I achieved? The beginning of talent and a fatal illness. |
| DINA | Now you're being morbid. Tell me more about the exhibition. Were there any really good paintings apart from yours? Whose did you particularly like? |
| MARIE | Need you ask? Bastien-Lepage, without question, was the |

best. You must go and see for yourself. He towers above them all. And to think they were making a great fuss of an English painter. Sargent I think his name was. His paintings looked like fake Velázquez. [*yawns*] Oh, and —

DINA  Haven't you had enough excitement for one day?

MARIE  Let me tell you about the picture I'm planning to start. It's going to be an allegorical subject. On the pointlessness of human endeavour. Have you heard of an ornamental tree called the monkey puzzle? There were a few outside the clinic at Soden. I was quite taken with them. My picture is going to consist of a very large one with dark, heavy, inviting leaves, promising the safest haven.

[*The lights begin to fade.*]

In reality its leaves are close set and savagely prickly. Not even the most agile of monkeys could ever hope to climb it.

[*Fadeout.*]


## SEVENTEEN

*Two chairs at either end of the stage.* MARIE *is sitting on one. The* NARRATOR *will presently sit on the other as* GUY DE MAUPASSANT.

*The* NARRATOR *enters.*

NARRATOR  As her health declined, her activity increased. During the first months of 1883 she worked feverishly, painting in oils, modelling wet clay, improvising tunes on the piano and mandolin, reading Homer, Livy and Dante.

MARIE  I am like a candle cut in four and burning at all ends. If I could keep a little quieter I might live another twenty years.

NARRATOR  Against all her doctors' advice she stayed on in Paris working through the winter months, with the windows of her studio shut tight, a fierce charcoal stove burning, eating only scraps in the indescribable smell of paint, turpentine and oil.

MARIE  Here are my plans: to begin with, I shall make a start on the

Sèvres picture, then I'll tackle the statue in the morning and work on studies from the nude in the afternoon. This will take me up to July. In July I shall begin *Le Soir*, a highway without trees ... a plain, with a road merging in the distance with the sky at sunset. When I've finished that, I shall go and winter in Jerusalem, and paint another landscape. And in May of next year Bastien-Lepage will declare me a great artist.

NARRATOR   As if all that were not enough, she embarked on a correspondence with Guy de Maupassant, who was then thirty-three and a celebrity, pursued, flattered and lionised. [*He walks up to the trolley and begins to change into a different coat.*] He was intrigued by Marie's letters, the more so since she began writing to him under various pseudonyms of uncertain gender. He was never to discover her real identity.

> [*The* NARRATOR *sits down and assumes* GUY DE MAUPASSANT's *role.*]

MAUPASSANT   Madame, You ask to be my confidante. What right have you to ask me that? I do not know you at all. Why should I say to you, a stranger, poste-restante, whose mind and inclinations may not accord with mine, what I might say verbally, in much more ... intimate circumstances to the women who are truly my friends? What can mystery add to the charm of a relationship by correspondence, in itself somewhat unsatisfactory? Does not all the sweetness of affection between man and woman stem from the pleasure of close companionship, of talking face to face, or even as one writes to one's friend ... in imagining the lines of her face floating between one's eyes and the paper? Forgive me, madame, for these thoughts of a man altogether more practical than poetical, and believe me, your grateful and devoted Guy de Maupassant.

MARIE   Monsieur, I did not ask to be your confidante — if you have time to read my letter over again you will see that the tone I employed was in fact ironical and irreverent. You obviously did not understand what I was driving at. Still, please do not excuse yourself for your lack of poetry or gallantry. Decidedly, my letter was foolish. By way of reparation and if a vague description only is necessary to satisfy you ... one might say of me: fair hair, middle height, born between the years 1812 and 1863. But now, shall I tell you how my imagination sketches you? — As a fairly stout gentleman, dozing on a bench under a palm tree at the seaside. A table, a glass of beer, a cigar. Am I right? Who are your favourite painters and musicians? Your foolish friend, Miss Hastings.

MAUPASSANT Madame, I fear I may not be the man you seek. I have not a ha'porth of poetry. I take everything with indifference and spend two thirds of my time in profound boredom. I spend a third of my time writing lines which I sell to the highest bidder. As for your portrait of me, yes, it is a likeness, but I have detected some errors: I am not really stout. [*He pauses to light a cigar.*] I never smoke. I drink neither beer nor wine, nor any kind of alcohol. [*He drinks a glass of what looks like brandy from a balloon glass in one gulp.*] Nothing but water. I rarely sit on benches. My favourite posture is squatting on a divan in Eastern fashion. You ask who is my favourite painter. Among the moderns, Millet. My favourite musicians? I have a horror of music. I really prefer a pretty woman to all the arts. And I put a good dinner, a real dinner, almost in the same rank with a pretty woman. I used to have two passions. It was necessary to sacrifice one, and I have to some extent sacrificed gluttony. But please, please tell me more about yourself. Are you worldly? Sentimental? Or again are you merely bored and in search of diversions? I pray the divine Homer to ask for you, from the God you adore, all the blessings of the earth. Guy de Maupassant.

MARIE Monsieur, I have profited by the leisure of Holy Week to re-read your complete works. I had never read you en bloc and right through. It was enough to damage my sight and upset all the nunneries in Christendom. — How can you possibly abhor music? No music, no tobacco? Are you telling me the truth? Millet is good, but I advise you to look at a young modern called Bastien-Lepage. Go to the Rue de Sèze. How old are you, really? Do you seriously pretend that you prefer pretty women to all the arts? I think you have been hiding behind a screen of pretence — and I am deeply hurt you could not bring sincerity into our correspondence. I remain, puzzled and in a sad perplexity, Yours, Miss Hastings.

MAUPASSANT   Madame, So I have deeply wounded you. Do not deny it. I like it, I like it, and beg your pardon for it very humbly. I asked myself: who is she? She wrote me at the outset a sentimental letter, the letter of a dreamer, an enthusiast. It is a pose common among girls — is she a girl? Then, madame, I replied in a sceptical vein. You were quicker than I and the letter before your last contained singular things. I kept saying to myself all the time: is this a masked woman having fun at my expense? Do you know the way to recognise women of easy virtue at the Opera? One pinches them. The girls are used to that, and simply say 'Stop it'. The others get angry. I pinched you in a similarly improper way, I confess, and you are angry. Again, pardon. I kiss the unknown hand that writes to me. Guy de Maupassant.

MARIE   Monsieur, How can I prove to you that I am neither a joker nor an enemy? And what's the good? Impossible any longer to swear to you that we were made to understand each other. You are not on a par with me. I regret it. Nothing would have been more agreeable than to recognise in you all superiority — in you or indeed in another. I found your last story interesting, and I should like to put a question to you on the subject of the girl. But — never mind. A delicate trifle in your letter has set me wondering. You are troubled at having given me pain. Well, well, I think you had there an attack of romanticism like Stendhal, but be easy — you will not die of it this time. Incidentally, I quite understand your suspicions. It is unlikely, is it, that a young and pretty woman of fashion should amuse herself by writing to you? But monsieur, how ... But no — I am forgetting that all is over between us. If you have them still, please return my letters. As for yours, I have already sold them to some Americans at an insane price. Goodbye!

   [*Fadeout.*]

## EIGHTEEN

*Paris, 1883.* MARIE *is sitting on a sofa, a blanket on her shoulders.*

BASTIEN-LEPAGE *enters.*

BASTIEN-LEPAGE     You've done it, Marie!

MARIE     What have I done now?

BASTIEN-LEPAGE     The Salon is at your feet. Ollendorf said yesterday that if it had been a Frenchman's work the state would have bought it. 'A very strong man, this Mr Bashkirtseff'.

MARIE     Mr Bashkirtseff?

BASTIEN-LEPAGE     That's how you appear on the catalogue. No matter. I told him you were a young girl and a pretty one. He was quite taken aback.

MARIE     Have the judges had their say?

BASTIEN-LEPAGE     Not yet. But the prize is as good as yours. Not quite the Prix de Rome, but you're well on the way. They're all talking about you.

[DINA *rushes in.*]

DINA     Marie! [*to* BASTIEN-LEPAGE *and then to* MARIE] Sorry to interrupt, but there's a gentleman from the *Monde Illustré* who'd like to photograph you and engrave your picture in his paper.

BASTIEN-LEPAGE     Tell him to come back this afternoon. There'll be others, Marie, and you may as well see them all at the same time.

DINA     I'll see to it. [*She goes.*]

MARIE     I had a telegram from Duesseldorf yesterday, asking for permission to engrave some of my pictures in a German paper, if I have no objection ...

BASTIEN-LEPAGE     [*spreads out his arms*] Marie. Success. At last.
    [*Fadeout.*]

## NINETEEN

*Paris, 1884.* MARIE *is lying in bed.* DINA *is sitting at her bedside.*

MARIE   Dina! Dina ... Where is Bastien-Lepage?

DINA   [*quietly*] Your mama is seeing him to the door.

MARIE   He was here a moment ago ... Did I doze off?

DINA   Yes.

MARIE   [*petulantly*] But why is he going?

DINA   The doctor says you're to rest. And Bastien-Lepage isn't very well himself.

MARIE   No. Now there's a sick man for you. I've always said so.

> [MME BASHKIRTSEFF *comes into the room and makes a silent gesture at* DINA, *who tiptoes out of the room.*]

MARIE   Dina ... Are you still here, Dina?

MME BASHKIRTSEFF   No, darling, it's me.

MARIE   Who? Is my hearing getting worse again? My neck hurts so much I can hardly turn my head ...

MME BASHKIRTSEFF   [*raising her voice a little*] It's me, darling.

> [*She sits by the side of the bed where she is visible to* MARIE *and takes her hand in hers, stroking it from time to time.*]

MARIE   Oh, it's you, mama. One moment it's Bastien-Lepage, then Dina, then you ... so confusing. I'm tired, tired ... and there's so much I have to do. So much.

MME BASHKIRTSEFF   The doctor says you're to rest. It's the best cure, he says. As soon as you're better you'll go South.

MARIE   No, mama. I'll never go South. To go South is to give in. No. I must get back to my studio the moment I'm a little stronger. When I was last there ... was it two or three days ago ...? I felt so incapable of work that I turned all my canvases to the wall ... I felt I'd never paint another picture in my life.

But then ... nothing happens either as you fear or as you hope. Does it?

MME BASHKIRTSEFF [*goes on holding and stroking* MARIE's *hand*] Whatever you say, darling. You're so clever. But try to rest now. There's no sense in tiring yourself out.

MARIE  I think when I'm better ... if I ever do get better ... I'll go North instead of South. Much more chic, don't you think? To Moscow and Gavrontsy and St Petersburg ... preferably in midwinter. [*Pause.*] At the Galitzines' house by the Neva there's a beautiful lifesize portrait of the Grand Duke Vladimir... I couldn't tear myself away from it ... I remember it in every detail to this day. You can't imagine a more perfect and entrancing beauty. I ended by kissing the portrait on the lips. Have you ever noticed how much pleasure a portrait's kiss gives? [*Pause.*] I was so ... moved I wanted to sing a love song there and then to the Grand Duke ... I still had a voice then ... remember how you all thought I was going to be a great singer? But my voice went ... and then my hearing ... What a pity! It really is a tragedy for someone like me never to have sung like Patti. And here I am ... quite possibly on my deathbed ... and only twenty-two. Am I twenty-two, mama?

MME BASHKIRTSEFF  Twenty-four, darling.

MARIE  Twenty-four. Oh dear. Well, I only feel twenty-two. I'm convinced I'd only feel eighteen but for this wretched consumption. To think there was a time when it was considered the height of fashion to be consumptive ... every woman in society tried to get her doctor to diagnose it ... provided it was the curable, milder variety. It was supposed to be good for the complexion. [*She coughs.*] If only it weren't real blood that I keep spitting.

> [*Until so instructed by* MARIE, *MME BASHKIRTSEFF will sit motionless and expressionless, holding her daughter's hand.*]

If only my illness were an imaginary one! You see, mama, I want to live. I don't suffer from unrequited love or some silly sentimental mania. It's really quite simple: I want to live and be famous and enjoy what's good in the world. [*Pause.*] And please remember, in case anything should go wrong ... my will ... you won't forget, I hope ... my instructions are quite clear. You know where everything is. And my journals ... will they be any good, I wonder? I think I'll write today's entry now, even if it is a little early in the day. Nothing's likely to happen before tomorrow. We're not expecting visitors ... I get so exhausted at night, even if I have spent the whole day in bed. Help me up a little ...

> [MME BASHKIRTSEFF *helps* MARIE *into a semi-sitting position and rearranges her pillows. At a gesture from her daughter she hands her a small writing box she will pick up from a side table with her current journal and writing materials.* MME BASHKIRTSEFF *then resumes her sitting position and will remain as motionless as before, looking at* MARIE *who begins to write.*]

MARIE   Monday 20th October 1884. Julien Bastien-Lepage came here today instead of going to the Bois, which would be so good for his health. He can scarcely walk any more, the poor boy. And here at home they're all so devoted to me ... My bed has been in the drawing room these last two days. It's too difficult for me to struggle upstairs. I do hope aunt Romanoff and mama will respect the terms of my will. I suppose there will be enough money to carry out my wishes. They are a little extravagant — I'll be the first to admit it. Perhaps I should have married someone rich who could have looked after me as grandly after death as in my lifetime ... endless requiem masses on each anniversary with full orchestras and the very best singers from the Opera ... someone ... yes! — someone like Monsieur de Lesseps. I met him last spring ... dear, dear Monsieur de Lesseps ... he took quite a fancy to me ... [*She smiles at the recollection.*] ... and told me a long story of nurses and babies and Suez Canal shares ...

> [*The lights begin to fade.*]

Mama is right. I must rest.

> [*The lights fade to partial darkness and she stops writing.*]

I won't write any more tonight.

[*The* NARRATOR *enters softly, a single spotlight on him.*]

NARRATOR   Not that night or any other night. Eleven days later Marie Bashkirtseff was dead.

[MME BASHKIRTSEFF *quits the room silently in an attitude of conventional sorrow. The* NARRATOR *approaches* MARIE's *bed and expertly removes the writing box, gently crosses her arms over her breast and covers her with a sheet. He snaps his fingers and* DINA *and* MISHA *bring in four tall funeral candles on stands, place one at each corner of the bed and leave. The* NARRATOR *begins to light the candles from a lit taper handed to him by* MISHA.]

It's probably fair to say that as Marie gradually realised she hadn't long to live she began to long for a suitably romantic early death ... hence her tendency to drop one or two years from her age, an innocent deception in which her mother occasionally aided and abetted her. It is nevertheless widely accepted that she died shortly before her twenty-fourth birthday — a premature death by any standard.   The instructions she left concerning her funeral, interment and subsequent anniversaries were little short of imperial. They included the erection of a chapel large enough for eighteen to forty people, to be designed by Julien's brother, the architect Emile Bastien-Lepage; an annual memorial service to be held in perpetuity with music by Pergolesi and Verdi performed by musicians of renown;  a statue of herself by the celebrated sculptor Saint Marceau; an annual prize for young painters to be endowed in her name; and the preservation of her ashes in an urn of pure gold — a wish which could not be granted, cremation being contrary to both Russian Orthodox and Roman Catholic practice. She also left minute instructions for mortuary attire to be supplied by her favourite shopgirl at Doucet's so that her own dear Bastien-Lepage might do a portrait of her lying dead in white drapery... but as the painter was dying himself at the time it was one Gustave Courtois who had the harrowing experience of being roused at dawn to paint without delay the picture which now hangs in the chapel of her tomb at Passy. Alas, few ... very few of her instructions were eventually carried out. [*Pause.*] In her short lifetime, hard though she tried, great fame eluded her. True, she impressed eminent singing teachers with the purity of her voice and its promise, intrigued Maupassant into corresponding with her, blossomed into quite a beauty and made a modest name for herself as a painter: to this day many of her works hang in French, American and Russian galleries but that hardly counts as renown. Ironically it was her death which in the end proved to be her best career move. Within months of the publication of her diaries in 1890 her fame spread like wildfire throughout Europe and beyond. She had finally made it. She was famous. Maria Kostantinovna Bashkirtseva had arrived.

[*The curtain falls.*]


[*As the play clearly ends on an upbeat note, the 'Radetzky March' should again be played after the final curtain as the actors take their bows, and played out as the audience leaves the theatre.*]

# STONEY BOWES

## THE FORTUNE HUNTER

---

My theme is alwey oon, and ever was, —
Radix malorum est Cupiditas.
(Chaucer, Preamble to 'The Pardoner's Tale')

## CHARACTERS

Stoney Bowes

Mary Eleanor Bowes

Dr Foot / A masked ruffian / A judge

Septimus Bland, a soldier servant / A voter / A judge

William Stamp, a footman / Monsieur Calostro / A constable/ A warder

Lord Strathmore / George Grey / Parson Bate

Hanna Stoney / Bella / Jenny

(A cast of seven will play various roles as indicated.)

The action of the play takes place during the latter part of the eighteenth century and the early nineteenth century at various locations in the North-East and London. Unless lavish and full production values are contemplated, each scene could be sparingly and economically staged; black-and-white slide projections of the front elevation of Gibside and a few interiors will suffice as backdrops. The scene number and caption could be displayed on large flip-cards stacked on an easel and turned over for each scene transition.

## SCENE 1:
## MUCKY TALK

*1776. An open space on the Gibside estate. In the far background the front elevation of the house. As the curtain rises the stage is empty save for the baleful figure of* DR FOOT, *who stands still on a small dais-like natural eminence upstage right, operatically wrapped in his cloak, his features barely visible under a wide-brimmed hat. He does in fact bear some resemblance to the figure on the Sandeman Port label. The audience could easily mistake* DR FOOT *for a piece of statuary placed in the grounds for decorative purposes, so motionless is he and almost part of the natural background.*

SEPTIMUS *and* WILLIAM *rush onto the stage like an enthusiastic variety act, and begin to sing.*

SEPTIMUS/WILLIAM [*to the tune of* The Miller of Dee]
When Andrew first from Ireland came,
Robinson Stoney was his name;
His income being rather low,
Into the army he did go:
It's true a Lieutenant he became
(of Captain he had but the name);
For three and sixpence was the pay
The bugger got from day to day.

> [*The song over,* SEPTIMUS *and* WILLIAM *settle down to a stroll round the estate. They both have Geordie accents.*]

SEPTIMUS I tell you, Bill, the bugger's after yer mistress.

WILLIAM Ye're fucking joking, Sep! Captain Stoney's after her ladyship, and him just a fucking captain?

SEPTIMUS A captain? He's a fucking lieutenant, that's what he is. He likes to be called cap'n. And if I doan' call him cap'n I'm in for a flogging. And not a penny to his name. Stoney by name and stony broke.

WILLIAM  By! Broke you say?

SEPTIMUS  Not a pot to piss in.

WILLIAM  What aboot Hanna Newton's money? Don't tell me he's been through all her brass? And her not dead a year...

SEPTIMUS  Aye. Ah reckon he helped her on her way an' all.

WILLIAM  Fucking murdered her you mean?

SEPTIMUS  Aye.

WILLIAM  An' you reckon he's after shafting Lady Strathmore?

SEPTIMUS  Aye. More bollocks than brains, man. He'll be up her flue afore the summer's oot, mark me words lad.

WILLIAM  Like as not, if I know her ladyship. Her's been a widder these fahwer months...

SEPTIMUS  Fancies a bit o' movement in her cockpit, does she?

WILLIAM  A bit? It's perpetual motion she'd like.

SEPTIMUS  Partial to a bit o' late milking is she?

WILLIAM  Aye. An' a mouthful of new bread fer good measure.

SEPTIMUS  Champion! That's what the cap'n likes.

WILLIAM  Then your master's the coming man.

SEPTIMUS  Aye. Comes all the time, does the bugger.

WILLIAM  Is he after her brass as well?

SEPTIMUS  Aye.

WILLIAM  He won't be so lucky.

SEPTIMUS  Is her ladyship a bit near?

WILLIAM  Aye. A tight purse and a slack grip: that's her.

SEPTIMUS  [*wistfully*] Fuck me!

WILLIAM  [*sceptically*] Who would?

[*They walk away, as* DR FOOT *comes to life and slowly and deliberately moves centre stage, his eyes still following the departing pair.*]

DR FOOT  There they go. Two servants. Venal to the core and utterly unprincipled. Little do they realise that two hundred years later their simple exchanges, so refreshingly steeped in profanity, would have made them a fortune on the London stage.

[*Blackout.*]

## SCENE 2:
## HOW STONEY TREATED HANNA

*1775. At* STONEY's *and* HANNA's *house, Cold Pike Hill, Lanchester, County Durham.*

HANNA, *her back to the audience, and sobbing, pours something into a medicine glass and drinks it.*

SEPTIMUS *enters carrying a chair, which he places somewhere in the room. He is clearly used to* HANNA's *tears, and he quietly arranges the furniture and begins to leave the room.*

HANNA [*whose back is turned on* SEPTIMUS, *stops crying.*] Is that you, Septimus?

SEPTIMUS Aye, missus.

> [HANNA *turns round, and a shaft of sunlight catches her features dramatically: she has bruises on her face and arms, and a black eye.*]

HANNA Has my husband come back?

SEPTIMUS Not that I know of.

HANNA He's been away three days.

SEPTIMUS Aye, that he has.

HANNA I've been very sick, Sep.

SEPTIMUS Aye. Dr Foot was telling us.

HANNA You know I lost the baby ...

SEPTIMUS I'm that sorry, Mrs Stoney.

HANNA Three days ago. My third miscarriage.

SEPTIMUS Aye.

HANNA I was at death's door, you know.

SEPTIMUS You warn't well. Dr Foot was telling us —

HANNA [*interrupting*] I nearly died.

SEPTIMUS You were that poorly. Aye.

HANNA When my husband was told it was a still birth he had the church bells rung. As if the infant'd been born alive.

SEPTIMUS [*embarrassed*] Aye, missus. But don't take on —

HANNA Then he hit me. [*She begins to sob again.*]

SEPTIMUS Look, missus ...

HANNA Then he went hunting. And he hasn't been back these three days.

SEPTIMUS D'ye need anything?

HANNA I'm in pain, Septimus.

SEPTIMUS Shall I fetch Dr Foot?

HANNA What'd be the good of that?

SEPTIMUS He'll look at them bruises. Put some ointment on.

HANNA Dr Foot is his friend.

    [SEPTIMUS *makes no reply, but stares at the floor.*]

I have no friends.

SEPTIMUS Shall I fetch your maid? She'll help you to bed.

STONEY [*Off. He has a slight Irish brogue.*] Bland! Septimus Bland! Corporal Bland! Where are you, you dog?

SEPTIMUS In here, sir!

STONEY [*enters, in riding clothes, sweating and in a towering rage.*] Ah there you are! Go and take care of my horse. This instant!

    [*As* SEPTIMUS *leaves,* STONEY *whacks him on his back with his riding crop.*]

Lazy bastard! [*He collapses onto an armchair and looks around.*] Oh...! What have we here — Ah, the mother of my dead children!

HANNA Please, Andrew...

STONEY You infertile slut! How dare you look me in the eye!

    [*He viciously pinches and twists the lobe of* HANNA's *ear. She stifles a cry of pain.*]

HANNA I'm not well... I think I'm going to die...

STONEY Good riddance, madam! Hurry up and die! Then I can re-marry and have heirs.

HANNA They tell me that you and Mrs Phipps —

| STONEY | What? Spying on me again? Yes, Mrs Phipps has thrown pups — two Stoney twin bastards, if you must know. |
|---|---|
| HANNA | How could you ...? |

[STONEY *goes up to her and begins to beat her savagely about the face with the open palm of his right hand, tearing off her clothes with his left, as he pushes towards a broom cupboard. By the time they reach it she is virtually naked.* STONEY *opens the cupboard door and pushes her into it. He then kicks the door shut and bolts it.*]

[*A knock at the door.*]

| STONEY | Who is it? |
|---|---|
| SEPTIMUS | [*opening the door*] Dr Foot, captain. |
| STONEY | Show him in. |
| SEPTIMUS | Sir. This way, doctor. |
| DR FOOT | You're back, Captain Stoney. |
| STONEY | I am, doctor. And not in need of your services. |
| DR FOOT | I'll grant you that. Though you are a little grey about the gills. But I hear your wife is poorly. |
| STONEY | Is she? |
| DR FOOT | She had a miscarriage not four days ago. |

[STONEY *grunts.*]

| DR FOOT | And three months ago I treated her for a broken jaw. |
|---|---|
| STONEY | The woman's unsteady on her legs. |
| DR FOOT | Could it be due to the laudanum you encourage her to take? |
| STONEY | Come doctor, you know perfectly well it helps keep her quiet. |
| DR FOOT | You treat her harshly, sir. |
| STONEY | I'm a soldier, doctor. |
| DR FOOT | You seldom show mercy to her. |
| STONEY | That's my business. |
| DR FOOT | The whole county knows about it. There is such a thing as the law. |
| STONEY | I am an officer and a gentleman. The woman's been |

disobedient. She goes about in rags. She has failed to bear children. She has brought me nothing but trouble.

DR FOOT   She brought you a fortune of thirty thousand pounds.

STONEY   There's not much of it left. Besides, that's something I told you in confidence, sir.

DR FOOT   And in confidence, sir, I tell you Mrs Stoney will not live long if you continue to treat her as you do. She is seriously ill.

STONEY   Nonsense! Besides, it's entirely her fault. Women, my dear doctor, are like dogs: they should respond to training and jump to their master's commands. My wife does neither. She must take the consequences.

DR FOOT   My dear sir, I beg you —

> [*He stops as whimpers issue from the bolted cupboard, followed by a dull thud.*]

What's that?

STONEY   [*unconcerned*] Mice?

> [*Slow fadeout, as a funeral bell tolls.*]


## SCENE 3:
## THE GAME OF THE NAME: NAME-SWAPPING AND OTHER ACQUISITIVE CUSTOMS OF THE BRITISH NOBILITY

*1767: London. The Park.*

*The opening Prelude of Charpentier's* Te Deum. *As it is played out, and during the subsequent song,* MARY ELEANOR BOWES, *flanked by* JOHN LYON, 9TH EARL OF STRATHMORE AND KINGHORNE, *both in court dress, promenade with great pomp along a path with a changing background.* SEPTIMUS, WILLIAM *and* BELLA, *attired as court singers, are grouped as a trio upstage left and begin to sing after the opening bars of the Prelude.*

SEPTIMUS/WILLIAM/BELLA   [*to the tune of the Prelude of Charpentier's* Te Deum]

See each face, with smiles look gay,
'Tis Mary Eleanor's Natal Day!

Fortune, we defy thy frown,
Mary comes to bless the town:
Jocund spirit and merry glee
Hail this Queen of Liberty!
Sound the trumpet, fill the bowl,
Revel all without control;
Phoebus! thy resplendent Ray
Shine upon her Natal Day;
Fill with shouts the ambient air,
Happy, happy, happy pair!

[*A final flourish of trumpets and the singers exit.*]

STRATHMORE   I saw you at Almack's the other night. You danced divinely.

MARY   You did, my lord? Did I?

STRATHMORE   Hm... You were dancing with young Cunningham-Hogg.

MARY   I had such a full programme! A great many gentlemen claimed my attention.

STRATHMORE   I'd hardly describe Cunningham-Hogg as a gentleman. Is he paying his addresses to you?

MARY   If he is, I certainly haven't noticed. Besides, my mama has warned me never to trust a man with a hyphen.

STRATHMORE   Very sensible advice. Especially in Cunningham-Hogg's case. But surely her warning doesn't extend to the nobility?

MARY   What do you mean, my lord?

STRATHMORE   As luck would have it, most of us, alas, are simply deluged with compound names through our titles of honour ... and hyphens often intrude.

MARY   I am sure mama would be bound to make an exception in such cases.

STRATHMORE   I feel I must speak to Mrs Bowes. Very soon. In fact, this very day. Is she in London?

MARY   You will find her at number forty, Grosvenor Square.

STRATHMORE   Capital! But first, Miss Bowes ... may I call you Mary?

MARY   [*coquettishly*] Mmm ... oh, very well.

STRATHMORE  Mary ... I ... [*He takes her hand and squeezes it, looking at her with longing.*] Mary, will you — ?

MARY  Lord Strathmore, if a formal proposal is what you have in mind, pray go no further. All such declarations must be lodged with my mother in the first place. I must warn you though that she may raise objections.

STRATHMORE  What might they be?

MARY  The number of your relations ... your mother ... and so many brothers and sisters. Your delicate state of health. But chiefly, I fear, your being a Scotsman. I hasten to add that none of these obstacles is insurmountable.

STRATHMORE  In that case I will call on your mother directly. But please don't deny me the opportunity of ... testing the waters.

MARY  But sir —

STRATHMORE  [*holds up his hand*] Please. Mary: I, John Lyon, Baron Glamis, Baron Tannadyce, Baron Sidlaw, Baron Strathdichtie, Viscount Lyon, 9th Earl of Strathmore and Kinghorne in the peerage of Scotland do hereby propose ... nay beseech you, Mary Eleanor Bowes, to become my lawful wedded wife —

MARY  [*cutting in*] Yes — but will you change your name?

STRATHMORE  [*in some astonishment*] What?

MARY  You are clearly not familiar with the terms of my late papa's last will and testament.

STRATHMORE  Well, rumour has it it was somewhat eccentric.

MARY  Papa was a cautious man. You are not unaware I am a woman of some substance?

STRATHMORE  Not entirely.

MARY  Yours is a glorious name, my lord, but your estates hardly match mine.

STRATHMORE  You are well informed, Mary.

MARY  I make it my business to be. Papa decided long ago that whoever married me should adopt Bowes as a family name.

STRATHMORE  But it'll require an Act of Parliament!

MARY [*triumphantly*] And what a splendid sign of devotion that will be on your part! The whole world will be made aware of your love for me!

STRATHMORE But ... we can prove royal descent in the female line! We bear the royal bearings — the tressure, the unicorn and the garlanded maid — to this day. Why, the name of Lyon has been in the family for centuries!

MARY Then drop the mangy old beast and add a Bowes to your string!

[*Pause, as they continue their walk.*]

STRATHMORE Perhaps Mrs Bowes will allow me to spend a few days at Gibside once our engagement has been announced. I am told your father worked wonders with the grounds.

MARY Papa was a genius with gardens. He wouldn't dream of asking Capability Brown to lend a hand, though he offered. But when you do come, get your man to pack lots of changes of clothes.

STRATHMORE Why, pray?

MARY Gibside is straddling all those boring coalmines ... So much coal dust about ... I can't think why they call it black gold.

STRATHMORE [*an anticipatory smile*] Indeed!

MARY According to a recent survey, our mines are larger than the entire county, and burrow simply miles deep into the earth.

STRATHMORE How fascinating!

MARY Have no fear. If the wind raises too much coal dust at Gibside, mama will spirit us away to Streatlam Castle, or even as far south as our place at St Paul's Walden.

STRATHMORE Mary Eleanor, you have made me a happy man.

MARY My lord, welcome to the family!

[*They embrace and kiss with great formality, to the accompaniment of the closing triumphal phrase of the Prelude to Charpentier's* Te Deum.]

[*Fadeout.*]

## SCENE 4:
## GIBSIDE — ALL THE WEALTH OF THE NORTH

*Gibside. 1767.* DR FOOT *and* LORD STRATHMORE.

STRATHMORE   You'll let me have some of that physic, doctor, won't you?

DR FOOT   I'll make it up presently for you, my lord. I gather you enjoyed good weather on your nuptial journey to Glamis.

STRATHMORE   Yes. But the east wind was too much for me. [*He coughs.*] My wife agrees with you that Gibside and the north aren't suitable for my condition.

DR FOOT   No, my lord. You should travel south as soon as possible.

STRATHMORE   You forget, doctor, that family interests detain me here. It is my duty to assist Lady Strathmore in the administration of her not inconsiderable fortune.

[*He coughs.*]

DR FOOT   Surely her man of business could attend to that?

STRATHMORE   A mere employee. I promised my wife I would attend to business matters for her. It cannot be left to clerks. The cultivation of one's interests is akin to an agricultural endeavour: it requires constant fertilisation. And the best manure is the farmer's foot.

DR FOOT   A wise precept, my lord. I gather her ladyship's mother lavished the most remarkable presents on your bride.

STRATHMORE   She has been most generous. [ *He suddenly comes alive.*] Why, the diamond stomacher she gave her cost more than ten thousand pounds ... and she gave her other diamonds worth another ten thousand.

DR FOOT   Really, my lord!

STRATHMORE   She also gave her a green landau, a blue post coach and a stone-coloured post chaise ... And remind me to show you the rest of the plate and jewels ... There's a great deal to attend to merely listing these items ...

DR FOOT   I understand, my lord. But you should avoid taxing your strength.

STRATHMORE   You may not realise it, doctor, but there are thousands of acres here in Durham and in Yorkshire and Middlesex under cultivation ... not to mention ... [*He lowers his tone and raises an index finger.*] ... black gold. And you've no doubt heard of the new iron works at Blaydon — the most advanced in Europe, I'm told.

DR FOOT   Really!

STRATHMORE   [*with the innocent fervour of a child showing off his toys*] Doctor, in confidence, of course, have you any idea of the extent of Lady Strathmore's estate?

DR FOOT   Well, I —

STRATHMORE   It was valued at six hundred thousand pounds on her father's death.

DR FOOT   [*registers astonishment*] Well ... I ...

STRATHMORE   Quite so, doctor. And that's mostly on the surface, so to speak ... [*He taps his cane on the ground.*] We keep sinking new shafts and discovering fresh seams.

DR FOOT   [*with a knowing grimace*] Black gold?

STRATHMORE   Of the highest quality. [*relishing the thought*] I tell you I may have to spend the rest of my life cooped up in the counting house just to keep track of things.

DR FOOT   Take care, my lord. You need rest. Don't forget what I prescribed.

STRATHMORE   Ah, yes, doctor. Thank you for reminding me. First the waters at Bristol. Then Portugal. [*puzzled*] Why Portugal ...?

DR FOOT   [*loftily*] The dry climate.

STRATHMORE   Of course. I promise you I'll be off before the month is out. [*He coughs.*]

[*Fadeout.*]

## SCENE 5:
## 1776. AT ALMACK'S CLUB, ST JAMES'S.
## THE HOUR STRIKES FOR THE COUNTESS TO DALLY ...

    GEORGE GREY *and* DR FOOT *at a table. The sound of dance music in adjoining rooms.*

DR FOOT    Your very good health, Mr Grey.

GREY    [*raises his glass*] Yours, doctor. I was sorry to hear of Lord Strathmore's death. Patient of yours, I hear.

DR FOOT    Indeed. But there was little medical science could do to help. He was beyond the reach of my ministrations.

GREY    Literally so, I understand: he died at sea, did he not?

DR FOOT    Off Lisbon, to be precise. Five months ago to the day.

GREY    Lady Strathmore did say he was taking a cure in Portugal.

DR FOOT    On my advice. It did him a power of good.

GREY    Oh?

DR FOOT    Er ... initially, at any rate, judging from letters from a colleague of mine on the spot.

GREY    I see.

DR FOOT    His condition was too advanced to make recovery even a remote possibility. His appetite began to fail.

GREY    Not so his thirst, I'll wager: as I remember on slight acquaintance, his lordship was ever a good bottle companion.

DR FOOT    And that probably extended his life. I prescribed four bottles of claret and one pint of brandy as part of his daily intake, and he found no difficulty in following my instructions. Indeed he sometimes exceeded that measure.

GREY    Did he, by Jove?

DR FOOT    The late Lord Strathmore was an excellent patient.

GREY    A sad business. You may take it from me that his widow is inconsolable ... indeed has been since his death last April.

[DR FOOT *raises a sceptical eyebrow.*]

I've done my best to be in attendance whenever I was needed, given the circumstances ...

DR FOOT   Quite.

GREY   ... and I flatter myself I have been of some use to her.

DR FOOT   I've no doubt you have been, Mr Grey.

MARY   [*off*] George! George! Where are you?

> [*She sweeps into the room in an extravagant ball gown, the only hint of her recent bereavement a large artificial black rose embedded between her amply visible breasts.*]

Oh there you are, George.

> [*The two men rise.*]

GREY   Yes, my dear ...

MARY   They've danced me off my feet. [*She notices the* DOCTOR.] Dr Foot ...

DR FOOT   Your servant, Lady Strathmore. The black rose is most becoming.

MARY   Thank you. As you know I'm still in mourning. [*She fussily rearranges the flower.*] One must show some respect. What brings you here, doctor?

DR FOOT   I'm escorting Lord Westmorland ... one of my patients. He's not at all well, but insisted on coming. He used to be fond of dancing, but is now confined to a wheelchair.

MARY   You'd better go to him then. He got out of his contraption, desperate to join the last quadrille and has just collapsed. He gives no signs of life.

DR FOOT   Heavens! I'll attend to him immediately. If you'll excuse me ...

> [*He rushes out of the room.*]

MARY   George, take me home.

GREY   So early?

MARY   It's past midnight.

GREY   That's hardly late for you, my dear.

| | |
|---|---|
| MARY | [*in an amorous undertone*] We have things to talk about in private, George. |
| GREY | Again? It's barely two hours since our last conversazione. |
| MARY | You know how talkative dancing makes me, George! Don't tell me you're taking vows of silence ... |
| GREY | No, your ladyship. That would be impossible in your society. |
| MARY | Let's go, then. |
| GREY | I'll have your carriage called. [*He snaps his fingers at a passing* STEWARD.] Lady Strathmore's carriage, please! |
| | [*The* STEWARD *bows and exits, just as* STONEY *enters and sits at a table.*] |
| MARY | Who is that? |
| GREY | A neighbour of yours at Gibside. Captain Stoney. |
| MARY | I've heard of him. Hasn't he a place at Burnopfield? |
| GREY | Cold Pike Hill. |
| MARY | Is he a serving officer? |
| GREY | On half pay, I believe. |
| MARY | He looks interesting. Haven't I heard something about him? |
| GREY | He has a bad reputation. He lost his wife not long ago. |
| MARY | Now I remember. He married poor Hanna Newton! |
| GREY | Yes. |
| MARY | Introduce me, George ... |
| GREY | I don't think I should. |
| MARY | [*petulantly*] And why not? |
| GREY | He's hardly a gentleman. Besides, your carriage is at the door. |
| MARY | [*imperiously*] Let it wait, and do as I ask. |
| GREY | Must I? |
| MARY | [*in a gentler tone*] Please. If you're good, tomorrow we'll start making plans about marriage. |
| GREY | Mary ... will you really? |
| MARY | A decent interval must elapse, of course. Then you'll be able to take a hand in running the estate. |

| | |
|---|---|
| GREY | You'll let me? |
| MARY | Provided the trustees allow me to. |
| GREY | They've got things pretty well tied up ... And so have you. |
| MARY | It was papa's idea. To keep big grey sharks at bay ... |
| GREY | Really, Mary! How could you think — |
| MARY | Shh! More of this tomorrow. [*She pats* GEORGE's *hand.*] And now introduce me to this gallant officer. |
| GREY | Very well. [*He rises and walks over to* STONEY's *table.*] Captain Stoney, I presume. |
| STONEY | [*a glimmer of recognition*] Mr Grey? Mr George Grey? |
| GREY | We've met before, sir. Lady Strathmore would like to make your acquaintance. Won't you join us? |
| STONEY | [*rises*] Lady Strathmore's wishes are my command, Mr Grey. |
| | [*The two men bow to each other and make their way to* MARY's *table.*] |
| GREY | Your ladyship, allow me to introduce Captain Stoney ... |
| STONEY | ... of the 30th Regiment of Foot. [*He bows.*] Your servant, ma'am. |
| MARY | I understand we're neighbours, Captain. Cold Pig Hill ...? |
| STONEY | Cold Pike Hill. Neighbours, you say? In the sense that the sun is close to the moon I dare say we are neighbours. Alas, Cold Pike Hill could never hope to rival the splendour of Gibside. |
| MARY | You know Gibside? |
| STONEY | From a distance. The column topped by the statue of liberty in the park is a beacon to the whole county. |
| MARY | You must pay us a visit, Captain. George will you arrange it? |
| GREY | [*grudgingly*] Mm. Very well. |
| MARY | In fact, come and stay. |
| STONEY | Thank you. |
| MARY | Do you hunt? |
| STONEY | Whenever possible. |
| MARY | Splendid! That's settled then. George ... my carriage is wait- |

ing? [GREY *rises and nods.*] Then good night, Captain Stoney. You will be hearing from me.

STONEY [*bows*] Your ladyship.

> [LADY STRATHMORE *and* GREY *leave the room.* STONEY *sits at the table they've just vacated and drinks from* LADY STRATHMORE's glass. *He refills it and drinks again.*]
>
> [*Fadeout.*]


## SCENE 6:
## ... AND WITH THE HOUR COMES THE MAN.
## STONEY PRESSES HIS SUIT

*Gibside. Autumn 1776.* DR FOOT *and* STONEY *are taking a turn in the grounds.*

DR FOOT  Will you be staying long?

STONEY  Lady Strathmore has been most hospitable. But I shall have to leave in a day or so. I have business at Cold Pike Hill.

DR FOOT  [*turns to admire the front elevation of the house*] Magnificent, don't you think?

STONEY  [*also turns to look at the house. He is silent for a few seconds, then as if to himself*] What a fine place to plunder!

DR FOOT  I beg your pardon?

STONEY  [*matter-of-fact*] Magnificent? So it is, by thunder!

DR FOOT  Is young George Grey staying too?

STONEY  Young George Grey? He's more than ten years my senior, doctor. India aged him before his time.

DR FOOT  Quite. But ... is he staying?

STONEY  He is not. Her ladyship does not find his society congenial any longer.

DR FOOT  I see. I must say I am surprised.

STONEY  Why?

| | |
|---|---|
| DR FOOT | There was talk of a closer future relationship with her ladyship. |
| STONEY | There are always rumours of the kind. Trust the gazettes to spread them. |
| DR FOOT | You are I take it referring to the *Morning Post*. Why, only the other day her ladyship was abused and vilified in that very paper over her possible contemplation of marriage with Mr Grey. |
| STONEY | You will find that accusation refuted in tomorrow's issue. |
| DR FOOT | Tomorrow's ....? How do you — ? Oh, I see. |
| STONEY | If any further smears of the kind should appear in that rag, the editor will have to answer to me, and take the consequences. |
| DR FOOT | The editor? You mean Parson Bate? |
| STONEY | I do indeed mean the Reverend Henry Bate, a disgrace to his cloth and a poor example to honest folk! |
| DR FOOT | As I remember, the article condemned her ladyship for considering remarriage so soon after the death of her husband. [*pointedly*] The precedent of Hamlet's mother was freely quoted. |
| STONEY | The cad will pay for it, I promise you, doctor. And mark my words, you will find another attack on Lady Strathmore in next Monday's issue. |
| DR FOOT | I'm at a loss to understand how you can predict all this. |
| STONEY | [*laughs*] That is not important, doctor. |
| DR FOOT | Wheels within wheels? |
| STONEY | Quite so. Lady Strathmore's reputation is sacred to me. I'll leave no stone unturned to defend it. I'll use fair means or foul! |
| DR FOOT | You speak of the subject with some warmth, sir. Are you by any chance ...? |
| STONEY | Suffice it to say, doctor, that I admire Lady Strathmore. |
| DR FOOT | As we all do. From a distance. |
| STONEY | Let us say that my admiration goes beyond the impersonal. |

| | |
|---|---|
| DR FOOT | [*ingratiatingly*] Why, I am delighted to hear it, sir... And here comes her ladyship ... |
| | [LADY STRATHMORE *enters. The black rose in her cleavage has been replaced by a more colourful bloom.*] |
| MARY | My dear Captain Stoney, I thought you were out riding. |
| STONEY | [*bows*] I was indeed, your ladyship. But earlier this morning. Much earlier. |
| MARY | You are an early bird, sir. Doctor ... one of my chambermaids has the vapours. Would you mind — ? |
| DR FOOT | I'll see her immediately, your ladyship. If you'll excuse me ... |
| | [*He raises his hat as he leaves.*] |
| MARY | Dear Doctor Foot ... he's getting old. We only keep him for the servants now. |
| STONEY | He's a good man to have around. |
| MARY | Was he not your personal physician? |
| STONEY | He still is. |
| MARY | I understand your late wife was one of his patients. |
| STONEY | She was. You knew Hanna? |
| MARY | When I was a little girl. She was brought up to my nursery to play with me. Then we ... inevitably... lost sight of each other. Did she grow up to be a beauty? |
| STONEY | I fear not. The late Mrs Stoney was short, dark, and not at all handsome. |
| MARY | Then her spiritual qualities must have attracted you ... |
| STONEY | [*darkly*] I dare say. |
| MARY | ... which shows you to be a man of great sensibility. |
| STONEY | You flatter me, Lady Strathmore. |
| MARY | Something tells me we're going to be great friends. I shall be able to confirm this next week in London. |
| STONEY | How so? |
| MARY | On Thursday next I have an appointment with Monsieur Calostro, the clairvoyant. He gives consultations in a private room at Almack's. [*She wags her finger at* STONEY.] |

|   | He'll be able to tell me who are my true or false friends. |
|---|---|
| STONEY | You believe in fortune tellers, Lady Strathmore? |
| MARY | Naturally. [*She offers her arm for him to take.*] But I think the time has come for you to call me Mary Eleanor. In private, that is. |
| STONEY | You are too kind. |
| MARY | Since we're going to be friends, may I call you ... Andrew? |
| STONEY | [*emboldened*] Indeed you may, Mary Eleanor. |
| MARY | It was only last month that we met at Almack's ... And yet I feel I've known you all my life. |
| STONEY | I share that feeling, Mary Eleanor. |

> [*He hazards an affectionate move, which is not rejected.*]

|   |   |
|---|---|
| MARY | I find it easy to talk to you. And I enjoy listening to you. Has anyone ever told you your conversation is exceptionally pleasing? |
| STONEY | Spare my blushes, please. |
| MARY | I am devoted to elevated talk. |
| STONEY | [*begins to kiss her neck and shoulders*] So am I, my dear. So am I. |
| MARY | [*reciprocating his attentions*] Oh ... yes. Yes! |
| STONEY | Mary Eleanor! |
| MARY | Shall we continue this conversazione in the folly over there? I feel you're going to be very talkative ... |

[*Blackout.*]

## SCENE 7:
## STONEY BRIBES A FORTUNE TELLER

*A dimly lit private room at Almack's. Winter 1776.*

MONSIEUR CALOSTRO, *in a multicoloured Eastern robe and turban, and what looks suspiciously like a false beard and moustache, is sitting at a table polishing a crystal ball with a silk bandanna.*

SEPTIMUS BLAND *enters on tiptoe and approaches* CALOSTRO, *who raises his head from his task.*

SEPTIMUS *is about to speak but* CALOSTRO *raises a hand enjoining silence.* SEPTIMUS *whispers in* CALOSTRO*'s ear.*

CALOSTRO *listens, then shakes his head vigorously, and resumes polishing the crystal ball.*

SEPTIMUS *taps* CALOSTRO *on the shoulder, smiles, bends down to whisper something again, and eventually produces a purse, which he dangles before* CALOSTRO*'s eyes.*

CALOSTRO *hesitates, then takes the purse and examines its contents. He sighs, shrugs his shoulders, and pockets the purse within an inner garment. Then he slowly takes off his robe, turban, and with surprising ease his beard and moustache. He hands these items one by one to* SEPTIMUS, *who places them on the table.* CALOSTRO *leaves the room by one door just as* STONEY *enters through another. Silently, he approaches the table and begins to put on robe, turban and beard. Having completed his disguise, he sits down at the table, and* SEPTIMUS *bows to his master and leaves the room.*

*A knock at the door.*

STONEY   Enter.

MARY   Monsieur Calostro, I am —

STONEY   [*in a disembodied voice*] I know who you are, madam. Please sit down.

    [MARY *complies.*]

Have we not met before?

MARY   No. Madame Belinda, who has a consulting room in Crown Court, told me you could help me.

STONEY   To advise you on a possible matrimonial adventure?

MARY   You knew!

STONEY   Of course.

MARY   There are two men, you see —

STONEY   [*nods knowingly*] The younger one, from across the Irish sea, seems the more suitable.

| | |
|---|---|
| MARY | You know about Mr Grey too? |
| STONEY | I do. |
| MARY | And about the fact that I am carrying his child? |
| | [STONEY *involuntarily betrays shocked surprise by a sudden movement, but quickly recovers his composure.*] |
| STONEY | Yes. |
| MARY | I am greatly concerned. |
| STONEY | I am not surprised. |
| MARY | You see, though Strathmore and I were married for some years, we latterly led separate lives. Mr Grey has been a great comfort to me. |
| STONEY | So it seems. |
| MARY | I need a great deal of affection. |
| STONEY | You intend to continue your liaison with him? |
| MARY | What do you advise? |
| STONEY | All I can do is echo your innermost feelings, of which you are not consciously aware. Among other things, you feel he has shown an excessive interest in your wealth. |
| MARY | So he has. |
| STONEY | I said it before: deep down, you wish to end your dealings with Mr Grey. He is therefore to be dismissed. There is another who loves you. You may rely on him. |
| MARY | The Irish officer? |
| STONEY | The same. You have granted him your favours, I think. |
| MARY | He's a most attractive man. I am very susceptible to masculine charm. |
| STONEY | I am aware of that. |
| MARY | He is ... reliable, you think? |
| STONEY | He is the soul of probity, Lady Strathmore. |
| MARY | I feel greatly reassured. |
| STONEY | You may embark with him on life's uncertain voyage with perfect confidence. |

[MARY *fumbles in her purse and produces a coin.*]

MARY     Thank you, Monsieur Calostro!

> [*She places the coin on a bowl on the table.* STONEY *raises his hand in respectful leavetaking and bows his head without rising.*]

STONEY     Milady ....

> [MARY *leaves.*]
>
> [*Fadeout.*]


## SCENE 8:
## THE COUNTESS HAS A LOOSE LEG

*A room at 40, Grosvenor Square. Winter 1776.*

MARY *is sitting at a writing-table.* GREY *dashes in unannounced.*

GREY     Mary!

MARY     [*turns to face him with cold formality*] Mr Grey. I don't think you were announced. Or expected.

GREY     Never mind all that. Why won't you answer my letters?

MARY     We have said to each other all that there is to say.

GREY     You mean you have said all you wanted to say.

MARY     It's over, George.

GREY     But your mother thinks we're going to be married.

MARY     She's been informed the engagement has been ended.

GREY     But ... announcements have been made ...

MARY     We'll issue new ones.

GREY     Aren't you concerned about the papers?

MARY     Papers? What papers?

GREY     All of them. The *Morning Post* in particular. About you and me. About you and Stoney. [*He lowers his voice to an angry hiss.*] About you and one of your servants!

MARY     I think it's rather charming of them to pay so much atten-

|        | tion. Why, the *Post* refers to this house as The Temple of Folly. Isn't it amusing? |
|--------|---|
| GREY   | Mary, this cannot go on. Don't you mind all the gossip? |
| MARY   | One cannot avoid being a victim to rumour if one is at all prominent. |
| GREY   | Rumour? There seems to be a great deal of truth in all those anonymous letters to the press. |
| MARY   | I wonder who could possibly be responsible for them. |
| GREY   | I can tell you that: the Irishman. |
| MARY   | Captain Stoney? Don't be absurd. It is just possible, though, that he could be the one who wrote the letters in my defence. |
| GREY   | As well as the ones attacking you! |
| MARY   | You're beginning to bore me, George. |
| GREY   | I tell you Stoney is in league with the papers. And with your Strathmore relations. He's trying to ruin my reputation! |
| MARY   | Your reputation, George? Have you one? Now, go to your club and play with your friends. |
| GREY   | I will not be treated like a junior clerk in the East India Company! |
| MARY   | [*sarcastically*] Which of course you once were. |
| GREY   | You wish to add humiliation to my distress? |
| MARY   | Why not go back to India, George? Remember those dancing girls you told me about during our more intimate moments? I'm sure you miss their athletic contortions. |
| GREY   | Must you be coarse? |
| MARY   | You once found it stimulating. |
| GREY   | Mary, this is intolerable! |
| MARY   | [*in final dismissal*] Goodbye, Mr Grey. |

[GREY *storms out of the room.* WILLIAM STAMP *enters.*]

| WILLIAM | Forgive me, milady. I couldn't stop him when he arrived. He rushed past me as I opened the door. |
|---------|---|
| MARY    | Never mind, William. But please remember he is not to be admitted ever again. |

| | |
|---|---|
| WILLIAM | Very good, milady. |
| MARY | Tell the other members of the household, won't you? |
| WILLIAM | I will. |
| MARY | And send Bella to me. I think I'll go to bed soon. |
| WILLIAM | [*respectfully, though with quiet complicity*] Will you be wanting anything ... later on? |
| MARY | I don't think so. |
| WILLIAM | Very good, your ladyship. [*He leaves.*] |
| MARY | Goodnight. |

[MARY *begins to write some letters.* BELLA *enters.*]

| | |
|---|---|
| BELLA | You sent for me, milady? |
| MARY | Yes Bella. I think I'll retire soon. Is my room ready? |
| BELLA | It is. |
| MARY | Remember that Mr Grey is not to be admitted from today on. I've already told William. |
| BELLA | Very well. |
| MARY | See to it that Mr Grey's personal effects are returned to him. From Grosvenor Square and Gibside. |
| BELLA | It will be done. |

[*A knock at the door.*]

| | |
|---|---|
| MARY | Yes? |
| WILLIAM | [*enters*] Captain Stoney is here to see you. |
| MARY | At this hour? Show him in. That'll be all, Bella. |

[STONEY *enters, as* BELLA *exits.*]

| | |
|---|---|
| STONEY | Your ladyship ... |
| MARY | Why, Captain Stoney — |

[*The moment they are alone, she rushes to embrace him.*]

Andrew! How did you know I was longing for you!

| | |
|---|---|
| STONEY | It's the second sight we have, your ladyship, across the water. [*They kiss passionately. Then, without further ado:*] Here ...? |
| MARY | Andrew! Won't you have some refreshment first? |

STONEY   [*pours himself a drink from a decanter on a side table*] There have been developments.

MARY   Oh?

STONEY   I've warned Mr Bate, the editor of the *Morning Post*, I will not countenance the gossip about you.

MARY   But Andrew, I find it all quite amusing!

STONEY   No, Mary, it's unforgivable. Think of your standing in society. Of your children.

MARY   I'm not concerned with the Strathmore brats.

STONEY   Yes, but think of Lord Strathmore. Or his family.

MARY   I loathe his family. My money's all they're interested in. As he was. The late Lord Strathmore was fortunate that all my five children were his. Not every wife in my position — bored to distraction by her husband — could claim he was the father of all her children.

STONEY   Even so, my dear, I won't have your name traduced.

MARY   What do you intend to do, my gallant knight?

STONEY   I shall challenge the blackguard to a duel.

MARY   To a duel? Parson Bate? He's a clergyman.

STONEY   A clergyman indeed! They call him the fighting parson: he'll pick a fight at the slightest excuse — and I'll give him one.

MARY   Andrew, you're not to take risks on my behalf.

STONEY   You know I'd lay down my life for you.

MARY   A few paragraphs in the prints are hardly worth the danger.

STONEY   You forget I'm a soldier!

MARY   How could I forget? But I prefer to decide where the field of battle should be. Your gallantry is exclusively my preserve.

STONEY   My mind's made up. You shall not be insulted.

MARY   Please, my dear ...

STONEY   I promise you, though, I shall let him live provided he apologises and desists from publishing any further attacks on you, or indeed prints any letters, for or against.

MARY   Come here.

STONEY  [*goes to her*] Yes?

MARY  Sit down.

STONEY  [*sits next to her*] Well?

MARY  [*wagging an admonishing finger*] I shall have to talk to you very severely.

STONEY  Oh? Now?

MARY  Now.

STONEY  Here?

MARY  [*begins to recline on the sofa, pulling* STONEY *towards her*] Here. Now!

[*Blackout.*]


## SCENE 9:
## THE DUEL WITH PARSON BATE

*At the Adelphi Tavern. 13th January 1777.*

STONEY *and* PARSON BATE *are sharing a table in a private room. Several jugs of wine are on the table. The two are on the best of terms and have clearly been sitting here convivially for some time. On another table by the entrance door, clearly visible to the audience, are two duelling swords and two pistols.*

BATE  [*laughs*] By Jove, you're a character, Captain Stoney. And a good host — and a good host, I'll grant you that.

STONEY  Thank you, Bate.

BATE  You've a way with people, you Irish. I doubt I can bring myself to fight you, sir, even if it's all a masquerade.

STONEY  Which reminds me — this should help you decide.

[*He throws him a purse, which* BATE *fails to catch and picks up from the floor.*]

BATE  [*briefly examines contents*] I'll fight you, captain. I'll even inflict the slight wound you require.

STONEY  [*alarmed*] Just a nick or two, Bate — draw a little blood, but that's to be all.

| | |
|---|---|
| BATE | Fine. Then ... you'll fire a pistol ... in the air ... |
| STONEY | ... and that will be the signal for my man Septimus to break into the room and stop the fight. |
| BATE | Just when I'll be starting to have fun! |
| STONEY | To err on the side of safety, Dr Foot will be on hand. He's on the premises now. |
| BATE | You've thought of everything. |
| STONEY | Mind you do stop the moment he comes in. I've heard stories about your duels. Few come out alive. |
| BATE | I'll admit I like a good scrap. |
| STONEY | And you a man of the cloth! |
| BATE | It's a way of meting out God's punishment to unworthy mortals. |
| STONEY | [*laughs drunkenly*] Ah! That's what it is, is it? |
| BATE | Yes. [*Pause.*] Now, about the correspondence in the *Post*: you want to end it once our little rencontre has taken place? |
| STONEY | Absolutely. No point in carrying on. |
| BATE | I congratulate you, my good sir, on your ability as a penman. You've created quite a stir with those letters. |
| STONEY | For which you are to take the blame, don't forget. |
| BATE | [*holding up the purse appreciatively*] Of course ... But I can't quite see the point of it all. |
| STONEY | [*with a chuckle*] Wheels within wheels, don't you know! But briefly, your articles against Lady Strathmore, and the correspondence I've devised has provoked me to challenge you to a duel to defend the lady's honour. This should please the bitch, and quite possibly bring about an alliance between her and myself with the blessing of your church. |
| BATE | Neat. Very neat, captain. Oh yes ... I recall your saying all this to me ... [*He belches.*] ... before. |
| STONEY | Quite so. Let us swear eternal friendship then, sir. |
| | [*He pours* BATE *a drink with an unsteady hand.*] |
| BATE | Dare I drink to that? |
| STONEY | Remember ... I'll forgive you publicly after the fight ... but you're to attack me in your paper just one more time. |

| | |
|---|---|
| BATE | Let me note that down. |
| | [*Although fairly intoxicated at this point, he awkwardly produces pen and paper, and scribbles something down.*] |
| STONEY | Mind you, nothing too outrageous. |
| BATE | Leave it to me, sir. |
| | [*He drinks and replenishes his own and* STONEY*'s glass, spilling some over the table.*] |
| STONEY | Easy now, Bate. We don't want you to prick me to the quick with your sword! |
| BATE | You question my ability as a swordsman? |
| STONEY | Certainly not — only your tolerance for strong drink! |
| | [*He hiccoughs.*] |
| BATE | [*affronted*] I don't think you're in a fit state to question my sobriety! |
| STONEY | [*conciliatory*] Shh ... let's be friends, Bate. We've work ahead of us yet ... |
| | [*He coughs, then belches. He follows up with a convulsive sneeze, then farts loudly.*] |
| BATE | [*intrigued*] Tell me, Stoney: can you make a noise with your navel? |
| STONEY | Give me time, parson ... Hm ... time. [*rises, unsteady on his legs*] Time we went to war ... |
| | [STONEY *makes for the other table and picks up a pistol with his right hand and a sword with his left.* BATE *also rises and staggers to the table. He picks up the other sword.*] |
| BATE | [*laughs uncontrollably*] En garde! |
| | [*He flourishes his sword in the air and accidentally puts out a number of candles.* STONEY *seems to find* BATE*'s action entertaining, and joins in the fun. He puts out several more candles with his weapon, laughing hysterically. The room is soon in total darkness, as laughter and the sound of bodies and metal bump-* |

*ing into furniture gathers in volume. A shot is heard, followed by a scream.*]

BATE  You've got me in the bum, you fool!

STONEY  There's marksmanship for you!

[*All is now noise and confusion.*]

BATE  [*enraged*] Take that then — !

STONEY  Ouch! I said just a nick!

BATE  — and that!

STONEY  Stop it you insane priest!

BATE  [*out of control*] — and that!

[*A scream, followed by the thud of a body noisily hitting the ground.*]

[*The door opens, and* SEPTIMUS BLAND *enters, carrying a lantern which gradually illuminates the stage, now littered with overturned furniture, glass and bottles.* STONEY *lies on the floor, bleeding profusely from the chest.* BATE *is standing, his left hand pressed awkwardly against his buttock to staunch the blood, and waving his sword with the other.*]

[SEPTIMUS *is also quite clearly drunk, but succeeds in remembering the instructions previously imparted by his master.*]

SEPTIMUS  Gentlemen ... gentlemen: I urge you to keep the King's peace.

STONEY  You're late! Get the doctor, you lout!

SEPTIMUS  But cap'n —

[DR FOOT *enters.*]

DR FOOT  What's happening here?

STONEY  And you're late as well! I'm bleeding like a pig!

DR FOOT  [*rushes to* STONEY, *and examines him*] This is more than I expected ...

STONEY  The fool nearly killed me!

BATE  You've shot me, you knave!

DR FOOT  [*in an urgent undertone to* STONEY] Compose yourself: her

|  |  |
|---|---|
|  | ladyship's on her way. She should be here by now ... It's all been carefully timed. |
| BATE | Could you attend to me, doctor? I shall faint presently. |

> [DR FOOT, *having bandaged* STONEY's *wound, moves over to* BATE, *lowers his breeches and bends him over the table by the entrance door to examine his wound. His naked buttocks are thus the first thing anyone entering the room would see.*]
>
> [*Hurried steps and the sound of a new arrival.* MARY *enters, out of breath.*]

|  |  |
|---|---|
| MARY | Is he dead? [*She notices* BATE's *exposed rump, recoils and shrieks with horror.*] |
| STONEY | [*feebly, from the far end of the room*] Your ladyship ... Is it you? |
| MARY | [*dashes to* STONEY, *kneels by his side and cradles his head with great reverence*] My hero! |

> [*Blackout, to the strains of Handel's 'See the Conquering Hero Comes'.*]


## SCENE 10:
## A WEDDING AND MORE NAME-SWAPPING

*St James's Church, Piccadilly. 17th January 1777.*

*Nuptial organ music.* PARSON BATE, *in full canonicals, is conducting the marriage service between* MARY ELEANOR *and* STONEY. *The service is in progress.*

SEPTIMUS *and* BELLA, *in choir singers' robes, upstage left.*

SEPTIMUS/BELLA [*to the tune of* See The Conquering Hero Comes]
Unmoved, Maria saw the splendid suite
Of rival captives sighing at her feet,
Till in her cause, his sword young Stoney drew,
And to revenge, the gallant wooer flew!
Bravest among the brave! — and first to prove
By death! or conquest! Who best knew to love!
But pale, and faint, the wounded lover lies,
While more than pity fills young Mary's eyes!

In her soft breast, where passion long had strove
Resistless sorrow fixed the reign of love!
"Dear youth," she cries, " we meet no more to part!
Then take thy honour's due — my bleeding heart!"

[*As the song ends, the marriage service resumes.*]

BATE  Wilt thou, Andrew Robinson Stoney, take this woman —

STONEY  [*cutting in*] Andrew Robinson Bowes.

MARY  [*nodding enthusiastically*] Andrew Robinson Bowes.

[BATE *registers surprise and irritation at the interruption, and looks from one to the other.*]

STONEY  [*hisses impatiently*] I have petitioned Parliament to allow me to adopt the name of Bowes. Get on with it!

BATE  Wilt thou, Andrew Robinson Bowes ... [MARY *and* STONEY *nod to each other with smug complicity.*] ... take this woman to thy wedded wife, to live together after God's ordinance in the holy estate of matrimony? Wilt thou love her, comfort her, honour, and keep her in sickness and in health; and forsaking all other, keep thee only unto her, so long as ye both shall live?

[*The rest of the service is drowned by organ music while* MARY *and* STONEY *exchange vows and* PARSON BATE *drones on.*]

[*Fadeout.*]

[INTERVAL]

## SCENE 11:
## TRUSTS AND MISTRUST

*Grosvenor Square. February 1777.*

STONEY *and* MARY, *who is visibly pregnant. Their relationship has undergone a change. What little charm* STONEY *had displayed towards her in the past is now no longer in evidence, and* MARY *shows she is plainly under* STONEY's *thumb.* MARY *pours a liquid from a bottle into a medicine glass and takes a sip.*

STONEY [*without lifting his head from the newspaper he is reading*] I'd go easy on the laudanum. That's your third glass.

MARY You got Dr Foot to mix it for me. You said it would do me good.

STONEY It's a wholesome drug, if taken in moderate quantities.

MARY Very good, dear.

STONEY [*lifts his head and lowers the newspaper he has been reading*] Beckett's dead, I see.

MARY Beckett?

STONEY The member for Newcastle.

MARY Oh, yes. I see.

STONEY Do you?

MARY I beg your pardon?

STONEY Do you see what that means?

MARY It means that Sir Walter Beckett's dead ...

STONEY ... and that there's a vacancy in that constituency.

MARY You're interested?

STONEY Given my new position in the area, I feel it's my duty to put my name forward.

MARY But Andrew, we've only been married one month, and —

STONEY [*cutting in, his tone now subtly menacing*] — and you're clearly pregnant by another man. Is that what you were going to say?

MARY Andrew, you promised you weren't going to mention it again.

STONEY How can I, when the manifest signs of your dissipations are before me every minute of the day and night?

MARY You said you'd forgive me.

STONEY Forgive — yes. Forget or condone, never! And now that scoundrel Grey is threatening to sue you for breach of promise!

MARY My lawyers tell me he'll take a sum of money.

| | |
|---|---|
| STONEY | *Your* lawyers! It's your husband who should be handling these matters. Your lawyers will probably hand a fortune over to him. |
| MARY | The sum of twelve thousand pounds has been mentioned. |
| STONEY | Why not let me take care of the whole affair? |
| MARY | The trustees won't allow it. |
| STONEY | What have I married you for then? Why did you execute the ante-nuptial trust behind my back? |
| MARY | The deeds were signed before you and I met. You know perfectly well I had to protect my assets from Grey. I was warned about him. |
| STONEY | You call that protection? You're now going to hand twelve thousand pounds over to him! If you'd let me handle your affairs I could have saved you that sum, and more beside. |
| MARY | Andrew, let's not talk about this. |
| STONEY | Surely a husband in this day and age should be in charge of his wife's income. The fact I was kept in ignorance about your ante-nuptial trust constitutes a fraud on me! |
| MARY | Mama says — |
| STONEY | Damn your mother! And while we're on the subject, I forbid you to see her without my express permission. She's been poisoning your mind against me. |
| MARY | She has my best interests at heart! |
| STONEY | Any person of intelligence will tell you that it is only reasonable and natural that a husband should have complete control of his wife's estates. |
| MARY | Andrew, please — first Strathmore and his horrid family, then Grey ... and now you. I love you, my dear, but I've only known you a few months. Give me time. The lawyers and mama will listen to me ... eventually. |
| STONEY | Why not write this very day to the lawyers and revoke the trust? |

> [MARY *is plainly unwilling to fall in with his wishes, and despite his hold over her, vainly casts about for excuses.*]

| | |
|---|---|
| MARY | The time isn't ripe, yet. The opposition to change won't be quite so great a little later ... |
| STONEY | Meanwhile I feel like a lackey in your house! |
| MARY | Please don't be quite so sensitive. If you're really interested, I'm sure we could do something about the Newcastle constituency. |
| STONEY | [*momentarily appeased*] You'll support me? |
| MARY | If that's what you really want. |
| STONEY | I've long been interested in politics. Yes. There's a great deal of corruption in the governance of the nation. A festering boil waiting to be lanced by the right man. We must restore liberty to every citizen in the land! [*He rises and stares self-importantly into space.*] Bowes and Freedom! Yes. That'll be my battle-cry! |
| MARY | [*happier now at the turn the conversation has taken*] Oh, Andrew, I can see a glittering career ahead for you! |
| STONEY | It'll take a great deal of money. |
| MARY | I'm sure the trustees will rally to the cause. I'll campaign with you. |
| STONEY | We shall make Gibside our campaign headquarters. |
| MARY | How wonderful! You know how much I love Gibside. |
| STONEY | The electorate's made up of two thousand voters ... |
| MARY | [*optimistically*] ... who will be only too anxious to elect you! |
| STONEY | ... each of whom has his price. We shall need funds immediately nominations close. |
| MARY | Will that be soon? |
| STONEY | Next week. |
| MARY | That soon? Will there be time for me to raise the money? |
| STONEY | [*aggressively*] Are you looking for excuses? |
| MARY | No, dear but — |
| STONEY | [*cutting in*] Timber. There's lots of timber at Gibside. |
| MARY | [*alarmed*] The woodland? But — |
| STONEY | We'll cut it down and sell it. There's money in timber. |

MARY  Papa said —

STONEY  [*cutting in frostily*] I'm not interested in what the cursed man said!

MARY  [*in her befuddled state, induced by laudanum and fear, she summons up what little confidence she has left, but only succeeds in sounding petulant and tentative*] Papa said the woodland should be left untouched. And you have no authority!

STONEY  Oh, no?

> [*He rises and approaches her.* MARY *cowers in her armchair, as* STONEY *pinches and twists the lobe of her ear in what is now one of his characteristically vicious practices. She cries out in pain.*]

I've no authority you say?

> [MARY *cries out again, and* STONEY *releases her and storms out of the room.* MARY, *her head bent, bursts into tears, then slowly composes herself. She pours more laudanum from the bottle.*]
>
> [*Fadeout.*]


## SCENE 12:
## ELECTIONEERING

*Newcastle. A public house. March 1777.*

*A first floor room. An open window.* STONEY *is at the window, as if delivering a speech with his back to us, though in a frozen attitude.* MARY, *lavishly attired and bejewelled, is sitting motionless.*

WILLIAM, *dressed as an election campaigner, walks up to the footlights line and sings.*

WILLIAM  [*to the tune of* The Blaydon Races]

Sir Walter being dead,
And the writ it came doon,
I offered meself, lads,
For Newcastle Toon.

Suppose that we lost it, lads,
Never mind that;
We lost it with honour
But Sir John's a rat!

Now Gibside's me own, lads,
You very well know
I've wood for to cut,
And coals for to hew!
And if it please providence
For to spare me wife,
I intend to lead a proper moral life!

> [*The scene comes to life and* STONEY *enters into the closing stages of what must have been a rousing election address to the voters outside.* MARY *fidgets with her bracelets and brooches.*]

STONEY ... yes, my friends: Sir Walter, now tragically no longer with us, was indeed 'The Patriot' and 'The Father of the Poor', and I intend to replace him in your trust and affection. You've known me long enough to recognise me for what I am ...

HECKLER [*off*] Aye: an upstart Irishman!

STONEY [*raises a hand*] Please, friends, please! Let us look at my opponent, nephew of the late Sir Walter, and draw your own conclusions. Sir John Trevelyan is a zealous foxhunter, true, and loves roast beef and claret as well as any fat-headed country squire in Somersetshire ... You are told by those who canvass for him that your late member on his death bed recommended his nephew Sir John.

HECKLER [*off*] He did an' all. And we're voting for him!

STONEY Is Newcastle then to be handed over as an heirloom? Has Sir Walter in his will bequeathed you to his nephew? Vote for me — and remember the rallying call of this most loyal of His Majesty's officers: Bowes and Freedom!

> [*He moves away from the window to the sound of cheers, and catcalls.*]

MARY You were wonderful, Andrew!

| | |
|---|---|
| STONEY | [*exhausted and irritable*] Hm. Time for you to do your stuff. |
| | [*He collapses on to a chair and mops the sweat off his face.*] |
| MARY | I'm ready. |
| | [*The noise outside has virtually ceased. She goes to the window, leans out shaking her hand downwards in awkward greeting and deliberately lets fall two of her bracelets. She comes back into the room and turns to* STONEY.] |
| | Was that all right, do you think? |
| STONEY | Let's see what happens. |
| | [*A knock at the door.*] |
| MARY | Come in. |
| | [*A* VOTER *enters, carrying the bracelets.*] |
| VOTER | Beggin' your pardon, milady. You dropped these bracelets just now from yon window. [*He hands them to* MARY.] |
| MARY | [*taking the bracelets*] How very kind of you ... I'm much obliged ... [*She takes a few gold coins out of a purse.*] Here, take this ... and I hope you'll vote for Stoney Bowes. |
| VOTER | [*taking the money*] Aye, I will your ladyship. An' God bless the bairn yer' carryin'. |
| | [*He exits, touching his forelock, as* MARY *goes back to the window to repeat the operation.*] |
| | [*Fadeout.*] |

## SCENE 13:
## A CUCKOO IN THE NEST

*Gibside. August 1777.*

*The muted strains of the first movement of Leopold Mozart's 'Toy' Symphony, with cuckoo calls.*

*A shaded corner of a garden.* MARY *is sitting, somewhat disconsolately nursing a baby.* STONEY *is walking morosely up and down, thrashing about with his riding crop in search of plants and flowers he can vent his spleen on.*

DR FOOT *enters.*

DR FOOT [*in an aside to the audience, as he approaches the pair*] In the quiet seclusion of Gibside, away from the prying eye of curiosity, Stoney Bowes may safely hear the cuckoo as a not unwelcome sound to the married ear.

STONEY [*sees* DR FOOT] There you are, doctor. Not before time.

DR FOOT [*bows to* MARY] Your ladyship. Sir: I am sorry about the election.

STONEY It was a close run thing.

DR FOOT So I heard. You'll stand again, of course.

STONEY Naturally. And I'll win. At the moment I'm petitioning Parliament against the result.

DR FOOT I wish you well, sir.

STONEY But to business, doctor. My wife gave birth without a midwife in attendance.

DR FOOT I gave express instructions —

STONEY The woman arrived well after the confinement, and I understand claimed and was paid a fee without my authority.

DR FOOT Well, I —

STONEY Please understand, doctor, that that sum will be deducted from your honorarium.

DR FOOT As you please, sir.

STONEY Since last month, when her ladyship annulled the antenuptial trust, I have been in complete charge of finances, and I mean to exercise the utmost economy.

DR FOOT Indeed sir, though I'd remind you I haven't been paid for several months.

STONEY Submit your claims in writing and I'll have my comptroller look into the matter.

DR FOOT I will, sir. What's the noise coming from Long Lands?

STONEY The sweetest sound in the world, doctor. The sound of axes felling trees.

| | |
|---|---|
| DR FOOT | It's fine woodland out there. |
| STONEY | The finest. You'll not find such timber anywhere in England, His Majesty's Docks excepted. |
| DR FOOT | So I've heard, sir. |
| STONEY | When my father-in-law died, timber on the estate was valued at fifty thousand pounds. |
| DR FOOT | Was it indeed? Will you be re-planting? |
| STONEY | For the moment I'm cutting down, doctor. Elections don't come cheap. |
| DR FOOT | You'll be fighting another one soon. |
| STONEY | The moment a seat is available. |
| DR FOOT | Your opponent will be running scared, I'll wager. |
| STONEY | He will — but I'll bide my time till I can bite, which I expect will be very soon. Till then it would be folly to show my teeth, eh? What do you say, doctor? |

[*Fadeout.*]


## SCENE 14:
## A MISMATCH?

*Gibside, 1780.*

STONEY *and* MARY *are sitting in the garden as in the previous scene.* MARY *is noticeably more subdued than at any other time.*

| | |
|---|---|
| SEPTIMUS | [*to the tune of* Spanish Ladies]<br>Her Ladyship's tenants first gained his attention<br>Whose treatment was cruel — most shocking to mention;<br>He raised all their rents, which if they could not pay<br>He craved them and seized them, then turned them away.<br>The helpless dependants — the labouring poor,<br>He removed from their work, or horse-whipped from his door.<br><br>Free schools he condemned, and of course did suppress,<br>As tending to cause and promote idleness.<br>The yearly, the weekly, the daily supply, |

                To orphans and widows he next did deny;
                Those acts of benevolence, whence Gibside was famed,
                Are wholly forbidden and must not be NAMED.

                [SEPTIMUS *exits.*]

                [DR FOOT *enters.*]

DR FOOT   [*approaches* STONEY *exultantly*] Congratulations, sir, on your election victory! [*turns to* MARY *and bows*] Milady...

STONEY    Thank you. I told you I'd succeed.

DR FOOT   With an excellent majority.

STONEY    You have not heard of my other appointment?

DR FOOT   Sir?

STONEY    You are speaking to the new High Sheriff of Northumberland.

DR FOOT   This is wonderful news! [*to* MARY] You must be very proud, your ladyship.

MARY      [*passively*] I am, doctor.

STONEY    Did you hear what my opponents called me during the campaign?

DR FOOT   No, sir. I was in London.

STONEY    [*laughs*] They called me a fortune hunter. A wolf in sheep's clothing.

DR FOOT   They wouldn't dare!

STONEY    Yes, they did. And that's not all. Apparently I am an unprincipled mock patriot. An upstart Hibernian.

DR FOOT   How insulting!

STONEY    I won, all the same, doctor. My purse was bigger than theirs.

DR FOOT   A splendid outcome.

STONEY    There's more.

DR FOOT   You overwhelm me, sir.

STONEY    Provided my bankers don't foreclose on me, there's a real possibility of an Irish peerage coming my way.

DR FOOT   There's no stopping you, Mr Bowes.

| | |
|---|---|
| STONEY | Didn't I tell you I'd soon be ready to bite? |
| DR FOOT | You did, sir, but — |

> [*He takes* STONEY *aside. The conversation that follows takes place in an undertone, and* MARY *hardly seems to be listening.*]
>
> I confess I'm worried about your wife. She doesn't look at all well.

| | |
|---|---|
| STONEY | [*impatiently*] She's fine, fine. |
| DR FOOT | Is she still exceeding her dosage of laudanum? |
| STONEY | How would I know? You'd better ask her. |
| DR FOOT | I'd like to examine her. |
| STONEY | No need to do that. The woman's perfectly all right. |
| DR FOOT | Maybe she should be bled. |
| STONEY | [*laughs*] I attend to that quite regularly, believe me. Still — take a look at her if you must. When you've done that, see me again: there's a couple of nags I've just bought for the Streatlam stud — I'm worried about their water. In fact, look at them first. Mary can wait. [*louder*] You can wait, can't you dear? |
| MARY | [*apathetically*] What? |
| STONEY | There's nothing the matter with you that can't wait, is there? |
| MARY | No ... |
| STONEY | Off you go, doctor. She'll still be here when you've done with the horses. |

> [DR FOOT *leaves, shaking his head.*]

| | |
|---|---|
| MARY | [*in a far-off voice*] Andrew ... |
| STONEY | Yes? |
| MARY | What do you want of me? |
| STONEY | [*with calm finality*] I am determined to make every day of your life more miserable than the last. |
| MARY | [*quietly*] That's the only promise you'll ever keep. |

> [*Fadeout.*]

## SCENE 15:
## FLIGHT, AND THE SWEARING OF THE PEACE

*1785. Grosvenor Square.*

BELLA, MARY's *maid, is half bending on a table with her skirts gathered about her waist. Her partial nudity is masked by* STONEY's, *close behind her, his breeches about his knees. He is busy holding her down and at the same time copulating with her from the rear. His movements are unhurried and the usual grunts are emitted by the pair:* STONEY's *of savage enjoyment;* BELLA's *possibly those of a reluctant participant.*

MARY *enters quietly, not quite steady on her feet, her face bruised. She blinks as she surveys the scene, though not from shock or disbelief, since this is not the first time she has witnessed a scene of this kind.*

STONEY *at length completes the act, disengages himself from* BELLA *and drinks from a glass on a table. He notices* MARY, *laughs, slaps* BELLA *on the rump, hitches up his breeches and leaves the room.*

BELLA *notices* MARY *with some alarm and adjusts her skirts.*

BELLA     I'm sorry, your ladyship. He surprised me ...

MARY     [*lethargically*] I know.

BELLA     I was doing the dusting. He suddenly caught me and ... claimed me.

MARY     It's not the first time, is it, Bella?

BELLA     No, milady. But it's been worse for Agnes.

MARY     The kitchen maid?

BELLA     She's five months gone.

MARY     Oh, no!

BELLA     She swears 'twere the master. Forced her afore breakfast one morning.

MARY     [*sits down*] Bella, I want you to do something for me.

BELLA     Yes?

| | |
|---|---|
| MARY | I want you to send William in to me. Then check whether Mr Bowes is still in the house. If he is not, get me a cloak and send for my coach. |
| BELLA | You'll want to change first, milady? |
| MARY | No. There won't be time. |
| BELLA | Very well. [*She leaves the room.*] |

> [MARY *reaches for what is recognisably a laudanum bottle and glass on a side table, but having picked it up puts it down again and takes a deep breath.*]
>
> [WILLIAM *enters.*]

| | |
|---|---|
| WILLIAM | You sent for me, milady? |
| MARY | You know Mr Peeble? |
| WILLIAM | Your solicitor? |
| MARY | Yes. Do you know his address? |
| WILLIAM | Lincoln's Inn. I've often taken documents there. |
| MARY | Good. |

> [BELLA *enters.*]

| | |
|---|---|
| BELLA | He's gone, milady. To a gaming house, his man Septimus says. |
| MARY | [*with a sudden access of energy and growing confidence*] Fine. Get my cloak as I asked. And be ready to leave with me. |

> [*The pace of the action quickens from this point until the end of the scene.*]

| | |
|---|---|
| BELLA | Very good, mum. [*She goes.*] |
| MARY | Now William, where were we? |
| WILLIAM | You asked me whether I knew Mr Peeble's address. |
| MARY | You said you did. |
| WILLIAM | Yes. |
| MARY | This is what you're going to do. Go to Mr Peeble and ask to see him personally. You're not to speak to anyone else — my husband has spies everywhere. Understood? |
| WILLIAM | Yes, milady. |
| MARY | If he's not there wait for him, until tomorrow if necessary. |

| | |
|---|---|
| WILLIAM | As you wish. |
| MARY | When you do see him, tell him Lady Strathmore has left Grosvenor Square ... |
| WILLIAM | [*registers surprise*] What? |
| MARY | ... and gone to stay with Mrs Morgan. He'll know the address. As you do. Tell him I want him to call on me there. |
| WILLIAM | Very well. |
| MARY | Say I wish to follow his advice and exhibit Articles of Peace against my husband. Can you remember that? |
| WILLIAM | Articles of Peace, you said. |
| MARY | Just so. That's to stop him molesting me. Tell him to prepare the documents and call on me as soon as possible. Then join me at Mrs Morgan's directly you've done. |
| WILLIAM | Very well, milady. |
| MARY | You're not to talk to anyone about this — except Mr Peeble. No one's to know my whereabouts. Go now. Hurry. |
| WILLIAM | Your ladyship. [*He goes.*] |

[BELLA, *in outdoor clothes, returns with a cloak.*]

| | |
|---|---|
| BELLA | Here are your things, mum. |
| MARY | Have you sent for the coach? |
| BELLA | It's at the door. [*hesitates*] Your ladyship — |
| MARY | Yes? |
| BELLA | Do you think you should? |
| MARY | Let's go. |

[*Helped by* BELLA, *she hurriedly puts on her cloak. They leave.*]

[*Blackout.*]

## SCENE 16:
## THE ABDUCTION

*1786. London and a journey to the North.*

MARY *is sitting in a room when* STONEY *and a masked henchman break in, both armed with swords and pistols, and kidnap her.*

SEPTIMUS *and* BELLA *are standing downstage left.*

*The abduction will encompass a journey to the North of England,* MARY's *imprisonment at Streatlam Castle, and the subsequent criss-cross rides until* STONEY's *capture near Darlington.*

*The kidnapping is mimed to the recitation of the verse to be spoken by* SEPTIMUS *and* BELLA *in turn, with Vivaldi's 'Winter' movement from* The Four Seasons *in the background. The director may exercise freedom in choreographing the action up till the end of the recitation, when the background music will cease and dialogue take over. Lighting effects should play an important part in the entire scene.*

SEPTIMUS/BELLA

>Her ladyship was much alarmed
>To find the ruffians all were armed,
>And when she shouted for relief
>Her mouth they stopped with handkerchief:
>And on their route Bowes shewed a paper
>Which for to sign he said he'd make her.
>By the contents she was to stop —
>All further law proceedings drop;
>And also own she was his wife,
>Which if denied, he'd take her life!
>
>With threats he urged her to comply
>Which she as firmly did deny.
>Often, with pistol at her head,
>He said 'Do sign - or you are dead!'
>With blows both violent and base
>He beat her body and her face!

> From Streatlam when he'd her convey
> He used her in this cruel way:
> He wrapped her in a blanket first,
> Then through a window did her thrust
> And further still, to use her worse
> He thus conveyed her 'cross a horse,
> When they arrived where he designed
> In a dark room she was confined.
>
> But his pursuers drawing nigh,
> She was compelled with him to fly
> O'er heaths and mountains faced with snow.
> Through dreary, dismal roads they go!
> Still worse — in this severe retreat,
> No shoes nor stockings to her feet!
> Her hat was also tied with straw,
> Thus spent that night, both cold and raw.
> His treatment still prevailing not,
> The poker once he made red hot!
> Then his request again renewed.
> But she maintained what she had vowed,
> At last he said he did intend
> And would her to a madhouse send,
> Where also in straight jacket, he
> Would order her confined to be!
> As all his efforts still did fail,
> Nor threats nor promises prevail;
> 'FOR DEATH,' he cried, 'FOR DEATH PREPARE,
> YOUR TIME IS SHORT — SAY YOUR LAST PRAYER!'

> [SEPTIMUS *and* BELLA *withdraw, as* WILLIAM, *in the uniform of a constable, enters.* MARY *breaks free from* STONEY *and intercepts him.*]

MARY  Please, sir! I am Lady Strathmore. For God's sake assist me!

CONSTABLE  [*produces a pistol*] Are you indeed Lady Strathmore?

MARY  I am, I am, and have been apprehended against my inclination by that man — [*pointing to* STONEY] Andrew Robinson Bowes!

CONSTABLE  I will secure your person, milady, and arrest your assailant. I have authority and will convey him to a magistrate. [*to* STONEY, *presenting his pistol*] My men will be here presently and place you under restraint, sir, in the name of His Majesty King George.

[STONEY, *with a defiant gesture, makes no answer.*]

I would not advise resistance, sir. My gun is cocked.

MARY   [*overcome by relief*] At last!

[*Fadeout.*]


## SCENE 17:
## THE ARRAIGNMENT

*1787. The Court of King's Bench.*

DR FOOT *and* SEPTIMUS *as two judges sit on tall chairs.* STONEY *sits on a low stool below them.*

JUDGE 1   [*in a pedantic tone, and shuffling parchments myopically*] ... I see that a placard was placed on the walls of various northern parts, notably in the County Palatine of Durham, offering a reward of fifty pounds to anyone who would rescue the lady and apprehend the accused and his armed henchmen.

JUDGE 2   As a result a constable did arrest Andrew Robinson Bowes, who denies having kidnapped his wife.

JUDGE 1   At present the Marshal of the King's Bench Prison has been able to accommodate the accused within the precincts of the said prison, and has allowed him three rooms and his own plate so that he may entertain.

JUDGE 2   For the purposes of this examination, is the accused satisfied with his present accommodation?

STONEY   I am not, my lord. Furthermore —

JUDGE 2   That will do as an answer. Please remain silent until addressed by the bench.

JUDGE 1   Apart from other more serious charges, you also stand accused of forcing your wife within one year of your marriage

|         | to write what we shall call her Confessions, supposedly written for your eyes only, and you have since published them for sale at a profit to the general public knowing them to have been written under duress. These Confessions, given the vile and abominable nature of their revelations, contain passages that could never have been written by a lady, and are possibly quite untrue — |
|---------|---|
| STONEY  | [*interrupting*] They're true all right! |
| JUDGE 2 | Silence in court! |
| JUDGE 1 | Andrew Robinson Bowes, you are further charged with forcing the Countess of Strathmore to cancel a pre-nuptial trust by the terrors of personal violence. How say you to this charge? |
| STONEY  | Not guilty. |
| JUDGE 2 | Your accusers describe you as a man of a savage and tormenting disposition, who would fly into the most violent passions on the most frivolous occasions. The Reverend Samuel Markham once said grace over dinner in your presence and he alleges that you shouted 'Damn your mercies, I want none of them' and proceeded to call him a villain and a rascal, and knocked him down and struck him many violent blows. |
| STONEY  | The man was drunk! |
| JUDGE 2 | Silence! |
| JUDGE 1 | We now come to the much graver charges of violence upon the person of your wife, the Countess of Strathmore. Miss Dorothy Stevenson has deposed that in her presence you gave Lady Strathmore many violent blows on her face, head and other parts of her body. You often kicked her and sometimes pinched her ears nearly through. |
| JUDGE 2 | Indeed on one occasion, at dinner, you threw a dish of hot potatoes at your wife, and then made her eat the resulting mess until she was sick, throwing a glass of wine in her face to wash the potatoes off. |
| JUDGE 1 | Your wife's maid Bella, whom you raped on various occasions, states that you pursued the Countess of Strathmore |

into a corner of her drawing room, where you kept her for about half an hour, beating her incessantly all the time with the hilt of your sword and a heavy silver candlestick, on the head, arms, and shoulders, in such a manner as obliged her to keep to her bed for the greater part of the next day — a very shocking spectacle, one of her eyes being almost closed, her face swollen, and her body covered with black marks. And you did all this for no other reason than her ladyship's inability to find your gold-topped cane.

JUDGE 2   Her ladyship also states that when annoyed by money matters, or out of humour with your mistresses, you would come home and begin to beat, pinch and kick her, sometimes varying the punishment by pulling her ears and nose, and occasionally spitting in her face. You would then inform her that you had married her only to correct her.

STONEY   That last statement is perfectly true!

JUDGE 1   Silence!

JUDGE 2   The Countess of Strathmore has initiated proceedings for divorce with the Bishop of London's Consistory Court, and her legal advisers have set down a comprehensive list of her husband's offences as follows: beating, scratching, biting, pinching, whipping, kicking, imprisoning, insulting, provoking, tormenting, mortifying, degrading, tyrannising, cajoling, deceiving, lying, starving, forcing, compelling and wringing of the heart — as well as a long record of the said husband's adultery and illegitimate progeny added to the petition as appendices. How say you to these charges, Andrew Robinson Bowes?

STONEY   I say read her Confessions — and make the most of them!

JUDGE 1   Finally I am instructed that another charge has been filed against you since your recent arrest — alleging that during your confinement in the King's Bench prison you did ingratiate yourself with one Elizabeth Waite, having promised to pay her father's debts and obtain his release from prison. You failed to honour this promise and raped the said Elizabeth Waite who has now ended up in the Magdalen Hospital in St George's Field.

STONEY [*rises from his stool and points an accusatory forefinger into space, shouting*] I gave the whore five shillings!

[*Blackout.*]

## SCENE 18:
## THE TRIALS

*1788 to 1800. The Court of King's Bench.*

*The passage of time to be indicated by lighting changes.*

DR FOOT *and* SEPTIMUS *as two judges, and* STONEY, *set as in Scene 17.*

JUDGE 1  Andrew Robinson Bowes, it is the decision of this court that you be bound over to keep the peace for a term of fourteen years, in your own security of ten thousand pounds, and in two securities of five thousand pounds each. The prisoner may now make a statement.

STONEY  I protest against the length of the term, my lord.

JUDGE 2  I would remind the prisoner that this is but the first of a number of trials, and advise him to reserve any appeal for the more serious charges, such as that of abducting your wife ...

STONEY  I will reserve my defence for the next trial, my lord.

JUDGE 1  You are well advised so to do. Take him away ...

[*The lights vary in intensity to denote the passage of time.*]

JUDGE 2  In this second trial, we rule that the crime of which you have been found guilty does appear to be of as atrocious and daring a nature as ever appeared in a Court of Justice, and had not the facts been made out by the most incontestable proofs, one would hardly have thought that in a civilised country, governed by such law, any man — even a husband — would have been found foolish enough to take away a lady of rank and fortune from one of the most public streets of this great town, namely Oxford Street, in defiance of all law, order and government, and to drag her through the heart of the kingdom two hundred and forty miles; and what is a high aggravation of the offence is that it was meant and intended to impede the current of public justice; and by force and violence to put a stop to a prosecution legally instituted by her against you, for cruelty and adultery.

JUDGE 1  Andrew Robinson Bowes, it is the verdict of this court that you be fined three hundred pounds and sentenced to three years' imprisonment in the King's Bench prison, at the expiration of the said term to find securities for fourteen years, as previously ruled, in the sum of ten thousand pounds.

*[The lights again vary in intensity.]*

JUDGE 2  This court finds that the Deed of Revocation signed by your wife giving you control of her income and estates was signed under duress. It is therefore the decision of this court that the Countess of Strathmore have her income and estates returned to her from the control of the said Andrew Robinson Bowes. The accused may make a statement.

STONEY  I would submit, my lord, that one of the rights a husband acquires by marriage is to take the profits of estates of which the wife is in possession.

JUDGE 1  Nevertheless, given that by various ruses and stratagems, among them the sham duel you fought — in itself unlawful and a flagrant breach of His Majesty's peace — this court finds that the original Deed of Revocation in favour of Andrew Robinson Bowes be declared null and void. The said Andrew Robinson Bowes is therefore not entitled to any consideration in this court of law.

STONEY  My lord, marriage, by the law of England, gives the husband the whole dominion over the property and the person of his wife, except as to murder, for by the old law the husband cannot be punished for cruelty to her. He is head of the family: to make another would be against the policy of the law. If the wife could, by her own act, and against the consent of the husband, make herself independent of him, it would destroy the subordination so necessary in families. If Lady Strathmore is right in what she has done, then the husband becomes a cypher in his own house.

| | |
|---|---|
| JUDGE 2 | As a felon, Andrew Robinson Bowes, you are denied such considerations. You are further ordered to pay an amount owed by you in the sum of ten thousand two hundred and ninety five pounds, eleven shillings and twopence. If in default, you will be sentenced to a further term of imprisonment. |
| JUDGE 1 | Andrew Robinson Bowes, have you anything to say before this court passes sentence? |
| | [STONEY *rises slowly from his stool to address the court. The lights will dim on the stage except for* STONEY's *immediate area. As he moves about the stage he will be tracked by a follow spot which will bathe him in a lurid light at the climax of his speech.*] |
| STONEY | I have argued, my lords, that a wife by virtue of a marriage contract becomes extinct for several civil purposes, in that she has merged with her husband. Or would you have a man who married without a marriage treaty be content to take the wife as he found her? You have arrested me, shackled me, imprisoned me, deprived me of my worldly goods and other inalienable rights on the strength of accusations by Lady Strathmore. I would beg the court to remember that when I married Mary Eleanor Bowes, Countess of Strathmore, she had had criminal intercourse and connection with George Grey, and was pregnant by him on our wedding day. I later found that she had had criminal intercourse with one of her footmen, George Walker, and with Thompson, a gardener at Gibside. I dismissed them both, and I endeavoured to instil discipline into my wife as any caring and God-fearing husband would. You have heard witnesses testifying to Lady Strathmore's dissipated and extravagant ways — you have heard others tell of her lustful and wicked behaviour. She'd stop at nothing to indulge in the gratification of her appetites. Soon after our marriage she behaved towards me with the utmost insolent contempt and disobedience and with the greatest impropriety and indecency. I submit that I had to place such restraints on her conduct as would be invoked by any husband. You have heard others say that Lady Strathmore was a woman without any sense of religion or |

morality, much addicted to the gratification of the flesh, drinking frequently to excess, and once succeeding in setting her clothes on fire. She told me personally that Lord Strathmore's death had been a release, and that she loved cats better than her own children. Some of you may be acquainted with Mr Gillray's cartoons depicting my wife: they speak louder than words. [*Pause.*] I have been accused of greed and avarice in disposing of the income from Lady Strathmore's estates. I submit that throughout our marriage I attempted to conserve her fortune and promote its growth. [*At this point he pulls out all the stops to win our hearts and minds.*] You call me greedy, my lords, yet all I did was what any person of rank is expected to do in this kingdom: I looked after my interests and those of my family and dependants. Though born in a province you subjugated, I have served with honour in His Majesty's armies and in Parliament as Member for Newcastle. Did I not discharge my duties as High Sheriff of Northumberland with distinction? It was said I hankered after a peerage: can there be any objection to a man's legitimate aspirations to a title of honour? I think not, my lords. [*in an impassioned tone*] Is it because of my humble origins that you hold me in contempt? Others far lowlier than I have risen higher, to universal acclaim and approbation. Does not society encourage social advancement? Remember, my lords: I am what you ... what this country ... made me, and am wholly innocent of the charges laid at my door. [*with great fervour and striking a heroic pose, a shaft of white light lending spirituality to his stance*] I say: let justice prevail!

> [*The lights gradually revert to normal, and* STONEY *resumes his seat.*]

JUDGE 2 [*matter-of-fact, and wholly unaffected by* STONEY'*s tirade*] Sentence will be passed presently. You are a thoroughly bad lot, Andrew Robinson Bowes, and I have no doubt you will go to prison for a great many years. The court will rise.

> [*The* JUDGES *rise and leave.*]

STONEY [*now alone on the stage, turns to the audience with a wicked grin*] Well, it was worth a try!

> [*Blackout.*]

## SCENE 19:
## THE IMPRISONMENT

*1800.* STONEY's *rooms in the King's Bench Prison.*

STONEY *and* DR FOOT *are playing cards as* JENNY SUTTON, STONEY's *pregnant mistress, pours them drinks from a crystal decanter. The setting is far from spartan, and though certain obvious signs confirm this is a prison, we are reminded of the furnishings of a comfortable inn.* STONEY *has aged somewhat, his hair greyer; he is fifty-three.*

WILLIAM STAMP, *dressed as a* WARDER, *enters and sings from a song sheet. A bunch of outsize keys hangs from his waist.*

WARDER [*set to the last bars of Bartolo's Aria 'La Vendetta' from* The Marriage of Figaro]

So thought the crowd, with groans and hissing
They did him safe conduct to prison.
Thus he who might all peace enjoy
And many mansions occupy
Doomed to a room twelve feet by eight,
Who could but say — They served him right?

> [STONEY *rises from the table, walks up to the* WARDER *and snatches the song sheet from him.*]

STONEY What's this? Twelve feet by eight? Trust the journals to get it wrong! Did you hear that, doctor?

DR FOOT I did.

STONEY [*glancing round at the room*] It's at least five times the size. And that's not taking into account my bedroom and dressing-room. It's all costing me a fortune!

DR FOOT It's a scandal, I agree.

STONEY I detect Parson Bate's poisoned quill.

DR FOOT The *Morning Post* will stop at nothing.

STONEY I've a mind to teach Bate another lesson.

| | |
|---|---|
| DR FOOT | You'd have to arrange the meeting within the precincts of this prison. |
| WARDER | A duel, cap'n? |
| STONEY | Yes. |
| WARDER | It could be arranged. |
| STONEY | We'll see. Has my claret arrived? |
| WARDER | It's in one of the inner courtyards. |
| STONEY | How many barrels? |
| WARDER | Two, sir. |
| STONEY | Lock them in the vault, clearly marked with my name. |
| WARDER | [*begins to leave*] Very good, sir. [*He goes.*] |
| STONEY | [*shouts after him*] And don't you or the Marshal touch a drop of it! [*He sits down to resume the card game.*] You can't trust the blackguards, doctor! [*to* JENNY] Go and make sure it's done properly, Jenny. And bring us another flagon of claret. |
| JENNY | Very well, dear. [*She goes.*] |
| DR FOOT | I see Jenny's with child again. |
| STONEY | Yes. [*shuffling the cards*] A fulfilling experience for a woman, I always say. |
| DR FOOT | You expect to serve out your sentence? |
| STONEY | I've irons in the fire. A number of appeals. I'm not resigned to another ten years. |
| DR FOOT | What if your creditors continue to sue? |
| STONEY | Ah, well, then I'd be here indefinitely. [*puts down the cards*] I need to raise funds, doctor. Will you help me? |
| DR FOOT | My means are limited. |
| STONEY | When I say help I mean ... you could carry out a few errands for me ... |
| DR FOOT | If you think it would help — |
| STONEY | The timber. At Gibside. |
| DR FOOT | What of it? |
| STONEY | You remember my grand act of deforestation? |

DR FOOT   How could I forget? It was the talk of the county!

STONEY    Indeed. A civilising gesture; a great step forward for humanity! Ours is justly called the age of reason! [*Pause.*] Tell me, doctor, is there a sound sweeter than axe against willow? Ah! Most of that timber's still there. Through a clerk at His Majesty's Docks who is ... temporarily sheltering within these walls I think I could sell it. He assures me it'd fetch a good price, even allowing for his commission. And there'd be something in it for you too, naturally.

DR FOOT   But ... is the timber yours to sell?

STONEY    Why not? I cut it down, didn't I?

DR FOOT   Has not every single estate reverted to the Countess? Including Gibside?

STONEY    Ah. That's where you come in. I want you to go to Gibside and arrange for the removal of the timber. Under cover of darkness, naturally.

DR FOOT   Well, I'll have to see if —

STONEY    Good! It's settled then. I'll give you the details later. If I'm to succeed in the number of cases I intend to present before the courts, I must keep my lawyers happy. Greedy bunch that they are! Is there no honest practitioner of the law left in this world? They've skinned me alive!

[*The* WARDER *enters.*]

WARDER    There's a messenger here to see you, cap'n.

STONEY    Who is it?

WARDER    Says he used to be a servant of yours. One ... [*glances at a piece of paper*] ... Septimus Bland.

STONEY    Show him in.

WARDER    [*turning round to the entrance*] Come in, you...

[SEPTIMUS *enters.*]

SEPTIMUS  Evenin', captain. You're looking champion!

STONEY    What brings you here, man? Out with it. I haven't got all day!

SEPTIMUS  I've come straight from Grosvenor Square.

STONEY    Aah! [*puts a finger to the tip of his nose*] The Countess is relenting!

SEPTIMUS  [*his head bowed*] Her ladyship died of a fever in the night.

[*There is a hush.*]

STONEY    [*begins in a quiet, subdued manner*] It is truly remarkable, doctor, how mysterious the ways of providence can be. It is at moments such as this that I become aware of the power for good exercised by Almighty God. [*oracularly*] In her death lies my salvation. [*shouting, at fever-pitch and manically, his arms outstretched in exultation*] The bitch is dead! D'you hear, all of you? I shall go to law without delay for the restitution of my fortune!

[*Fadeout.*]


SCENE 20:
BOWES MORIBUND


*1810.* STONEY's *rooms in the King's Bench Prison.*

STONEY, *now sixty-three, has aged a great deal. He is lying on a makeshift sofa in the same room as in the previous scene. The furnishings are tatty and threadbare, an indication that* STONEY's *fortunes have suffered many reverses in the intervening decade. He is clearly gravely ill, and* DR FOOT *is mixing some medicine.* STONEY's *arms and legs are bandaged as a result of the application of leeches.*

*The room is in semi-darkness, a tallow candle or two providing the only lighting.*

DR FOOT   Drink this. You'll feel better.

STONEY    [*his voice hoarse, attempts to introduce a little humour*] None of your mixtures of mercury now, doctor!

DR FOOT   You may rest assured, sir, that I wouldn't —

STONEY    Come, come, man: have you no sense of humour? Many's the claps you cured me of! And worse!

DR FOOT   Drink this, please, captain.

| | |
|---|---|
| STONEY | If I must. [*He drinks and grimaces with disgust.*] This is even worse than mercury. And far less fun than Venus! |
| DR FOOT | As your physician, sir, I must inform you that you are not at all well. |
| STONEY | I don't need you to tell me that. What I need to know is ... am I at death's door? |
| DR FOOT | I must reserve my prognosis until your temperature subsides and you've been bled. |
| STONEY | Again? |
| DR FOOT | I am concerned about the girl Jenny. |
| STONEY | Is anything the matter with her? |
| DR FOOT | She has been your devoted companion within these walls for many years. She has borne your children. |
| STONEY | Don't remind me of them, please, doctor — or I shall take a turn for the worse. |
| DR FOOT | Have you made provisions for her maintenance? |
| STONEY | [*surprised at the question*] Provisions? For her maintenance? |
| DR FOOT | Sir, you owe it to her. She has served you faithfully for many years. |
| STONEY | I doubt I could raise any money at all. You forget I am a bankrupt. |
| DR FOOT | You have some trinkets and jewels I could dispose of for you. |

[*Pause.*]

| | |
|---|---|
| STONEY | [*almost inaudibly*] So this is the end. |
| DR FOOT | Will you allow me to make the necessary arrangements for Jenny Sutton? |
| STONEY | [*his voice weaker, he is close to tears*] But doctor ... me? Make arrangements to provide for ... a woman? |
| DR FOOT | It would be the gesture of a truly generous man. |
| STONEY | [*with one last desperate effort sits up in bed, his hand shaking menacingly at* DR FOOT, *shouting*] I'm damned if I do anything of the kind! Let her find her own — |

[*With a sharp intake of breath he falls back onto the sofa. He is dead.*]

[DR FOOT *quietly closes* STONEY'*s eyelids, and sets about removing* STONEY'*s pocket watch from his waistcoat, as well as other pieces of jewellery such as rings and fobs. He puts them in a leather purse and tiptoes out of the room.*]

[*Hold before fadeout.*]

THE END

# DA PONTE'S LAST STAND

CHARACTERS

Rickenbacker
Louella van Pick
Lorenzo da Ponte
Baron Wetzlar
Salieri
Mozart
Joseph II
Prince Babenberg
Casanova
Adriana
Steward

The action of the play takes place in August 1838 in New York, with flashbacks to other locations: Vienna, 1785; Dux Castle in Bohemia, 1790s. Apart from da Ponte's rooms in New York, which may be a fixed set consisting of chairs, a table and a sofa, the other venues may be sparingly depicted by a simple arrangement of a few pieces of furniture. The billiards room scene in Mozart's rooms may be achieved by a back-projection of just a corner of a billiard table, with recorded sound effects of the shots which Mozart or da Ponte in turn will pretend to be taking on stage. In that particular scene a harpsichord or a virginal (or a mock-up of either of these instruments) will be essential, and should be placed a few feet from the projection of the billiard table, although the sounds issuing from both will of course be recordings. As to da Ponte's age changes, the director may think fit to use a number of disguises such as wigs and moustaches to be used and discarded according to need.

The musical passages where indicated should be regarded as an integral part of the play, and the relevant extracts may be obtained from the many recordings available.

## ONE

RICKENBACKER's *office. New York. Autumn 1838.*

RICKENBACKER  You ... killed him?

LOUELLA  I did. But not ... intentionally.

RICKENBACKER  This is incredible. The gazettes ... his friends and family reported that he died peacefully in his bed. You mean to tell me it happened with you ... at the Opera?

LOUELLA  In the retiring room of Box 42. As I describe in my journals, if only you'll take the trouble of reading right through them. Poor Lorenzo! [*She sobs.*] There was, of course, a cover-up.

RICKENBACKER  You don't say!

LOUELLA  There was. Lorenzo da Ponte had enemies who'd be only too pleased to blacken his name. I can just hear them: look at the way he died! If he acted like that at the age of eighty-nine ...

RICKENBACKER  Was he that old?

LOUELLA  ... what was he like as a younger man?

RICKENBACKER  At the risk of sounding indelicate in front of a lady, Miss van Pick, why the man was a libertine!

LOUELLA  [*passionately*] He was an American citizen! Don't you forget that! He lived among us for thirty-three years, an ornament to our up-and-coming culture.

RICKENBACKER  Spoken like the literary correspondent of the *New York Enquirer!* Miss van Pick: I'm a publisher, not a moralist. Nevertheless the reputation that followed him from Europe was unsavoury, to say the least ...

LOUELLA  Typical European envy. Lies. They were all of them jealous of a superior talent. He was hated by the Austrians, ignored by the French, banished by the Italians and vilified by the rest of Europe. He came to America in search of freedom and belated recognition ...

RICKENBACKER  Which eluded him.

LOUELLA  Yes, to the very last ... until, that is, two months ago. When I met him.

RICKENBACKER  [*riffling through manuscript*] Ah yes, your journals.

LOUELLA  Precisely. Mr Rickenbacker, will you publish?

RICKENBACKER  Don't hustle me, Miss van Pick. I haven't read your manuscript yet. Apart from the few details you've given me, I don't know a thing about this guy da Ponte. Besides, didn't he bring out his own memoirs some fifteen years ago?

LOUELLA  [*dismissively*] The memoirs were an exercise in self-defence as well as an attempt to make some money. He told me so himself. He simply couldn't tell the whole truth in his book. But look through those papers and you'll find disclosures that'll send ripples through the rotten European establishment. I tell you Mr Rickenbacker, you could make history by publishing my story.

RICKENBACKER  Why don't you publish it in your paper?

LOUELLA  That's what I thought of doing at first, but the subject is too big for a weekly. It deserves hard covers.

RICKENBACKER  Yes, but ...

LOUELLA  And if it's Lorenzo da Ponte's amatory disposition that worries you ... [*nostalgically*] ... isn't that a sure sign of exuberance in creative artists the world over?

RICKENBACKER  [*in an undertone*] It's the first time I've heard it called that ... [*businesslike*] I guess this is 1838, and I know you hold advanced views ... but maybe the world isn't ready to share your outlook.

LOUELLA  The rest of the world may not be ready, Mr Rickenbacker, but America most definitely is!

RICKENBACKER  Yes ... Well, I'll read your manuscript and talk to you again.

LOUELLA  When?

RICKENBACKER  Let me see ... The day after tomorrow? Here, at my office?

LOUELLA  I'll be here, Mr Rickenbacker. Good day. [*She begins to leave.*]

RICKENBACKER  Good day to you, Miss van Pick.

> [*She goes.* RICKENBACKER *heaves a sigh of relief.*]

Let's see now... [*He begins to read.*] The circumstances of my first meeting with Lorenzo da Ponte can only be described as extraordinary, even by modern, 1838 standards. Yes, quite ...

> [*His voice fades out.* LOUELLA*'s voice takes up the narration.*]

LOUELLA  ... extraordinary, and I use the word advisedly. As extraordinary as the man himself. For do we not use the word of ambassadors, who are deemed to be both extraordinary and plenipotentiary — and dear Lorenzo's plenitude of powers, incidentally, was beyond doubt despite his advanced age, as we shall see. Can I ever forget that evening at the Opera?

## TWO

*Park Theatre, New York. First the auditorium, then a refreshment concourse.*

LOUELLA*'s narration.*

LOUELLA  All the best people in New York were there and within the confines of red plush and baroque curlicues, romantically lit by the most scientifically advanced gas-fired chandeliers in the world, the old and the new seemed to meet in glittering display, surely a harbinger of the exciting future in store for our great nation. I might never have spotted him, so enraptured I was by Mozart's truly divine *Marriage of Figaro* and the marvellous singing of the entire company. And then during the concluding strains of the opera ...

> [LOUELLA *sits next to* DA PONTE *in the auditorium of the Opera House. Fade up closing bars of* The Marriage of Figaro *over the next speech.*]
>
> [LOUELLA*'s narration.*]

LOUELLA  ... then I noticed this man sitting next to me. A very striking appearance. Flowing locks of snow-white hair, tall, handsome. Yes — and leaning on a pearl-handled cane. I simply had to talk to someone about the opera!

[*Prolonged applause.*]

LOUELLA  Bra – vo! Bra – vo! Oh, this is too enchanting! Sir! Don't you think it was ... well ... just great?

DA PONTE  [*polite but on his guard*] It would be churlish of me to disagree, madam.

LOUELLA  To think this masterpiece was written over fifty years ago, before the French Revolution and just after our own great struggle for independence ... and here it is, in New York. Didn't you find it a great experience?

DA PONTE  Yes.

LOUELLA  Oh but ... didn't you just love it?

DA PONTE  In point of fact, madam ... [*He clears his throat.*] I wrote the words.

LOUELLA  No!

DA PONTE  For my sins ... I did.

LOUELLA  [*gasping for breath*] You mean to say ... the libretto ... that you ... you ...

DA PONTE  Yes.

LOUELLA  So ... so you've just got to be ... the legendary Abbé ...

DA PONTE  Lorenzo da Ponte, at your service.

LOUELLA  [*breathlessly*] Louella van Pick ... of the *New York Enquirer*. Glad to know you ... My, what a scoop! But this can't be possible ... It's got to be some kind of dream!

DA PONTE  Miss van Pick, I believe they are serving excellent chocolate in the main concourse of the theatre. May I offer you a cup?

LOUELLA  Why ... yes ... I'm so excited I don't know what to say ...

DA PONTE  You'll find hot chocolate has remarkable sedative properties. I've often recommended it. This way.

[*They rise and stroll to the refreshment area.*]

... the perfect sedative, as I was saying ... [*He takes a noisy sip of chocolate.*] ... when taken neat. However, I occasionally

|            | lace it with a little schnapps. It then turns into a most agreeable stimulant ... Is it to your taste? |
|---|---|
| LOUELLA | The chocolate's fine ... but ... Mr da Ponte, I still can't get over the fact you're here ... in New York ... in America ... and still ... |
| DA PONTE | ... alive? |
| LOUELLA | I didn't mean that. Of course, I've read your memoirs, but that was years ago ... and as I said, I'd no idea you were over here ... now ... |
| DA PONTE | [*flattered, his interest in* LOUELLA *beginning to grow*] You've read my book? I'm delighted to hear it. You've obviously read the volume that deals with my life prior to my arrival in America. [*gravely*] I'm afraid it didn't do very well. I have latterly translated it into Italian ... but I doubt whether people'll be interested. |
| LOUELLA | How long have you been in America? |
| DA PONTE | Let me see ... since 1805 ... thirty-three years. And before that I spent ten years in London ... which I had to leave ... with unseemly haste ... |
| LOUELLA | Oh ...? |
| DA PONTE | ... owing to pressures not unconnected with financial matters ... Still: you read my memoirs, eh? Good. Good. |
| LOUELLA | What a fascinating book! Especially the account of your years in Vienna. I really am sorry it didn't enjoy the wide circulation it obviously deserved. |
| DA PONTE | Alas, it didn't. The printers and I lost heavily. Enemies and scarcity of funds seem to have haunted me all my life ... |
| LOUELLA | Never mind, Mr da Ponte: you said what had to be said. After all, you stated in the book that your object in writing it was a desire to set the record straight ... and to tell the whole truth ... |
| DA PONTE | The whole truth? My dear young lady: I run a modest lodging house in Greenwich Street which hardly pays the rent. I trade a little in rare books ... As professor of Italian at Columbia University I receive no salary. All I'm trying to tell |

you is that my object in writing my memoirs was indeed to make a profit ... as large a profit as possible.

LOUELLA  You've got to be kidding. You — Mozart's librettist, the author of the finest operas of our time ... you wrote for ... profit?

DA PONTE  A very sensible Englishman once said that no man but a blockhead ever wrote except for money. I entirely agree with this view. As for truth, Miss ... er ... Miss ...

LOUELLA  Van Pick.

DA PONTE  ... Miss van Pick, don't ever go looking for it in memoirs or biographies. There's hardly a word of truth in the whole of my autobiography, whichever volume you care to tackle.

LOUELLA  Hardly a word of truth? Now I know you're kidding.

DA PONTE  I'm not. You see, the only way to confound my enemies ... and they were ... and are ... legion ... was to write the kind of book you've read. It was what you would call ... a whitewash ... [*He sighs.*] ... on a crumbling edifice.

LOUELLA  I don't understand.

DA PONTE  No matter. I didn't expect you to. You're obviously a stranger to the world of intrigue. Besides, it's a long story. Why should a pretty young lady like you take an interest in me? I'll wager these pretty white gloves conceal still whiter hands?

> [DA PONTE *begins from this point on to accompany his old-world gallantry with typically Mediterranean pawings, to which* LOUELLA *reacts with surprise.*]

LOUELLA  Er ... They won't come off if you pull like that ... they go right up to my elbow.

DA PONTE  I do beg your pardon. [*Pause.*] As I was saying, yes ... why so much interest in ... a relic of the past?

LOUELLA  Mr da Ponte ...

DA PONTE  I should be flattered if you'd call me Lorenzo. It'd make me feel ... younger ...

LOUELLA  Well, then ... Lorenzo: I'm a journalist. And in my book, why, you're a great big hunk of history. Lorenzo, you were Mozart's librettist!

DA PONTE [*coldly*] I was his poet, not his librettist. He set my dramas to music.

LOUELLA  Of course ... naturally.

DA PONTE  Many other composers set my dramas to music ... Martin, Weigl ... Salieri ... Thanks to my work some of their music was moderately successful.

LOUELLA  I'd really love to hear more about your work.

DA PONTE  And you shall, my dear, you shall ... Hm ... You begin to interest me ...

LOUELLA  Oooooh! What was that!

DA PONTE  I am most terribly sorry. My walking stick ... It's a new one ... I'm not quite used to it.

LOUELLA  About your work Mr da ... er ... Lorenzo. It occurs to me that ... with your permission, naturally, I could feature you in a number of essays.

DA PONTE  I beg your pardon?

LOUELLA  I could write about you in my paper.

DA PONTE  [*haughtily*] Am I to understand you wish to publish a reportage about me in your ... gazette?

LOUELLA  Only as part of a general review of the arts in the latter part of the eighteenth century ... But of course if you have any objections ...

DA PONTE  What I would have to say to you would be in the strictest confidence. Off ... Off ...

LOUELLA  ... the record?

DA PONTE  Precisely.

LOUELLA  [*disappointed*] You wouldn't want me to print it.

DA PONTE  Let us say ... not in my lifetime. [*Pause.*] Well, are you still interested?

LOUELLA  Would you ... would you allow me to take notes? Not for immediate publication ... but for ... well ...

DA PONTE  Posterity?

LOUELLA  Well, if that's the way you want to put it. I'd really appreciate it.

DA PONTE  Can I trust you, I wonder?

LOUELLA  One hundred per cent, Lorenzo. And call me Louella.

DA PONTE  Very well, Louella. I'll ... I'll take a chance.

LOUELLA  Oh, thank you! Thank you!

DA PONTE  I suggest you call on me ... I have notes and papers in my study I could dip into ... Would you care to pay me an initial visit?

LOUELLA  That sounds just great. When?

DA PONTE  Whenever you like.

LOUELLA  [*eagerly*] Tomorrow?

DA PONTE  Tomorrow? Indeed, why not tomorrow. Say about three o'clock?

LOUELLA  Perfect.

DA PONTE  [*suddenly anxious*] You'll come then ...

LOUELLA  I've just said I would.

DA PONTE  At three. Without fail, mind you.

LOUELLA  I'll be there.

> [*Fade up 'Dunque in giardin verrai' under the next five speeches.*]

DA PONTE  You won't forget?

LOUELLA  Yes ...

DA PONTE  Yes?

LOUELLA  I mean ... no.

DA PONTE  Good! Three o'clock tomorrow. I'll be expecting you. [*Begin to fade out.*] I live at ...

> [*Fade out and cut into* LOUELLA*'s narration.*]

LOUELLA  It was with considerable trepidation that on the following day I made my way to Lorenzo da Ponte's residence in Greenwich Street. The approach to his house was in sharp contrast to what he must have been accustomed to in the days when he sauntered into the Royal Palace in Schoenbrunn for one of his many exciting talks with Joseph II, arm-in-arm maybe with one of his composer friends such as Salieri

... or even Mozart. Alas, no marble nymphs or liveried footmen in powdered wigs greeted the eye here. No. Only pigs which wallowed in the mud, drawn by the garbage in the gutters. 'How are the mighty fallen' is the phrase that came to mind as one picked one's way through the mean side streets, conjuring up pictures of past glories in imperial Vienna over fifty years ago ... As I knocked boldly at his door, a rheumy-eyed sow nibbling at my feet, I felt a twinge of anxiety. With da Ponte's public fame I was — as who is not? — well acquainted already, but what of him in a private setting? His ... endearing courtliness when we first met was not unmixed with a ... physical effusiveness which I must confess I found a little ... disturbing ... though not altogether unwelc– ... surprising. His eventual appearance as he opened the door, however, immediately dispelled any doubts or fears on my part. He greeted me like a long-lost friend, and even if the pressure of both his hands on mine as he bent to kiss them was somewhat excessive for a quarter after three in the afternoon, I felt reassured the moment he straightened up again and pointed to the interior of the house with a flourish of his hands and a truly patrician bow ...

THREE

DA PONTE'*s rooms. Chairs, a table with books scattered on it. A sofa. Another side table with cups etc.*

DA PONTE  You are here! Excellent. Come in. My house, Louella, is yours ...

        [LOUELLA *enters.*]

And this, my dear, is my little den. Sit down. This sofa is quite comfortable.

LOUELLA  It's really cosy here. May I look around first?

DA PONTE  Certainly.

LOUELLA  What charming books you have ... Hm ... I see no music among them.

DA PONTE  No music? Ah: musical scores. No, you won't find any here.

LOUELLA  Why?

DA PONTE  I deal in words. [*gently*] My music's in the words.

LOUELLA  I'll remember that. Look at all these books ... Dante ... [*pronouncing with some difficulty*] Pet ... rar ... ca. Oh, that's Petrarch I guess.

DA PONTE  These few books are about all I could bring with me from Europe. The only things I could salvage from the greed of my creditors.

LOUELLA  What superb bindings. Tasso. [*uncertain of her pronunciation*] Ari... ari - osto?

DA PONTE  [*pronouncing correctly and with some impatience*] Ariosto. Ariosto.

LOUELLA  And look at this one ... Am I allowed to handle this?

DA PONTE  Please, go ahead.

LOUELLA  I've never seen tooled leather like this. It's a masterpiece of binding.

DA PONTE  [*casually*] Florentine. Late seventeenth century.

LOUELLA  Aret ... aret ... ino?

DA PONTE  Aretino. The sonnets. Yes. Charming. Very ... stimulating.

LOUELLA  Sonnets. Sonnets. How I wish I knew Italian.

DA PONTE  I will teach you if you like.

LOUELLA  So well printed, too. Hey: it's illustrated.

DA PONTE  Charming compositions, don't you think?

LOUELLA  Yes. I'm ... trying to figure out what all those people are doing ... Oh my God!!

DA PONTE  Hm?

LOUELLA  [*snapping the book shut in some alarm*] They're just too ... too ...

DA PONTE  You find them a little too ... athletic perhaps? Let me assure you they're only a pale approximation of the poet's text ...

LOUELLA  Lorenzo, I never ...

DA PONTE  In that case you've missed a great deal.

LOUELLA  I didn't mean ... It's inconceivable to me that people could act like that ...

| | |
|---|---|
| DA PONTE | Come now. They're merely giving expression to mutual feelings of attraction, no more and no less. |
| LOUELLA | You call that a subject fit for poetry? |
| DA PONTE | Possibly the only one. A sign of exuberance in creative artists the world over. Even my landlady's daughter in Vienna was extremely fond of Aretino. Yes. So she was. |
| LOUELLA | [*tetchily*] Well, that was Vienna. |
| DA PONTE | [*nostalgically*] Yes, that was dear, dear Vienna. The sonnets ... I translated most of them for little Helga. |
| LOUELLA | Into German? |
| DA PONTE | Into action. [*quickly*] But let me offer you some refreshment. |
| LOUELLA | Please don't go to any trouble. |
| DA PONTE | I insist. I know you like hot chocolate. My housekeeper has prepared us a steaming pot. [*He pours out chocolate.*] Please be seated. |
| LOUELLA | Thank you. |
| DA PONTE | Well, I'm ready to be questioned. |
| LOUELLA | [*taking a sip of chocolate*] It's hot ... Mmm ... It tastes as if ... |
| DA PONTE | I've ... spiked it with a little schnapps, to sustain us through the rigours of this interview. |
| LOUELLA | I see. [*She puts the cup down.*] I think I've had enough for the moment. [*Pause.*] Er ... how is Mrs da Ponte? |
| DA PONTE | My poor wife passed away over seven years ago. |
| LOUELLA | I am so sorry. |
| | [*Fade up instrumental accompaniment to 'Aprite un pó quegli occhi' to underlie the next seven speeches.*] |
| DA PONTE | Don't be. Nancy was a splendid woman in her way, but over the years we failed to achieve ... compatibility. In fact, it was hell on earth. |
| LOUELLA | Please, I didn't mean to ... |
| DA PONTE | Hell on earth. She never understood me. Cold as a fish and cunning as a fox. |
| LOUELLA | I don't really want to pry ... |
| DA PONTE | [*with mounting irritation*] Like so many others, she intrigued |

against me. I nurtured a viper in my bosom. Nancy. Nancy. Of each stage of my downfall the ruthless initiator.

LOUELLA   Don't go on, Lorenzo. It's obviously upsetting you.

DA PONTE   A millstone. A millstone round my neck. [*louder*] And she dared accuse me of lacking a sense of humour. Me! Why, I must have had a sense of humour to marry her at all! [*Pause.*] Forgive me. I'm not being a very good host.

LOUELLA   You're being perfect. Don't worry.

DA PONTE   Well now, all those questions you wanted to ask me. Are you going to take notes?

LOUELLA   Yes. I've brought some paper.

DA PONTE   Is the sofa comfortable enough?

LOUELLA   It's ... fine ... One of the springs is trying to break through ... but it's all right where I'm sitting.

DA PONTE   Why not ... recline on it?

LOUELLA   I'm fine as I am.

DA PONTE   [*suddenly animated*] I'm convinced you'd be more comfortable if only you'd lie down ... like this ...

> [DA PONTE *clumsily attempts to make her lie down, and a scuffle ensues.*]

LOUELLA   Lorenzo! How do you imagine I could write in this position, with you pinning my arms down ...

DA PONTE   Forgive me.

LOUELLA   ... and that broken spring in the small of my back.

DA PONTE   This sofa has seen better days ...

LOUELLA   Let go of me!

DA PONTE   ... and kinder women.

LOUELLA   Why not sit down opposite me and be a good boy...

DA PONTE   If I must. Well, proceed.

LOUELLA   [*relieved*] Thanks. Let's see. I think you cover most of your childhood and adolescence in your memoirs.

DA PONTE   I do.

LOUELLA   I take it they're reliable.

DA PONTE  Up to my departure from Venice for Austria ... yes. Utterly.

LOUELLA  Of course I know you became an Abbé — that's some sort of preacher isn't it?

DA PONTE  I took minor orders as an Abbé and thereafter dedicated myself to poetry. You'll find all that in the memoirs, quite reliable as I said up to this point.

LOUELLA  Fine. Could we maybe jump ahead a little ... would you tell me how you came to be in Vienna ... and how you first met Mozart?

DA PONTE  To start with, just before Vienna, I spent some time in Dresden, where I produced some acceptable verses, and where diversions were not lacking. Circumstances, however, made a hasty departure imperative, and depart I did, with a letter of recommendation to Maestro Salieri in Vienna.

LOUELLA  Wait. I did hear a rumour... about Dresden.

DA PONTE  [*suspiciously*] Slanders?

LOUELLA  Something to the effect that you'd formed an attachment with two young ladies ... and their mother.

DA PONTE  Oh that. Yes. [*relishing the memory*] My detractors couldn't even get that right. [*He chuckles.*] Yes, as I recall, it was put about that I was caught in flagrante with the mother — a handsome creature incidentally — and her two daughters ...

LOUELLA  That couldn't possibly have been true.

[*'Catalogue' aria from* Don Giovanni *to underlie the next eleven speeches without drowning them.*]

DA PONTE  It was not. It was palpably untrue. We'd be much closer to unmasking the truth if to the three charmers already mentioned we were to add the girls' French governess ... and a frisky Dalmatian housekeeper. And that was but one household. [*He begins to warm to the memory.*] Yes, Dresden was full of diversions. A noble city, filled to its quaint rooftops with still nobler, superbly nubile beauties. I was happy there. I could compile a long list of ... [*He crosses over close to* LOUELLA.] Would you care to hear more about Dresden? Let me sit next to you ...

LOUELLA  I'd rather you didn't.

DA PONTE   [*conspiratorially*] It's all coming back to me ...

>   [*He sits next to her, upsetting some china.* LOUELLA *rises with a shrill cry and hurries off to the back of the sofa.* DA PONTE *follows in hot pursuit and a spirited chase round the sofa ensues.*]

[*short of breath*] How can I tell you all about Dresden chasing you round this sofa ...

LOUELLA   [*still running*] You must calm yourself, Lorenzo.

DA PONTE   [*still running*] I just wanted to tell you my Dresden story.

LOUELLA   [*still running*] Compose yourself! Remember you were ... for all I know you still are ... in holy orders ...

DA PONTE   [*still running and very nearly out of breath*] My dear ... they ... were ... very minor orders.

>   [LOUELLA *stops dead.*]

LOUELLA   [*emphatically*] This is ridiculous! Let's both sit down.

DA PONTE   That's exactly what I was about to suggest.

LOUELLA   You over there — and I here.

>   [DA PONTE *grudgingly complies as the 'Catalogue' aria in the background comes to an abrupt stop.*]

That's better. Now I'll pour you a cup of chocolate ... and one for me.

DA PONTE   Thank you.

LOUELLA   Quite frankly I think we've covered Dresden pretty extensively.

DA PONTE   [*disappointed*] Oh.

LOUELLA   Tell me rather ... [*She takes a sip of chocolate.*] My, this chocolate's sure got a kick ... tell me about your first meeting with Mozart.

DA PONTE   [*drinking noisily*] Ah! That's better. Mozart, did you say?

LOUELLA   Can you remember when ... where you first met him?

DA PONTE   Let me think. Where was it we met? Yes, in 1783. Was it really fifty-five years ago? So it was, by Jove, at the house of —

>   [*Blackout.*]

## FOUR

BARON WETZLAR's *town house, 1785. Suggest entrance to sumptuous state rooms. A Mozart divertimento plays softly in the background.*

WETZLAR ... Raimund Wetzlar von Plankenstern! [*The click of his heels rings out like a pistol shot.*] Delighted to meet you, Signor da Ponte. And congratulations on your appointment as Poet to the Italian theatre here in Vienna. So glad you could come to my little soirée.

DA PONTE Sir.

WETZLAR I hear the post carries a salary of twelve hundred florins a year.

DA PONTE His Imperial Majesty has been most generous, Herr Baron.

WETZLAR You won't find me ungenerous either, da Ponte. I might contribute another five hundred per annum from my own purse were you to perform services for me ... not unlike those you've rendered His Imperial Majesty.

DA PONTE I'm yours to command, Herr Baron. Is it an ode you require? Or an epithalamium for your daughter's forthcoming marriage?

WETZLAR No. Nothing like that.

DA PONTE An epic on your illustrious House perhaps?

WETZLAR [*in an undertone*] I hear you're familiar with the charming Italian sopranos who grace our theatre ...

DA PONTE Well ...

WETZLAR ... and that you've made it possible for the King to attend certain intimate ... er ... performances you occasionally devise ...

DA PONTE Really, Herr Baron...

WETZLAR Could I ... with the utmost discretion, it goes without saying — Damn! Here's Salieri. More of this later, da Ponte. My dear Salieri, you know our friend da Ponte, I take it?

SALIERI  Indeed I do. He is my protégé and friend. How are you, Lorenzo?

DA PONTE  Very well, maestro.

SALIERI  I've been dying to tell you I'm more than satisfied with the libretto you've just written for me.

DA PONTE  Thank you. Thank you.

SALIERI  Not at all. You know, Baron, da Ponte is a superlative poet. He's been a great help to me.

WETZLAR  I don't doubt it for a moment, Salieri. I only hope he'll oblige me too at some point ... Ah, there you are, Duke ... Excuse me, gentlemen ... [*He moves off.*]

SALIERI  You must come and sup with me soon, da Ponte. I keep a good table. And we'll go through Act One together afterwards.

DA PONTE  I'd like that. Name the day, maestro.

SALIERI  Have you met Mozart yet?

DA PONTE  I haven't... but I'm longing to. His fame is beginning to spread.

SALIERI  [*grudgingly*] A promising young man. Still has a long way to go, of course ... there he is ... [*He calls out.*] Mozart!

MOZART  Good evening, Maestro Salieri.

SALIERI  Are you having a good time?

MOZART  Oh, absolutely!

SALIERI  I want you to meet the poet da Ponte. He's just finished a libretto for me. — Wolfgang Mozart ...

[MOZART *and* DA PONTE *exchange civilities.*]

MOZART  I've heard so much about you, Signor da Ponte.

DA PONTE  [*darkly*] Not slanders, I hope and trust.

MOZART  Oh, absolutely ... not! In fact, I'd —

SALIERI  [*cutting in*] I see His Majesty's summoning me ... excuse me. [*He moves off.*] Come and sup with me soon, Mozart. I keep a good table as you know.

| | |
|---|---|
| MOZART | Thank you. |
| DA PONTE | You were saying, Herr Mozart? |
| MOZART | About your work ... yes. I'm told you excel at translation and adaptation. |
| DA PONTE | Is that a compliment, sir, or... |
| MOZART | Oh, absolutely! You see, there's this play by a Frenchman ... Beaumarchais or something ... I've just read it. I think it has definite possibilities as an *opera buffa*. Do you know the thing? |
| DA PONTE | I'm afraid I don't. |
| MOZART | Supposing you liked it, might you be tempted to adapt it for me? |
| DA PONTE | What's it called? |
| MOZART | You've got me there ... just a moment ... Yes: *Le Mariage de Figaro*. |
| DA PONTE | Oh yes. *Le Nozze di Figaro*. I've heard of it. I'll read it and give you an opinion if you like. |
| MOZART | I'd be most grateful if you would. I say, do you play billiards? |
| DA PONTE | I do. |
| MOZART | How absolutely splendid! I have a table at home. You must come and give me a game sometime. |
| DA PONTE | Thank you. I will. With pleasure. |
| MOZART | I'd really like to know what you think of the French play I've just mentioned. I'd love to write an Italian opera. |
| DA PONTE | I'll tell you the moment I've read it. We'll probably meet soon for supper at Salieri's. I'm told he keeps an excellent table. |
| MOZART | Oh, absolutely! Decent man, Salieri. I go whenever he asks me. Between ourselves, I can always do with a square meal. Trouble is, I seem to get the most awful stomach aches for days afterwards... Look out: here comes the King! |

> [JOSEPH II *approaches with his retinue. He has a heavy cold and will cough or sneeze at intervals.*]

| | |
|---|---|
| JOSEPH II | Ah: our beloved artists. Mozart ... |
| MOZART | Your Majesty. |

JOSEPH II   It is our royal command that you go on composing more of those brilliant divertimenti of yours.

MOZART   Oh, absol — As you command, Your Majesty.

JOSEPH II   Good. They're by far the best background music in Vienna.

MOZART   You flatter me, sir.

JOSEPH II   My dear da Ponte, Maestro Salieri tells us he's well pleased with your latest libretto.

DA PONTE   You honour me, sir.

JOSEPH II   We're looking forward to hearing the finished work. Very much. Yes indeed. Mozart — why don't you go and join your fellow musicians over there, there's a good chap ... we want a private word with da Ponte.

MOZART   Sir.

[*He bows and begins to withdraw, but cannot resist a last impulsive reminder to* DA PONTE.]

Signor da Ponte: don't forget about the French piece!

[ *He goes.*]

JOSEPH II   [*alarmed*] French piece, da Ponte? I thought most of your pretty little sopranos were Italian. [*reproachfully*] I sincerely hope you're not depriving me of a delightful newcomer in favour of Mozart ...

DA PONTE   With respect, Your Majesty... Mozart was merely intimating I should familiarise myself with a dramatic piece.

JOSEPH II   [*relieved*] I see, I see.

DA PONTE   A play.

JOSEPH II   Quite.

DA PONTE   Not a plaything.

JOSEPH II   [*with a high-pitched, mannered laugh*] Oh very droll, very droll indeed, da Ponte. You shall be appointed our court jester as well as poet. But seriously, I am most grateful for that little entertainment in the maze at Schoenbrunn the other night.

DA PONTE   I endeavour to please, sir.

JOSEPH II   Nevertheless, perhaps we should plan our next ... private performance ... under cover.

DA PONTE  As you wish, Majesty.

JOSEPH II  We caught the most awful chill ... And the maze was frightfully prickly...

DA PONTE  I am so sorry!

JOSEPH II  We're not complaining, mind you. The ... er ... nymphs were delightful. Skin like molten gold, my dear chap. Well done. [*He sneezes.*] But let the next venue be under cover.

DA PONTE  Your wish is my command.

JOSEPH II  [*louder*] Yes, you deserve well of us, da Ponte. Come gentlemen ... [*They begin to leave.*] He — he — he ... French piece indeed ...

[*Fade out on sneeze, and quick change to next scene.*]


## FIVE

DA PONTE's *rooms.*

LOUELLA  The King was sure keen on performances!

DA PONTE  [*pointedly*] Ensembles in particular.

LOUELLA  That then was the beginning of your collaboration with Mozart ...

DA PONTE  Yes. Would you care to read the three libretti I eventually wrote for him?

LOUELLA  I do so wish I could. But ... I've told you I don't understand Italian.

DA PONTE  That needn't stand in your way. If I could just get past you ... to these books ... [*He bumps into* LOUELLA, *who reacts with a cry.*] I beg your pardon! Here we are ... These are the English versions of my libretti ... translated I might add by me and published at my own expense. Borrow them and read them at your leisure.

LOUELLA  Oh but how exciting! *The Marriage of Figaro* ... which we saw the other night ... *Don Giovanni* ...

DA PONTE  Which will be staged in New York the week after next.

LOUELLA ... and ... *The School for Lovers?* I don't think I've heard of this one.

DA PONTE I originally called it *Cosí Fan Tutte*, but its subtitle seemed more suitable for an Anglo-Saxon audience ... a notoriously unimaginative one as a rule ... However, all this is academic as this opera has hardly ever been performed. Not even in London. But I live in hope.

LOUELLA I think I've taken up enough of your time for one day.

DA PONTE Please don't go yet ...

LOUELLA It's getting late.

DA PONTE Won't you stay to supper?

LOUELLA I'm sorry. I've simply got to fly. But I'd love to come again. May I?

DA PONTE You may. And as soon as you wish.

LOUELLA What about ... today week?

DA PONTE Not a moment too soon.

LOUELLA Fine. Today week, then. At the same time.

DA PONTE I'll see you to the door.

LOUELLA [*rising precipitately to avoid further close contact*] Don't bother ... no ... really, I'll see myself out ... [*She begins to leave.*] I'll see you today week ... and you take care, d'you hear? [*She goes.*]

[*Fadeout.*]

[LOUELLA's *narration.*]

LOUELLA So abundant was the material I'd gotten from Lorenzo at that first meeting that even the most sluggish pen would have been impelled to labour for days. And labour I did. For days and days, noting and sifting and fixing all that had issued so readily from Lorenzo's lips — his eyes aflame, his leonine mane of white hair flowing, his hands waving expressively and occasionally interf— ... the whole climaxing in a lasting hypnotic effect. Not since attending the inauguration of our own dear President van Buren — a cousin twice removed — had I been so impressed by the personality and sheer warmth of another human being. But there'd been more in store: my task became that much more rewarding when I'd read

Lorenzo's operatic libretti. Here it was indeed that his poetry was truly great. And how varied were his three great works, rich in all the human moods, as externalised by the airy lightness of *Figaro*, the dark broodiness of *Don Giovanni* and the exquisite wit of *Cosí Fan Tutte*. Having read them I now realised his poetry was truly representative of the genius of a man whose lesser failings — such as his exuberance — were just part of the common heritage of creative artists the world over. Yes. It had been a humbling experience, and one I couldn't wait to renew. As I hurried — I'm not ashamed to confess it — impatiently on the appointed day towards Greenwich Street, I felt not unlike a literary explorer, a kind of Christopher Columbus in reverse ... sensing the impending rediscovery of European glories of yesteryear in our own glorious United States of America. Which made me all the prouder and more impatient to reach my destination in good time. [*She knocks at the door.*] I was in good time. I was an hour early. [*She knocks again.*]

## SIX

DA PONTE's *rooms.*

DA PONTE  You're an hour early! Excellent! Please come in.

LOUELLA  Good afternoon, Lorenzo.

DA PONTE  Enter ...

LOUELLA  [*firmly*] No. After you.

DA PONTE  Oh but I ... — very well. [*Pause.*] You'll be pleased to hear that since last week I've had the spring of this sofa repaired. Please be seated. Some wine? [*He fetches a decanter and glasses.*]

LOUELLA  Not for me, Lorenzo.

DA PONTE  Just a little Italian wine to get us going, as it were. A classic vintage. Here's your glass ...

LOUELLA  Thank you.

DA PONTE [*pouring wine*] Look at it: don't you think it's a most striking amber colour? Bottled sunshine from across the Atlantic ... [*He spills some wine over* LOUELLA, *who reacts with a shout.*] How clumsy of me! Let me get a towel and some salt ... they say salt's the very thing for wine stains ...

LOUELLA  I've got something to mop it up with ...

DA PONTE  I hope it won't have stained the front of your dress. Such fine lace ...

LOUELLA  Never mind, it's ...

DA PONTE  Here, let me help ...

LOUELLA  Lorenzo!

DA PONTE  If I rub some of this salt firmly over this ...

LOUELLA  [*helplessly*] I wish you wouldn't ...

DA PONTE  ... magnificently intricate lace ...

LOUELLA  [*with a last desperate effort at self-defence*] That's quite enough!

DA PONTE  Very well. But I insist you sample the wine.

LOUELLA  OK. But try pouring it into the glass this time.

DA PONTE  [*pouring a fresh glass*] I can't think how it could have happened. My hands are as steady and active as ever.

LOUELLA  I'll say.

DA PONTE  And here we are. Your health, Louella.

LOUELLA  And yours. [*sips wine*] It's delicious.

DA PONTE  What did I tell you? I see you've got my libretti among your papers.

LOUELLA  [*enthusiastically*] Oh Lorenzo — I've read them: what superb dramas! You told me your *Figaro* was based on a play by Beaumarchais. Should I read the original?

DA PONTE  Do — if you enjoy political tracts.

LOUELLA  Oh ...

DA PONTE  The theme of my *Figaro*, on the other hand, is universal. I'm not saying Beaumarchais was not without a certain skill, but I've always maintained that with untalented artists, political writing has often been popular, since it enables them to blame society for the fact that nobody wants to hear what they have to say.

LOUELLA [*writing*] '... what they have to say.' Forgive me not looking at you, Lorenzo. I'm just taking notes.

DA PONTE But I am looking at you, Louella, and what do I behold? The wisdom of Minerva ... and the beauty of Venus.

LOUELLA You embarrass me, Lorenzo.

DA PONTE I have always admired a combination of beauty and scholarship in a woman. Yes. To my mind it's the ultimate aphrodisiac.

LOUELLA Now look: about *Figaro* ...

DA PONTE [*not to be deflected*] A most seductive mix. [*nostalgically*] I remember ... yes ... was it the Contessa Bragadin ... or was it? A most scholarly woman as well as a beauty. She carried learning so far that when divesting herself of her last garment she quoted St Clement of Alexandria in scriptural Greek on the relation between nudity and shame.

LOUELLA [*firmly*] About *Figaro*.

DA PONTE [*with a hint of irritation*] What about *Figaro*?

LOUELLA I've heard it said that your libretti for Mozart were the beginning of a new kind of opera.

DA PONTE There were — when I came on the scene — accepted rules for libretto-writing: the action was carried forward in blank verse, set as a recitative, interspersed with lyrics, usually solos, or at most duets. But what about trios, quartets, quintets, sextets? — virtually unknown. Well, Mozart and I helped sweep away those tired old conventions. We gave opera a new dimension.

LOUELLA There's a sextet in *Figaro*, isn't there?

DA PONTE Mozart's favourite. He found ensemble work in opera a challenge. And I provided him with the right amalgam of poetic lines. Those were exciting days.

LOUELLA Was Mozart fun to work with?

DA PONTE Fun? Hardly a way to describe our collaboration. It was stormy occasionally. Often tense. But it was life-enhancing at all times. And he recognised that my recitatives were as important as the arias. How shall I put it ... he understood perfectly the relationship between words and music. His balance was always right. Mind you, one had to push him.

LOUELLA  What do you mean?

DA PONTE  He needed my help. That is ... I had to guide him.

LOUELLA  Are you trying to tell me that Mozart needed guidance? From you?

DA PONTE  Guidance? I'll say he needed guidance. [*confidentially*] As a matter of fact *Figaro* very nearly didn't get written at all. But for a timely intervention on my part.

LOUELLA  What?

DA PONTE  It was I who first put it to Joseph II that Mozart should be commissioned to set my drama to music. 'What?' said the Emperor, 'Mozart's all right for instrumental music, but as for opera ... he's only written one as it is, and I didn't think much of it.' I said: 'Neither did I, sir, but look at it this way — without your patronage even I wouldn't have written you a libretto for Vienna.' 'True,' he said, 'but I've forbidden *Figaro*. Count Rosenberg and many others tell me it's ... rather radical.' 'Your Majesty,' I said, 'Leave it to me and I'll tone it down. And let young Mozart get on with the music.

LOUELLA  What did the King say to that?

DA PONTE  He said: 'My dear da Ponte, I'll rely on your taste where the music is concerned, and on your prudence as to the politics of the piece. Go ahead.'

LOUELLA  [*clapping her hands*] Well done, Lorenzo!

DA PONTE  Ah, but that was only half the battle.

LOUELLA  More obstacles?

DA PONTE  I fear so.

LOUELLA  Who caused them this time?

DA PONTE  Who but our dear composer? I had the devil's own job getting him to work on *Figaro*.

LOUELLA  What stopped him? Was it too big a job for him?

DA PONTE  No. He had ... other interests.

| | |
|---|---|
| LOUELLA | Oh ... Oh: women? He was married ... Don't tell me he too wandered off from time to time. |
| DA PONTE | No. It wasn't women. No. Believe it or not it was billiards. |
| LOUELLA | Billiards? |
| DA PONTE | Billiards. Glued to the green baize for days on end. I had to stand over him and goad him on like a slave-driver ... |

[*Fadeout.*]


## SEVEN

MOZART's *rooms. Vienna, 1785. The corner of a billiard table just visible. A harpsichord or virginal.*

| | |
|---|---|
| MOZART | [*at the billiard table*] Twenty-one ... [*Click.*] Twenty-three ... Now double the red into the middle pocket ... [*Click.*] Twenty-six ... [*He takes another shot as* DA PONTE *appears.*] |
| DA PONTE | [*breezing in*] Morning, Mozart ... [*disappointed*] Oh. I see you're busy improving your mind. |
| MOZART | Absolutely. Damn it, Lorenzo! You've spoilt my break! You shouldn't have done that. Not on the shot. I'd got as far as twenty-six ... |
| DA PONTE | More important: how far have you got with our little opera? |
| MOZART | You did say ... [*He takes another shot.*] Wasn't that a good one! You did say the other day we hadn't got clearance from the King yet. No point in writing an opera if it's not going to be put on. What's the hurry? |
| DA PONTE | No no no no no! [*patiently*] What I said was that ... yes, there is some opposition. Count Rosenberg told the King *Figaro*'s a bit subversive. I said I'd take care of that, which I've done. Toned it down a bit. His Majesty told me himself he'd judge our work on its merits. [*louder*] How on earth can he do that if you don't get on with the job? |
| MOZART | Well ... since I last saw you I've done one more aria. |
| DA PONTE | That was over a week ago. Just the one? |
| MOZART | I think you'll like it. It's the Countess's aria. It's over there by the harpsichord. [*He takes another shot.*] |

| | |
|---|---|
| DA PONTE | [*crosses over to the harpsichord*] Let's see ... Hm. 'Dove sono ...' [*dismissively*] You can play it to me later. I hardly call that rapid progress. Seriously, Wolfango, please press on with the next piece. You should enjoy working on it. It's a duet. |
| MOZART | That cannon's come off. |
| DA PONTE | [*severely*] Wolfango! Are you listening? |
| MOZART | You are a spoilsport, Lorenzo. What's that you said? The next piece ... Duet? What is it exactly that comes next? |
| DA PONTE | Maria Santissima! Your absent-mindedness borders on the amnesiac! I hope and trust you've read my libretto beyond the pieces you've set to music so far. |
| MOZART | Oh, absolutely! Duet? You mean the bit where the Countess dictates a letter to Susanna ... |
| DA PONTE | [*with mock relief*] You've remembered! Thank you. That's the one. Would you care to tell me when you intend coming to grips with it? |
| MOZART | I'll tell you what — let's play a hundred up, then I promise I'll jot down a few dots. |
| DA PONTE | No. |
| MOZART | Please, Lorenzo. |
| DA PONTE | I said no. And as the only way to get you off that billiard table is to practise a little myself ... hand over your cue. Don't let's have any nonsense. The cue I said. |
| MOZART | Oh ... |
| DA PONTE | Thank you. And now go and sit down by that sadly neglected instrument of yours and GET ON WITH IT! |

> [MOZART *crosses over to the harpsichord grumbling and strikes a petulant discord on the keyboard.*]

| | |
|---|---|
| MOZART | Serves me right for lumbering myself with an Italian librettist ... presto, presto, presto ... that's all you ever hear from them! Wretched duet. |
| DA PONTE | This table's pretty grubby... Still, I'll try a cannon and an in-off. [*A metronomic click of billiard balls to the time of the first four notes of 'Sull'aria'.*] That's a good five ... I'll try it again ... [*Exactly the same sound.*] Ha ha! Another five. |

MOZART [*suddenly attentive*] Lorenzo, do you think you could repeat that shot?

DA PONTE What? I can but try. I say, aren't you supposed to be working? [*He repeats the shot. Same sound.*] What do you know... another five.

MOZART I think I've got it ... [*He taps his knuckles four times on the harpsichord woodwork.*] ... and you've given me the melody ... [*He plays the first four notes of 'Sull'aria' on the harpsichord, tentatively at first, then goes on to complete the phrase. He repeats it with growing confidence, then gets stuck.*] Let's try again ... [*He repeats the short phrase on the harpsichord, this time humming or singing the vocal line.*] What does that sound like?

DA PONTE [*grudgingly*] Not bad ...

MOZART Let's see. What next ... I'd better look at the words ... Oh, it's Susanna's turn. [*with a weary sigh*] I don't feel like it today. Won't you give me a hand?

DA PONTE Play that bit again. And sing it. If you must.

[MOZART *complies.*]

MOZART Well?

DA PONTE I'd say you need singing lessons. Once more ...

[MOZART *complies.*]

DA PONTE What about — [*He hums Susanna's first phrase.*]

MOZART Yes. Yes! YES! That's it. [*He hums* DA PONTE'*s phrase, then repeats both phrases.*]

[*If technically possible, the fully orchestrated duet, having merged with* MOZART'*s opening bars, should now be faintly audible in the background over the ensuing speeches.*]

Thanks to your help I think this'll just about wrap it up. I say ... any ideas on the orchestration?

DA PONTE Orchestration, eh ... Look here: aren't you supposed to be the composer? Do I have to do all the work? Hm. Well ... orchestration. Let's see. Yes. Strings — one oboe — one bassoon.

MOZART But of course! What else? Thanks! You know, you sometimes make me feel quite inadequate, Lorenzo. Right. What about that hundred-up now? I swear I'll get on with *Figaro* the moment the game's over.

DA PONTE [*wearily*] Just this once. But it's straight back to work for you afterwards ...

> [*Fade out on click of billiard balls and louder continuation of duet up to its conclusion.*]

[INTERVAL]


## EIGHT

DA PONTE'*s rooms. Recall closing bars of 'Sull'aria' duet in background.*

LOUELLA Dear, dear Lorenzo! You never mentioned that in your memoirs! Just like you to hide your light under a bushel!

DA PONTE Hm. Well ...

LOUELLA I'd no idea you helped him so much ... and not only with his music, but with the orchestration as well.

DA PONTE One doesn't like to blow one's own trumpet ... but ... yes, I did make a modest contribution. Never mind. Er ... have you noted all this down?

LOUELLA You bet I have.

DA PONTE Splendid! Or rather ... perhaps you shouldn't have ... But since we are concerned with setting the record straight ... so be it ... even if it goes ever so slightly against the grain.

LOUELLA You're too modest.

DA PONTE No one could ever accuse me of having sought the limelight ... Poor Mozart! If only he'd listened to me his name would be one to conjure with ... As it is, I can't even remember whether he spelled it with one z or two.

> [*Blackout.*]

[LOUELLA's *narration.*]

LOUELLA  Humility. Industry. Perseverance. Those assay marks of true creative artists the world over were writ large on Lorenzo da Ponte. Worldly success had smiled but briefly on him — but oh how radiantly! — during that short halcyon spell in Vienna. The long years of penury and obscurity that followed had failed to embitter him. Nor had melancholy marked him for her own. Far from it. During my subsequent visits to him, ever and anon his boundless vigour still manifested itself in spirited chases round his now refurbished sofa ... Was it fate that eventually cast me as Diana to his Actaeon? But I'm anticipating ...


## NINE

DA PONTE's *rooms.*

LOUELLA  This miniature ...

DA PONTE  You like it?

LOUELLA  Such a handsome young man, Lorenzo. A ... kinsman of yours?

DA PONTE  The likeness is over sixty years old, of course. Don't you detect a certain resemblance?

LOUELLA  Well —

DA PONTE  Think — if that rather aggressive moustache weren't there.

LOUELLA  Yes ... but ... oh, Lorenzo: is it ... was it ... could it be ... you?

DA PONTE  The same, my dear, the same. In my late twenties.

LOUELLA  Yes! I see it now. The eyes, yes, the nose ... It was the moustache that misled me.

DA PONTE  It misled ... indeed it led astray quite a number of delightful creatures in its day ...

LOUELLA  No! Please Lorenzo. Sit over — there.

DA PONTE  Very well ... You find the moustache in the miniature ... becoming?

LOUELLA    Very.

DA PONTE   To please you ... I could easily grow another one ...

LOUELLA    Sit over there, Lorenzo. Please. We've been through all this before.

DA PONTE   Louella ...

LOUELLA    Yes?

DA PONTE   [*momentarily abandoning his attentions, gives himself over to reverie*] About that moustache.

LOUELLA    Go on.

DA PONTE   How does it ... strike you?

LOUELLA    What do you mean exactly?

DA PONTE   Does it ... do anything for you?

LOUELLA    All I can see is a big black moustache.

DA PONTE   No more than that?

LOUELLA    It's bushy. I'll say that for it.

DA PONTE   It was a most successful appendage in its day. The powers it displayed over ... the gentler sex were ... talismanic.

LOUELLA    Listen, Lorenzo ...

DA PONTE   It had a nickname, you know.

LOUELLA    [*resigned*] OK. Out with it.

DA PONTE   The best tickler in Venice.

LOUELLA    Fine. And now, if you don't mind, I'd like to talk about that last libretto for Mozart. *Così Fan* —

DA PONTE   [*triumphantly*] ... but it was in that very libretto that I went into the symbolic value of a man's moustache ... Act One, Scene Three ...

LOUELLA    Oh. Did you?

DA PONTE   Naturally you only read the English version. The original was quite explicit ... [*pensively*] You know, the girl who first sang Fiordiligi in that opera ...

LOUELLA    Yes?

DA PONTE   She was ... very attached to me.

LOUELLA    Was she?

DA PONTE  Yes. Adriana del Bene. A native of Ferrara.

LOUELLA  But you set the opera in Naples.

DA PONTE  So I did. There was no point in pandering to her every whim ... I did, however, point out in my stage directions by way of concession that the two sisters, Fiordiligi and Dorabella, were from Ferrara.

LOUELLA  That was sure big of you.

DA PONTE  Adriana sacrificed ... her life to me. Even Mozart felt that her passion for me was so ... obsessive that he tried to drive a wedge between us ... He nearly succeeded. He wrote one of his most difficult arias ever for her. Virtually unsingable. And d'you know why?

LOUELLA  I'm dying to know.

DA PONTE  To trap her into failure. But Adriana carried it off. Sensationally. Triumphantly.

LOUELLA  And did you make her happy?

DA PONTE  The nights we spent together should be imagined rather than described. [*He sighs.*] But she was a conventional girl. Her key to happiness was matrimony. Alas, in those days I clung to my independence as to a lifeline.

LOUELLA  That was very selfish of you.

DA PONTE  Perhaps it was. But as you know I yielded in the end — to another.

LOUELLA  Nancy?

DA PONTE  [*gloomily*] Yes. With disastrous consequences. Hm. Where was I?

LOUELLA  This singer ... Adriana. You were just saying she wanted to marry you.

DA PONTE  She did. She did. 'I shall marry you or I shall marry no other.' It became her favourite refrain. She turned down many an advantageous match. She even refused a proposal of marriage from one of the most powerful men in Austria. Prince Babenberg.

LOUELLA  She did? Tell me more.

DA PONTE  She refused Prince Babenberg ... because of me.

LOUELLA   Prince Babenberg? I'll take notes. Just a moment ... Go ahead.

DA PONTE   I can remember it all as clearly as if it were yesterday ...

> [*Blackout and fade up first two bars of orchestral introduction to opening trio of* Così Fan Tutte.]


TEN

ADRIANA's *bedroom.*

BABENBERG   What can this ... versifier da Ponte do for you, Adriana? Write you tinselly roles in musical dramas? Think carefully: for every imaginary role he can provide, I can furnish its actual fulfilment. You may not love me, but can you afford to refuse to become my wife? No — please don't interrupt. Hear me out. I, Franz Maximilian Adolphus Frederic Otto, Prince Babenberg, Archduke Hohenstaufen, Margrave of Steyr, Prince of Znaim, Baron Chiemgau, Baron Mautern, Count of St Polten and Stockerau in the peerage of Austria ... offer you my hand. The emperor has placed a wing of the Royal Palace at Schoenbrunn at my disposal, and the use of its gardens ... Do you enjoy riding? No fewer than eight Lipizzaner horses from the Spanish Riding School are groomed ready for my use. My summer palace in Salzburg would be yours and its staff of seventy-three stewards and maids yours to command. You would prefer to move from Austria to the milder climate of the South? Very well. On waiving the Archdukedom of Tuscany in favour of a Hapsburg princeling I was given the island of Strapurni in the Adriatic by way of compensation ... It boasts the finest, sandiest beaches: if you look out to sea I am told you can feast your eyes on mermaids sporting with playful dolphins most afternoons in early summer. Do you enjoy hunting? As a descendant in the female line of Humbert the White-handed of Savoy I have hunting rights just where the Alps straddle Savoy and Piedmont ... My alpine lodge is said to be the best appointed in the region. Does the East attract you? As Count Benckendorff in the peerage of Russia I was granted land near Ochakov and the steppe between the Dniester and the Bug by Catherine the Great ... whose favours I once enjoyed ... (my private suite at the Hermitage is still kept in readiness for me) ... I have noticed more than once that you appreciate the flavour of a goblet of Tokay: your supply would be endless — as Count Bathory in the peerage of Hungary I have title to the harvests of a dozen vineyards ... Be my wife and your bridal dress shall be woven in the finest Flanders lace — for in Bruges (I am hereditary falconer to the Dukes of Bouillon) I have an interest in a weaving guild — and to ensure the uniqueness of its design I would have the looms destroyed and the weavers exiled. It is possible that the lakes of upper Bavaria may attract you at certain times of the year: the Chiemsee, Tegernsee and Koenigsee would be your private bathrooms, for am I not Duke of Zweibruecken, Baron Windisch-Graetz and Count Wittlesbach in the Palatinate of Bavaria? If cattle and rolling farmland should be a further inducement to you, know then that I enjoy the perpetual usufruct of the bishoprics of Wuerzburg, Bamberg, Augsburg and Freising ... I fear you could not in the foreseeable future visit my French estates as there seems to be a revolution in progress there at the moment, but luckily the Committee of Public Safety still allows safe annual passage to two hundred barrels of my Chateau Babenberg into Austria ... a most sustaining Burgundy should you find yourself with child. Do accept me, Adriana, for I cannot answer for my actions otherwise: I am descended in the male line from Duke Frederick the Quarrelsome, whose uncertain temper I'm told I've inherited ... but be my bride and I will give you outright title to three of my castles in Transylvania ...

> [*We now discover that* DA PONTE *is hiding under the bed, its mattress rhythmically shaking under the activity of the couple above. He is listening intently.*]

... as well as Margrave of Bohemia and Elector of Moldavia I am a Prince of the Holy Roman Empire and a Knight of the Golden Spur. Most crowned heads in Europe with daughters of marriageable age would consider me an eligible ... and dare I say it ... a desirable match — why not you?

ADRIANA  Because I love Lorenzo da Ponte. I shall marry him or no other.

> [*His face projecting from under the bed or sofa,* DA PONTE *nods enthusiastic approval in appreciation of her loyalty, as the agitations of the springs increase in intensity. Fade out and immediate cut to:*]

## ELEVEN

DA PONTE's *rooms.*

LOUELLA  She turned all that down for you? And you wouldn't marry her?

DA PONTE  She did. And I wouldn't.

LOUELLA  What a sap!

DA PONTE  She was a foolish child. As I hid under her bed while Prince Babenberg ... pressed his suit ... I couldn't fail but be moved to tears by Adriana's unswerving loyalty and devotion.

LOUELLA  Well, I'm not sure that —

DA PONTE  [*moved by his own words*] Forgive my emotional state ... but the thought of Adriana to this day fills me with regret ...

LOUELLA  And no wonder.

DA PONTE  Her loyalty was total. Her passion ... volcanic. Her fund of generosity ...

LOUELLA  ... bottomless?

DA PONTE  No. [*reflectively*] I wouldn't care to use that word of Adriana. [*with fond remembrance*] Not in that context.

LOUELLA  What happened to her in the end?

DA PONTE  [*darkly*] Who knows. There were so many Adrianas ... So many images. After all these years they all seem to merge into one. Into one long eternity of ... unfulfilled longing ... [*quickly*] Why do you keep rejecting me, Louella?

LOUELLA  That line's no good and you know it, Lorenzo.

DA PONTE  Must I give up all hope then? Surely you know how I feel about you.

LOUELLA  Frequently.

DA PONTE  Louella, am I really to be denied that crowning ... ? Couldn't you accept me ... my ... hm ... as a signal proof of ... the warmth and vitality common to ...

LOUELLA  ... creative artists the world over? Yeah. I know.

DA PONTE  Then... you'll never ... ?

LOUELLA  Lorenzo: what do you expect me to say?

DA PONTE  What about ... yes?

LOUELLA  [*troubled*] For the moment you'll have to make do with ... [*Pause.*] Oh, I don't know ...

[*Fadeout.*]

[LOUELLA*'s narration.*]

LOUELLA  Aware as I've always been of how strange the byways of the human mind can be, I began to allow Lorenzo to ramble on at will about the past. True, his immediate and favourite recollections tended to be of a carnal rather than an artistic nature, but by injecting a note of firmness here and there I elicited the kind of information I considered relevant for my future monograph on his work. Today was to be no exception. He was telling me of his stay in London, England, and the subject was to lead to a most astonishing disclosure ...

## TWELVE

DA PONTE*'s rooms.*

LOUELLA  You were saying ... your first impressions of England?

DA PONTE  With hindsight I'd say that a foreigner arriving in England needs to be fortified with resignation.

LOUELLA  [*writing*] ... with resignation.

DA PONTE  Mind you, their women are not without ... certain qualities. Hm. I'd hardly been in London a week than I found myself with an idle evening on my hands. I made up my mind to take a conveyance to the Ranelagh.

LOUELLA  The ... Ranelagh? What's that?

DA PONTE  Pleasure gardens by the Thames. I went. I had some tea, danced some minuets ... but made no acquaintances. At about midnight I decided to return to my lodgings in Pall Mall. Alas, there wasn't a coach to be found. An extremely pretty woman who was waiting for her carriage by the Rotunda noticed my distress and said that if I lived anywhere near Whitehall she could give me a lift. I thanked her and accepted. Once in the carriage I renewed my expressions of ... indebtedness. I covered first her hands with kisses ... then her cheek ... She smiled all the time. In short, by the time we'd got to Whitehall I'd given her an unequivocal mark of my gratitude.

LOUELLA  That sounds like you all right ...

DA PONTE  However, a few days later at a rather grand party at Lady Betty German's, who should I spot on a chaise longue ... reading a book ... but our Ranelagh charmer? I made straight for her, bowed, and reminded her of our recent encounter. Do you know what she said?

LOUELLA  What did she say?

DA PONTE  She turned on me haughtily: 'Sir, a moment of folly is not an introduction.' Since I was plainly puzzled she added gently: 'A social ... introduction.' She then went back to the book she'd been reading and ignored me. Astounding woman — but typical of the English nobility.

LOUELLA  Wait a moment, Lorenzo ...

DA PONTE  Yes?

LOUELLA  That story has a familiar ring.

DA PONTE  Oh?

LOUELLA  Now I remember! Yes! Wasn't that one of Casanova's adventures? His memoirs have recently come out in French and German ... I've read extracts.

DA PONTE [*amused*] You have? Good.

LOUELLA But then ... is what you've just told me ... a fabrication?

DA PONTE No. It is not. But ... what I can tell you is that ... the deception is now complete.

LOUELLA I don't get you.

DA PONTE Louella, as you know, Casanova was a friend of mine. A close friend. There was a time when we saw a great deal of each other. He even attended the first performance of my *Don Giovanni* in Prague. Some of my enemies said he helped out with the script; I'd have been honoured if he had. He was a fine writer.

LOUELLA I still don't understand. Casanova ... was he the kind of ... libertine they all made him out to be?

DA PONTE [*vastly amused*] Giacomo? A libertine? Casanova was an indefatigable traveller, a mathematician, something of a philosopher and a dabbler in the occult. He published a number of learned books. He met and corresponded with Voltaire.

LOUELLA [*impressed*] With Volt ... did he really?

DA PONTE Yes. A scholar certainly. But never one for the ladies. [*He laughs.*] The very idea!

LOUELLA What so funny about it?

DA PONTE Where shall I start?

LOUELLA Try the beginning.

DA PONTE Casanova — like me as it happens — had a beautiful singing voice as a child.

LOUELLA Was he a choirboy?

DA PONTE Yes. The most angelic boy soprano I'm told. Well, before his voice broke it was put to him by his choirmaster that he could — if he wished — retain his high registers for ever. All that was involved was ... a little surgery ...

LOUELLA [*shocked*] Lorenzo! You can't possibly mean that they ...

DA PONTE Yes. A most cruel operation. Thank heaven they're no longer carrying it out. When I was a boy they wanted me to agree to it. Me! But I wouldn't. No, thank you, I said. [*He sings a bass arpeggio.*] A-a-a-ah! You see?

LOUELLA  How ... barbaric!

DA PONTE  No, I said. I didn't let them either. [*He repeats the bass arpeggio.*] A-a-a-ah! But poor Casanova on the other hand went through with it. He loved singing in the choir. In fact he formed quite close attachments with his angelic little fellow choristers ...

LOUELLA  [*suspiciously*] What are you driving at, Lorenzo?

DA PONTE  I'll ... I'll put it as delicately as I can. Casanova retained his high registers ... as well as a lifelong predilection for his own kind.

LOUELLA  I could do with some of that strong drink you keep offering me.

DA PONTE  A wise decision. I think I'll join you. [*He fetches the decanter and pours.*] You're not ... you're not shocked, my dear?

LOUELLA  Shocked? That's got to be the understatement of the century! [*She drinks at a gulp.*] Casanova ... a ... a ...

DA PONTE  He was a delightful man. Make no mistake — in an age when ... all was permissible ... he was discretion itself. The amours he describes in his memoirs ... were mine.

LOUELLA  You're trying to tell me that ... they all happened to you?

DA PONTE  [*suddenly animated*] They did, Louella, they did. [*He moves closer to her.*] They did. Could you ever doubt it?

[*A scuffle ensues.*]

LOUELLA  Hey! I asked for an explanation, not a demonstration. Sit — over there!

DA PONTE  If I must.

LOUELLA  How come these ... episodes ... found their way into his book?

DA PONTE  Quite simply because he asked me, as a favour. And I could hardly refuse. He was, after all, a friend. You see, towards the close of his life poor Casanova ended up as Count Waldstein's librarian at Dux Castle in Bohemia, and was bored to death most of the time. Consequently he decided to write his memoirs. I used to drop in on him occasionally.

Well, he told me that an enlightened eighteenth-century autobiography wouldn't fare well without its regulation number of ... adventures, so to speak. You see, he wanted his book to be the portrait of a well-rounded man.

LOUELLA And you let him have your experiences in ... that field?

DA PONTE Naturally. He was a friend. Yes, I gave him my experiences, as you call them. Partly by correspondence, occasionally in person. I well remember my last visit to him at Dux Castle before leaving for England in ... was it 1791 or '92?

[*Fadeout.*]


## THIRTEEN

*Dux Castle, Bohemia. The Library. Early 1790s.*

CASANOVA [*very camp*] Hel-lowe Lorenzo. Sorry I've kept you waiting.

DA PONTE Ah, there you are, Giacomo ... Where have you been?

CASANOVA I've been for a walk in the grounds ... I'm so glad to see they've given you some food ...

DA PONTE Yes. Thank you.

CASANOVA Who served you?

DA PONTE A very odd-looking footman, I must admit.

CASANOVA The rather soigné one in the pink wig?

DA PONTE That's the one.

CASANOVA That's Heinrich. He's my friend.

DA PONTE Yes ... How are you getting on with the book?

CASANOVA I'm having an utterly beastly time fitting in all those stories of yours ...

DA PONTE Now look here — you did ask me to make them over to you!

CASANOVA I'm not complaining, dear. Don't get all huffy! It's just that one isn't exactly adjusted to ... embodying all those ghastly females into one's very own memoirs.

DA PONTE  Well, *noblesse oblige*, Giacomo. Besides, even you must admit to having missed some experiences in life.

CASANOVA  I doubt it, dear. But there is something I'd like you to explain. It wasn't at all clear in your last letter.

DA PONTE  What was it?

CASANOVA  Your handwriting got ever so spidery ... as if you'd got all worked up remembering ... Shame on you, Lorenzo!

DA PONTE  Get to the point, man.

CASANOVA  That nun and her friend, you know, in that casino in Venice ...

DA PONTE  So?

CASANOVA  Well now, when the nun got her friend into the room ... let me think ... I expect it's all going to be perfectly disgusting ... was there just the one nun or were there two?

> [*Fadeout.*]

> [LOUELLA's *narration.*]

LOUELLA  My mind reeled at what I'd just heard. I was the only person on this earth privy to the fact that Lorenzo da Ponte was not only the greatest librettist, but also the most accomplished lover the world has ever known ... And yet, with the generosity typical of the creative artist ... he had deliberately handed over his ... achievements to another. There he sat opposite me, an ordinary human being at first sight. A genius to those who knew better. Yes, there he was, Lorenzo the strong, the generous. Open to some, inscrutable to most. Lorenzo ... Lorenzo ... the magnificent. Forgetting the tenets of conventional morality for a moment — and I've been trying hard to forget them now for quite a time — I suddenly became conscious of a feeling of inner agitation akin to ... yes ... [*She laughs hysterically.*] ... careless abandon ...

> [*As light fades, fade up 'Prenderó quel morettino' in background into the next scene.*]

## FOURTEEN

*New York, public gardens.* LOUELLA *and* DA PONTE *strolling.*

DA PONTE  You seem strangely quiet, my dear. Is anything the matter?

LOUELLA  [*starting*] Sorry. I ... [*alert*] I've got a surprise for you. Guess?

DA PONTE  My powers of divination aren't what they used to be.

LOUELLA  That new production of your *Don Giovanni* at the Opera ... I've reserved us a box. For tomorrow.

DA PONTE  How very thoughtful of you. You shouldn't have, really.

LOUELLA  Oh, but I wanted to. And ... [*impulsively*] I may as well tell you it's rather a fancy box we've got. With a retiring room.

DA PONTE  I see.

LOUELLA  Do you?

DA PONTE  [*matter-of-fact*] The box has a retiring room, you say.

LOUELLA  Retiring rooms are very private.

DA PONTE  [*somewhat put out, sensing an unexpected offer on* LOUELLA*'s part, and wholly unprepared for it*] Ah, yes. Good! Well — excellent!

LOUELLA  Is that all you can say?

DA PONTE  You really mean that you ... that I ... that we ... tomorrow ...

LOUELLA  What else, my... dearest?

[*Fade up briefly in background the opening orchestral bars of 'La ci darem la mano' with slow fadeout.*]


## FIFTEEN

*The interior of a coach-and-four driving through New York.* LOUELLA *is alone in the cab.*

LOUELLA  So tonight we were to see his *Don Giovanni* together, at the very theatre where we'd first met a few weeks earlier, and where he was to take a leaf out of his hero's book and obtain — albeit from a willing participant — an earnest of my affection for him. I had for the occasion hired a coach-and-four, which I thought he'd appreciate. On my way to fetch him the strangest thoughts crossed my mind, not least among them the recurring question: Did I love the man? ... followed by the ever-recurring answer: No. I did not. But I truly admired his talent. I thought highly of his appearance and was stimulated by his achievements and the accounts of the people he'd met so very long ago. And although I'd gotten myself into this fancy situation of my own free will ... although I'd promised him what he, in his old-fashioned way called my 'favours' — and no van Pick has ever failed to honour his or her pledge — I felt a twinge of reluctance at parting with that supreme gift which should have been reserved for a spouse and not lavished on an ... ageing lover. But I wasn't getting any young—but time's wingèd chariot was hurrying near ... and such a speculation was more in the nature of a hypothesis than a realisable possibility. So if Prince Charming isn't going to eventualise ... let it be Lorenzo da Ponte. As the horses picked their way disdainfully through the squalor of Greenwich Street I looked out the window ... and my heart leapt: there he stood ... erect, framed in his doorway, one of the most truly distinguished figures ever to grace our country — with the possible exception of our own dear President van Buren, related to the van Picks through a Dutch connection ...

LOUELLA  Stop here, coachman!

COACHMAN  Whoaah!

LOUELLA  [*opening carriage door*] Good evening, Lorenzo.

DA PONTE  [*climbing in, somewhat subdued*] Good evening, Louella.

[*The coach moves off.*]

LOUELLA  I can't tell you how much I'm looking forward to tonight's performance.

DA PONTE  [*distracted*] Eh? What?

LOUELLA   To the opera, Lorenzo. I've been through the libretto twice. I feel I know it already.

DA PONTE  I'm so glad ... [*He shivers.*] It's August, but there's a chill about tonight.

LOUELLA   We'll have some hot grog the moment we get to the theatre ... Sit a little closer to me. I'll warm you. How long is it since you saw *Don Giovanni?*

DA PONTE  Many, many years ...

LOUELLA   I'm so excited, Lorenzo ... I just want to burst into song ... [*She sings.*] It was a lover and his lass, with a hey, and a ho, and a hey nonino ...

   [*Pause.*]

DA PONTE  'Is it not strange that desire should so many years outlive performance ...'

LOUELLA   What's that?

DA PONTE  Something by the same author — written in later life, I should imagine.

LOUELLA   Are you sure you're all right, Lorenzo?

   [*To underlie next speech only: 'Dove sono'.*]

DA PONTE  [*with an effort*] Yes, Louella. You must forgive me. The past few weeks have brought back so many memories ... raised so many hopes ... They've been wonderful weeks.

LOUELLA   For me too.

DA PONTE  [*recovering*] Did I ever tell you how I settled down to writing *Don Giovanni?*

LOUELLA   You never gave me any notes on that. No.

DA PONTE  The king wouldn't believe I could tackle three libretti at the same time. But I did.

LOUELLA   Three?

DA PONTE  One for Martin, one for Salieri and one for Mozart. I wrote for Martin in the morning, for Salieri in the afternoon and for Mozart at night. That first night I sat at my writing desk — a bottle of Tokay on my right, the inkwell in the middle ... a box of Seville tobacco on my left. How vividly I remember it all! I spent twelve hours working ... and whenever inspiration sagged ... I rang the bell for my landlady's daughter ...

LOUELLA    [*flat*] Helga?

DA PONTE    Helga, whom I should have loved as a daughter ... however ... [*Begin to fade.*] She brought me biscuits ... coffee ... and helped me while away the uneasy intervals ...

[*Blackout.*]

## SIXTEEN

*Box 42 at the Opera House. Don Giovanni is reaching the point at which the statue of the Commendatore is about to drag the Don into hell.*

LOUELLA    [*whispering*] Let's hear the rest in the retiring room ...

DA PONTE    Very well.

[*They withdraw into the retiring room, which is in semi-darkness.*]

LOUELLA    [*giggly*] The grog's made me quite light-headed ...

DA PONTE    Louella ...

LOUELLA    ... and the music's filled me with longing, Lorenzo ...

DA PONTE    Louella ...

LOUELLA    Lorenzo ... Hold me ... hold me ...

DA PONTE    Carissima ...

LOUELLA    Oh ...

[*At this point* DA PONTE *clearly has a violent seizure, possibly to be suggested by grunts or other loud and strident sounds of distress, as the two are hardly visible. The closing chorus of* Don Giovanni *is to underlie the next six speeches.*]

Steward! Help ... Please ... help ...

[ *A* STEWARD *rushes in with a lantern. The retiring room is now much lighter.*]

STEWARD  What's the matter? Hey, lady ... is this old-timer bothering you?

LOUELLA  He's sick, can't you see? I think he's fainted ... Help me get him off me ...

STEWARD  Here ... How's that ... Got any salts, lady?

LOUELLA  [*fumbles in her reticule*] Here you are ... Wake up, Lorenzo ... Lorenzo!

    [*Pause.*]

STEWARD  You'd better sit down over there. I reckon your grandaddy's a goner.

    [LOUELLA *sobs disconsolately.*]
    [*Up music and blackout.*]


## SEVENTEEN

*RICKENBACKER's office. Two days after Scene One.*

RICKENBACKER  So that's how he went ...

LOUELLA  Yes, Mr Rickenbacker. We moved him ... under cover of darkness, back to Greenwich Street. It was there on the following day that his friends choreographed his last dignified exit. He lay in his bed, a revered patriarch, a few intimates kneeling reverently by his side, with all the comforts of religion ... his beautiful long white hands crossed over his chest ... and the air heavy with incense. And that's what we read in the papers and what the world has come to believe was the natural death of Lorenzo da Ponte. I nearly believed it myself when I read about it.

RICKENBACKER  What a cover-up! You can't beat the Italians when it comes to stagecraft!

LOUELLA  Let's say they have a sense of occasion.

RICKENBACKER  Yeah. But tell me: when he croaked — I mean when he passed on ... Had he actually... worked the trick?

LOUELLA  What are you trying to ask me, Mr Rickenbacker?

RICKENBACKER  [*embarrassed but pruriently curious*] Put it this way. When he launched his ... last attack ... did he ... fall before or after ... breaching the walls?

LOUELLA  I'm not a war correspondent ... but if you must cloak your nauseating curiosity in military analogies ... let's say he'd barely reached the outer defences when he fell. Valiantly!

RICKENBACKER  The poor guy. Must've gotten stuck in the moat.

LOUELLA  [*impatiently*] Listen Mr Rickenbacker, I've answered your questions and you've read my manuscript. What's your verdict? Will you publish?

RICKENBACKER  Nope.

LOUELLA  Your reasons?

RICKENBACKER  Quite simply, Miss van Pick, because I don't believe a word you've written. Now, if you'll excuse me ...

LOUELLA  Not so fast. Not so fast. Are you calling me a liar?

RICKENBACKER  Oh heck ... sorry. No. I guess you wrote what you heard. No. I won't call you a liar. I'll just say you're about the most gullible human being I've ever met. What's more ... d'you really want to commit those very ... intimate experiences of yours to the presses?

LOUELLA  Never mind me. I owe it to history and to Lorenzo.

RICKENBACKER  But can't you see the guy was just a horny old goat?

LOUELLA  Is that all you can say about him?

RICKENBACKER  So he did write a few good scripts ... by adapting other people's. Don't forget he wasn't above dipping into other writers' cookie jars! Why, the guy was the biggest chiseller since Michelangelo!

LOUELLA  [*on the verge of tears*] Damn you! Damn you to hell, Rickenbacker!

RICKENBACKER  Now just you watch your language, Miss van Pick!

LOUELLA  That's the only kind of language people like you will ever understand.

RICKENBACKER  You listen to me for a moment. Right — da Ponte never told a lie except when his lips were moving. Hell's bells, woman: he was a rake, a conman and a bankrupt in half a dozen countries. Why, he was an undesirable immigrant! He told you a few fancy tales to make you in the hay.

LOUELLA [*calmer*] No. Now I know you'll never understand. Not in a million years.

RICKENBACKER Try me.

LOUELLA Oh sure, all the things you've said about him are probably strictly as advertised. And he's had a bad press. Poor Lorenzo ...

RICKENBACKER Save the sob stuff. You haven't exactly helped.

LOUELLA Maybe not. What you ... all of you have missed, except the few who really understood, is that he knew the secret ... of the magic of words.

RICKENBACKER [*ironically*] So he was some kind of magician and alchemist as well?

LOUELLA You think he's good for a laugh, do you? Fine. Then I'll tell you something else that'll maybe make you laugh: he was the kind of man who could smelt the commonplace in a crucible of wonder and turn it into poetry. Yes, he was a kind of alchemist now you mention it.

RICKENBACKER You've lost me.

LOUELLA He knew how to ... how to do things with language. He was a genius.

[*Pause.*]

You see ... he knew about WORDS.

[*Fade up on the opening orchestral bars of 'Il mio tesoro'. Play out the entire aria, with a slow fadeout as the curtain falls.*]

# CONFESSIONS OF ZENO

———————

from the novel by Italo Svevo

## CHARACTERS

Zeno Cosini
Dr S.
A nurse
Alfio Cosini
Dr Coprosich
Enrico Copler
Giovanni Malfenti
Signora Malfenti
Augusta
Ada
Alberta
Anna
Guido
Carla
Carmen/Maria*

*double

The action of the play takes place in Trieste between the early 1890s and the initial stages of the First World War.

Two acting areas.

The first, Dr S's consulting room, may be a naturalistic set, conventionally furnished with desk, chairs, couch, book-lined walls, etc.

The second area will provide the various venues required throughout the play, and each scene will be indicated by a simple arrangement of easily movable items as required.

*Confessions of Zeno* was first performed in Great Britain at the Italian Cultural Institute, 39, Belgrave Square, London SW1 on 14 February 1995 with the following cast:

Zeno Cosini ... Jeffrey Perry
Dr S ... Norman Davie
Dr Coprosich ... Richard Pescud
A nurse ... Pauline Munro
Alfio Cosini ... Luigi de Angioy
Giovanni Malfenti ... Richard Pescud
Signora Malfenti ... Stella Quilley
Augusta ... Melanie Carson
Ada ... Patti Clare
Alberta ... Mandy Craig
Guido ... Matthew Morgan
Enrico Copler ... Luigi de Angioy
Carla ... Mandy Craig

Directed by Stella Quilley

*Confessions of Zeno* was first broadcast in Great Britain on BBC Radio 3 on 13 September 1978 with the following cast:

Zeno Cosini ... John Moffatt
Dr S ... Jack May
A nurse ... Hilda Kriseman
Alfio Cosini ... Lockwood West
Dr Coprosich ... Robert Trotter
Enrico Copler ... Peter Baldwin
Giovanni Malfenti ... Anthony Newlands
Signora Malfenti ... Maxine Audley
Augusta ... Jennifer Piercey
Ada ... Lisa Harrow
Alberta ... Amanda Murray
Anna ... Heather Bell
Guido ... Gary Bond
Carla ... Polly James
Carmen/Maria ... Petra Davies

Directed by Glyn Dearman

## ONE

*1914. DR S's consulting room. DR S is sitting at his desk examining notes. ZENO is sitting opposite him.*

*DR S lifts his eyes from his notes and looks at ZENO.*

DR S     So. You want to give up smoking.

ZENO     Yes.

DR S     Are you a heavy smoker?

ZENO     About sixty a day. I thought psychoanalysis might help.

DR S     One moment. Do you mean to tell me that you want to have a course of psychoanalysis just to give up smoking?

ZENO     No, no. Not just that. In fact I think I could give up smoking quite easily, without outside help that is, if only I put my mind to it. Of course I haven't succeeded yet. No. [*Pause.*] I'm a sick man, doctor.

DR S     I noticed you limp.

ZENO     Yes, I do. And that is only one of many —

DR S     [*cutting in as he examines a letter*] Now, your Dr Coprosich ... and his letter to me is quite recent ... 4th April 1914 ... let's see. Apart from the usual details — born in Trieste, happily married, in your late fifties. Two children. Hm. Successful businessman. — Apart from that he states that you're in good health.

ZENO     Organically... yes.

DR S     Then what made you decide to consult me?

ZENO     I'm a failure, doctor. That's it, in a nutshell. I've failed at all the things most men would achieve as a matter of course. At my studies, my relationship with my father, my marriage, my mistress, and my business career. I hope to be able to make it all clear to you by and by. [*Pause.*] Why have I come to you? — I happened to read a book on the interpretation of

DR S     dreams, heard that you were practising in Trieste, and — tell me: have you really worked with Sigmund Fr—

DR S     [*interrupting*] Yes. We collaborated over a short period in Vienna. [*Pause.*] Remarkable. You've read my colleague's book on dreams.

ZENO     Yes. A fascinating book. I dream incessantly you see. Does the treatment involve hypnosis?

DR S     No. And we may as well get this clear: we're not hypnotists or clairvoyants, my dear sir. In fact nowadays we analysts are sufficiently advanced to let our patients do most of the work. Imagine yourself as a field of battle, over which two enemies are fighting. I, the analyst, will help you find a way to prevail on the warring factions within you to come to a truce, an armistice, or — if we're lucky — to conclude a peace treaty.

ZENO     Is it going to be expensive?

DR S     [*laughs*] There you go. You tell me you're a sick man and yet you worry over the expense. Hm. That's a question I can't answer. The expense depends on the length of the treatment. You're not exactly a poor man, are you? Forget about the expense and the book you've read. Go and lie on that couch.

ZENO     [*moves to the couch*] Do I go on looking at you?

DR S     Not if you don't want to. Does looking at me make you nervous?

ZENO     No. Well, yes and no. You remind me ...

DR S     [*interested*] Yes, go on. Who do I remind you of?

ZENO     My father. Yes. My father used to look at me in exactly the same way.

DR S     [*well pleased*] Good. Good! Well, since you were nervous of your father, probably hated him ...

ZENO     [*protesting*] I never said ...

DR S     You needn't bother to look at me. Look up at the ceiling, or straight ahead, or better still close your eyes.

ZENO     [*complies*] Very well.

DR S     Good. Now tell me: how are you feeling at this particular moment? Are you at ease, or nervous, embarrassed, baffled?

| | |
|---|---|
| ZENO | [*yawning*] To be perfectly frank I feel like dozing off. I had rather a heavy lunch. |
| DR S | I see. I would now like you to tell me the first thing that comes to your mind. |
| ZENO | Something from my childhood? Personal? |
| DR S | No, no. That won't do. You've got hold of a smattering of psychoanalytical ideas and you're trying to meet me half way. Am I right? |
| ZENO | Well, it was a random answer to a random question. |
| DR S | Very well, if you must, think of your childhood. What do you see? |
| ZENO | A baby. Naked. On a marble-topped table. |
| DR S | Good. Good! Go on. |
| ZENO | Am I that baby, doctor? |
| DR S | [*severely*] I'm the one to ask the questions. We're not going to make much progress, if you carry on like this. |
| ZENO | Sorry. Yes, a baby. No, it can't be me. It's probably my sister-in-law's. I saw her put talcum powder on him after his bath last week. A revolting sight. |
| DR S | [*disappointed*] Quite. Well, tell me whatever it is you're thinking of now, as I'm asking you the question. Freeze whatever image is crossing your mind. What do you see? |
| ZENO | A locomotive. A steam engine puffing uphill, dragging an endless string of coaches up a steep gradient. |
| DR S | Does it remind you of anything? |
| ZENO | No. |
| DR S | Then it's a totally irrelevant image. Forget it. |
| ZENO | But am I not supposed to remember, to ... probe into my past? |
| DR S | I'll be the one to help you do that. How good are you at remembering past events? |
| ZENO | Quite good, I think. I may be absent-minded, but I've a very good memory. But what's the use of that — I remember everything and I understand nothing. |
| DR S | About your smoking. Sixty a day, eh? |

| ZENO | Yes. |
| --- | --- |
| DR S | Ever tried giving it up? |
| ZENO | I'm forever giving it up. I've resorted to the most elaborate schemes. |
| DR S | Have you? Good. Then let's start with your smoking. Give me a survey in depth, as it were, of your smoking habits. Can you remember your first cigarettes? |
| ZENO | Only too well. They don't make that brand any more. They were sold in small cardboard packets embossed with the double-headed eagle of the House of Austria. I was only a small boy then, back in the seventies. And before I even got on to cigarettes I used to smoke my father's cigar butts. |
| DR S | Did you indeed. Your father smoked cigars? |
| ZENO | Yes. |
| DR S | [*pointedly*] Cigars, you'll agree, are larger than cigarettes. |
| ZENO | Yes, of course they are. I say, is that supposed to be a significant factor? |
| DR S | Never mind about that. So. You were only a little boy when you started smoking. |
| ZENO | Yes. And I smoked whenever and wherever I could. Up in the attic, down in the cellar. I even held smoking competitions with other boys in the lavatory. |
| DR S | [*triumphantly*] The lavatory? |
| ZENO | [*matter-of-fact*] Yes. A most convenient place. It had a large window, and I could get rid of the smoke quite easily. |
| DR S | How did you get hold of cigarettes? |
| ZENO | Oh, I used to take small change from my father's waistcoat. He never noticed. |
| DR S | You stole from your father. Good. Good! Now we're beginning to get somewhere. Did he ever catch you? |
| ZENO | He very nearly did — once. I was fiddling with his waistcoat; he came into the room and asked what I was doing. I remember saying quite naturally that I was trying to count up the buttons on his waistcoat. He seemed quite satisfied with my answer. [*Pause.*] Do you mind if I smoke, doctor? |

| | |
|---|---|
| DR S | Go ahead. |
| ZENO | [*lighting a cigarette*] He was such a nice, uncomplicated, ordinary man. [*He chuckles.*] We had so little in common. He was placid, contented. I, on the other hand, have always hankered after self-improvement. I don't think he ever made the least effort to better himself. Never worried about a thing. No — I tell a lie: he did once confess that he often worried about me. |
| DR S | When did you first attempt to give up smoking? How many times have you tried giving up? |
| ZENO | Countless times. Yes. I used to make a note of it. Only the other day I turned up a note I made in my notebook: '15th April 1890. My father died. L.C.' — that stands for last cigarette. |
| DR S | So your father's death in effect gave you the opportunity to smoke a last cigarette. |
| ZENO | That had nothing to do with it. I'd already decided to give it up. You see, I've always felt that by writing down a resolution I'd stand a better chance of succeeding. And then dates have a magic all their own: take for instance the ninth day of the ninth month in eighteen ninety-nine — what a perfect concordance! I very nearly brought it off then. I think I didn't smoke for over four hours on that occasion. |
| DR S | You seem to have smoked a great many last cigarettes. |
| ZENO | Yes, indeed. Last cigarettes have their attractions. A cigarette tastes that much better, its aroma is that much headier when you feel it's going to be the last. Perhaps if I'd succeeded in giving up smoking I'd have become the strong, perfect man I've always wanted to be. Healthier, too. What do you think? |
| DR S | You tell me. |
| ZENO | Well, you see, if it is smoking that really stops me from being healthier, from fulfilling myself, perhaps I cling to it so that I can go on believing in my own latent potential. I suppose the same can be said of my attitude to women. |
| DR S | Are you very attracted to women? |
| ZENO | As you know, doctor, I'm a married man. A happily married |

| | man. But I'm not satisfied with one woman. Not even with many. I want them all. |
|---|---|
| DR S | All? |
| ZENO | I've come to regard it as a personal tragedy that I couldn't sleep with every woman I fancied. I'm fifty-seven, but I can assure you that unless I give up smoking — unless psychoanalysis cures me — why, I'll make a pass at the nurse by my death-bed — provided she's pretty. And as long as she isn't my wife. |
| DR S | Was your mother a beautiful woman? |
| ZENO | I suppose so, judging by her snapshots. I was very young when she died. |
| DR S | And your wife? |
| ZENO | What about my wife? |
| DR S | Is she ... was she ... attractive? |
| ZENO | Attractive? Oh ... er ... a perfect wife. [*matter-of-fact*] Luckily she doesn't object to my smoking. |
| DR S | Yes, let's get back to your smoking. I want you to tell me whether you ever really, and I mean seriously, meant to give it up. |
| ZENO | [*surprised*] But of course! Every resolution was meant to be the decisive one. Why, I even went so far as having myself locked up in a nursing home in order to give it up. It was over twenty years ago. Now that I think of it it was my wife who suggested it. As I've just said, she didn't mind my smoking so much as the worry it seemed to be causing me. So she suggested that I spend a few days in a nursing home, under supervision. The whole idea seemed to amuse her rather. We hadn't been married long, and maybe she was relieved that I didn't seem to mind the loss of my liberty. [*Pause.*] I suppose I was too busy regretting other things. We thought at first of picking a place in Switzerland, but then our family physician, Dr Coprosich, suggested a nursing home he knew of here in Trieste, so my wife packed a case for me and off we went ... |

[*Fadeout.*]

## TWO

*A private room in a nursing home. A bed, bedside table, chair. Evening.* ZENO *is sitting on the bed, fully dressed.*

DR COPROSICH   What a nice room! What do you think of it, Zeno? A home from home, eh?

ZENO   I suppose so.

DR COPROSICH   You'll be comfortable here, and out of harm's way. No temptations in this room. You won't be able to get out so easily, either. We're on the ground floor, but the only exit is through a second floor door, which is kept permanently locked. Only your nurse has a key to it. When you need her just ring. Her room's next to yours. Like this.

[*He presses a button and a bell rings next door.*]

ZENO   What's she like? Is she nice?

DR COPROSICH   Your nurse? A responsible, efficient woman. I wouldn't exactly call her nice. [*He laughs.*] I've known her for years. Bit of a dragon. But capable, my dear Zeno, extremely capable. Utterly impossible for you to escape from this place unless you use physical violence on her.

[*The* NURSE *enters.*]

NURSE   You rang, doctor?

DR COPROSICH   Yes, nurse. Here is your patient, Signor Zeno Cosini.

NURSE   Good evening, sir.

ZENO   Good evening.

DR COPROSICH   Look after him well, won't you, nurse. This is the first time he's been away from home since he got married.

NURSE   He's not to smoke at all, is that right?

DR COPROSICH   Correct. He can have anything he likes and wants except tobacco. [*jocularly*] I hope you won't come to blows with him. He can be very obstinate.

ZENO   Really, doctor!

NURSE     I'll carry out my duties, as I always do, but I can't stand violence. If he as much as lays a finger on me I'll call a male orderly...

DR COPROSICH   Don't worry, he's quite tame really. Zeno, you won't give nurse any trouble, will you?

ZENO     All I want is to be left in peace. I've got enough books with me to keep me occupied.

> [*He takes a cigarette packet out of his pocket and opens it.*]

DR COPROSICH   Must you?

ZENO     A last cigarette. The very last one in the packet as you can see.

> [DR COPROSICH *grunts.*]

[*lighting the cigarette*] You can search me if you like. It really is my last one. I'm not a child, you know.

DR COPROSICH   Of course you're not. Well, I'd better leave. Your wife is waiting for me downstairs. I promised I'd give her a lift home.

ZENO     [*suspiciously*] Oh ...?

DR COPROSICH   [*beginning to leave*] It's on my way.

ZENO     I see.

DR COPROSICH   [*going*] Well, Zeno, just think: the next time we meet you'll be rid of Milady Nicotine for good. Goodbye.

ZENO     [*absent-mindedly*] Er ... yes ... Goodbye.

> [DR COPROSICH *leaves.*]

I wonder why he's taking her home ...

NURSE     Did you say something?

ZENO     I beg your pardon? Oh. No. Sorry. Well, well: so you're my nurse.

NURSE     That's right.

ZENO     Quite. Well, here we are.

NURSE     You won't be difficult, will you, sir?

ZENO     Me? No, of course not. I'll just finish my last cigarette ... [*He drags and exhales.*] That's it. All over. [*He stubs it out.*] And now I'll be as docile as a well-trained child.

| | |
|---|---|
| NURSE | I'm glad to hear you say that. We never have any trouble here. Not with our gentlemen, anyway. |
| ZENO | You have women here as well? |
| NURSE | Didn't you know? This is really a maternity home. But this wing is for special cases. Like yours. |
| ZENO | Babies! I'm in a house full of babies! |
| NURSE | Oh, you won't hear them this side of the building if that's what's worrying you. We're cut off here. [*Pause.*] It's nearly your bed time, sir. Is there anything I can get you before you turn in? |
| ZENO | Am I allowed to have anything I like? |
| NURSE | Anything at all. To eat and drink, that is. Anything at all as long as it's not cigarettes. |
| ZENO | In that case ... bring me a bottle of brandy. |
| NURSE | Brandy? |
| ZENO | [*from a sitting position, still fully dressed, stretched out on the bed, his head on the pillow*] Strictly for medicinal purposes. |
| NURSE | Very well. [*She begins to leave.*] I won't be long. And remember what the doctor said — don't try to get out or do anything funny while I'm fetching the brandy. |
| ZENO | Don't worry. I'll catch up with some reading while you're gone. [*He picks up a book from the bedside table.*] |
| NURSE | I won't be long. |

> [*Short fadeout to denote a brief passage of time.*]
>
> [*The* NURSE *returns with a brandy bottle on a tray with a glass.*]

| | |
|---|---|
| | Here we are. I'll put it on your bedside table. Or would you like a drink now? |
| ZENO | I think I will have some now. The proverbial nightcap. |
| NURSE | [*pours him a brandy*] There. |
| ZENO | [*takes the glass and savours the drink*] Delicious. [*He drinks a little more.*] Ah! And now all that's missing is a cigarette. |
| NURSE | [*alarmed*] What? |

| | |
|---|---|
| ZENO | Just one. One last cigarette. After all, my cure hasn't started yet. |
| NURSE | [*on the verge of hysteria*] Do you want me to lose my job? |
| ZENO | I'd be quite willing to pay you ten crowns for just one cigarette. |
| NURSE | I'll go and fetch the house doctor this instant. See if I don't!<br>[*She makes for the door.*] |
| ZENO | [*placatory*] There, there. Not so loud. Please don't go. I was just testing you, that's all. |
| NURSE | Are you sure? |
| ZENO | Yes, yes. Calm down. I had to make sure you were ... well, incorruptible. I can see you'd never take a bribe. |
| NURSE | Never. Besides, I'd risk losing my job. |
| ZENO | I had to make sure. You see, I want the cure to work. This place is frightfully expensive. |
| NURSE | So I've heard. They don't pay us all that much, mind you. |
| ZENO | Don't they? Have a little brandy. Join me.<br>[*He pours her out a drink in a glass that had been on his bedside table.*] |
| NURSE | I don't mind if I do. They pay us a pittance. And I'm a widow. With two young children to support. |
| ZENO | Really? Here you are. [*He hands her the drink.*] |
| NURSE | Thank you. |
| ZENO | Sit down. Make yourself comfortable. Tell me about your family. |
| NURSE | There's not much to tell. |
| ZENO | You're a widow, you were saying. |
| NURSE | [*sipping her drink*] Yes. I've been a widow so long I can't remember what it's like being married. |
| ZENO | Were you happy? |
| NURSE | He was a good man, I suppose. But he used to knock me about a bit. |
| ZENO | You mean, he beat you? |

| | |
|---|---|
| NURSE | Now and again. Especially when we were first married. He was a jealous man, you see. |
| ZENO | I'm so sorry. Have some more brandy. [*He refills her glass.*] |
| NURSE | Just a little ... Thanks. Still. I didn't mind if he was a bit rough. It was so nice when we kissed and made up. I used to think it was almost worth going round with a black eye and a few bruises for a couple of days. |
| ZENO | Did you give him reason to be jealous? |
| NURSE | [*now a little light-headed from the brandy*] That'd be telling, wouldn't it? |
| ZENO | Go on. Were you unfaithful to him? |
| NURSE | Shh! Not so loud! Do you want everybody to hear? [*sips her drink*] Hm. This is the way to live. A little drink. A pleasant conversation with an educated gentleman. [*sips again, tipsily*] Lovely, just lovely! |
| ZENO | Have another ... and don't change the subject. I'm very interested. Were you unfaithful to your husband? |
| NURSE | [*coquettishly*] Hm ... Oh ... Well, yes — but only when we were first married. Then I got fonder of him. |
| ZENO | Was your first child by the other man? |
| NURSE | How on earth did you — ? I ... Yes. I think so. Their eyes are so alike. But I suffered for it, you know. [*She laughs.*] Cheating on my poor hubby like that. [*She laughs again.*] |
| ZENO | You find it funny? |
| NURSE | Yes. Let's face it, I'm sorry I did it, but these things are always a bit funny. Looking back on them I mean. [*in a more serious mood*] In a sense I've minded more since my husband died. I mean, when he was alive he never knew. I reckon now he's dead he probably knows all about it. [*She begins to sob.*] |
| ZENO | There, there ... Even supposing he does know ... now ... I don't think he'd bother his head about a thing like that. |
| NURSE | You think so? |
| ZENO | I'm absolutely sure. Have some more brandy. |

| | |
|---|---|
| NURSE | No, I'd better not. Well — perhaps just a teeny one ... |

[ZENO *pours. The* NURSE *giggles.*]

| | |
|---|---|
| ZENO | What's so funny now? |
| NURSE | I was just thinking. Why is it you want to give up smoking? I mean, you must want to very badly if you have yourself locked up in a place like this. And talking of locking up, I mustn't forget to take the key out of the second floor door before I go to bed. We don't want you to fly away in the night, do we? |
| ZENO | Nothing could be further from my mind. I'm quite happy with the brandy. |
| NURSE | [*cooing*] You never know ... Why do you want to give up smoking? There's nothing wrong with smoking. In moderation, I mean. |
| ZENO | Quite so. As a matter of fact it's my wife who wants me to give it up. |
| NURSE | [*laughs uproariously as if at an irresistible joke*] Your wife? It's your wife who wants you to give it up? |
| ZENO | Yes. [*He pours* NURSE *another drink.*] Look, I'm going to tell you something very confidential. Can you keep a secret? |
| NURSE | Cross my heart and hope to die. |
| ZENO | Well, it's like this. Whenever I've smoked about ten cigarettes I ... well, I'm a perfect terror ... well, you know ... with the ladies. |
| NURSE | I don't get you. |
| ZENO | To put it bluntly, after ten cigarettes I get all sexed up and ... there's no stopping me. |
| NURSE | [*giggling*] You mean to tell me your wife is trying to stop you smoking the ... vital ten cigarettes? |
| ZENO | That's it. At least, she used to try to stop me. |
| NURSE | [*laughing*] I can just picture you: ten cigarettes, say half an hour ... set the alarm clock ... and then ... |

[*She laughs uncontrollably.*]

| | |
|---|---|
| ZENO | [*didactically*] No. Ten cigarettes take me about an hour to |

smoke. Then another hour to produce the full effect, give or take a few minutes ...

NURSE [*as though suddenly sober*] Well, I can't stay here chatting all night. And this brandy's quite gone to my head. Time for me to turn in. Are you quite comfortable? You'd better get undressed and go to bed now. Your pyjamas are over there. Ring for me if there's anything you need. Remember I'm only next door.

[*Fadeout.*]

## THREE

ZENO *crosses over from the bed in the nursing home into* DR S*'s consulting room and resumes his position on the doctor's couch.*

DR S   What happened then? You fell asleep, had a bit of a hangover on the following morning, I shouldn't wonder.

ZENO   Far from it. I'd hardly touched the brandy. The nurse'd had most of it. No. As she left the room she gave me a look that made my blood run cold. And she left my door ajar. I started reading one of the books I'd taken along, and a few minutes later something fell in the middle of the floor. I picked it up. It was a packet of cigarettes with eleven cigarettes in it. Not ten, mind you, but eleven. She had thrown an extra one in for good measure.

DR S   Go on.

ZENO   I smoked them one after the other. They were a cheap Hungarian brand, but tasted marvellous to me. And then I started worrying about my wife.

DR S   Why?

ZENO   Dr Coprosich had offered her a lift home. Why? Were he and my wife having an affair? How convenient for them to have me shut away in a nursing home ... Wasn't it my wife who'd first suggested that if I wanted to give up cigarettes so badly, why not try the clinic? Anyway, I panicked. I decided

|  | I simply must get home. I got out quite easily, as the nurse, drunk as she was, had forgotten to take the key off the second floor door. She was snoring away as I passed her bedroom on my way out. |
|---|---|
| DR S | Were your suspicions about your wife justified? |
| ZENO | No. When I got home she was sewing quietly in our living room. She was very amused. |
| DR S | Did you carry on smoking after that? Or did you cut down a little? |
| ZENO | Not at all. My consumption went up. But I made a note in my little notebook that I'd have another try at giving up quite soon. |
| DR S | You kept a notebook? |
| ZENO | Yes. I did. It was my father who first suggested I should. |
| DR S | Ah. Your father. |
| ZENO | He thought I was terribly absent-minded, and told me I should keep a notebook. I used it mostly to jot down resolutions about last cigarettes. |
| DR S | As far as you can tell, did your father resent your absent-mindedness? |
| ZENO | He ... yes, he reproached me for it, as if it had been my fault. That and my tendency to laugh at what he called 'serious subjects'. |
| DR S | He doesn't seem to have had much confidence in you. |
| ZENO | No. And yet I must admit he was a very nice man. I suspect he had no confidence in me because I was his child, just as knowing I was his child was enough to undermine my confidence in him. He thought I was a bit of a butterfly, always switching subjects at university from law to chemistry and back to law again. He once said he entertained serious doubts on my sanity ... and ... just as a bit of a prank, you know, I got myself examined by a doctor who found me quite normal, and I got him to issue me with a certificate of sanity to show my father. |
| DR S | How did your father react to that? |

| | |
|---|---|
| ZENO | He was very upset. His eyes filled with tears. He said: You really are mad! [*plaintively*] That's all the thanks I got for an innocent prank, and ... |
| DR S | Yes? |
| ZENO | I think it was on that occasion that my father finally decided not to let me run our family business, but to leave it in the hands of his manager, Olivi. He told me a few days later that he'd made a new will, that Olivi would look after our affairs even after his death ... and that it was all for the best. |
| DR S | You accepted his decision? |
| ZENO | What else could I do? I told him I hoped my conduct in the years to come might make him change his mind. |
| DR S | And did he? |
| ZENO | No. He died not long after. And Olivi, his manager, nearly twenty years later ... is still running our business. On my behalf, of course. And very efficiently, mind you. |
| DR S | Do you blame your father for depriving you of the opportunity of managing your own affairs? |
| ZENO | No. I was very devoted to him. He was kind, uncomplicated. While I was constantly trying to improve myself, he was perfectly satisfied with himself. I was forever attempting to give up smoking, and he happily went on smoking his large cigars all day long — all night long when he couldn't sleep. |
| DR S | Did he drink? |
| ZENO | In moderation, as a gentleman should. Just enough at dinner to be sure of falling asleep the moment he went to bed. On the whole he regarded tobacco and alcohol as wholesome drugs. |
| DR S | A happy man indeed. [*insinuatingly*] Did that worry you? |
| ZENO | I suppose it must have done. For a start it added to my own feelings of inadequacy. He seemed so well integrated. I'm sure he coped with women far better than I ever could. |
| DR S | Was he fond of the ladies? |
| ZENO | He was totally loyal to my mother. Or so I've heard. Though ... yes, some kind relation or other once told me that he did |

| | |
|---|---|
| | once give my mother cause for jealousy. Apparently she once nearly caught him in the act with her dressmaker. |
| DR S | Interesting. How did he get out of that? |
| ZENO | I'm told he flatly denied that any impropriety had taken place. He pleaded a fit of distraction, and persisted so much that in the end my mother came to believe in his innocence. But mind you, it seems my mother never used that dressmaker again. Nor did my father. |
| DR S | In your father's place, how would you have acted? |
| ZENO | I'd have owned up and asked for forgiveness. But I'd probably have kept the dressmaker. |
| DR S | I see. Where you halt you take root. Quite. |
| ZENO | My father and I never really had a serious talk till the day he died. Pity. |
| DR S | Did your father's death upset you very much? |
| ZENO | Upset me? Why, it was an unmitigated catastrophe. I was thirty-three at the time, and with him gone I felt as if the most important, the really decisive part of my life was behind me, never to return. |
| DR S | Why? |
| ZENO | Right up to his death I'd lived from cigarette to cigarette as it were, switching subjects at university, with an indestructible faith in the possibilities that lay before me. And I can't help feeling that if he hadn't died I'd still have that faith. In some way his death destroyed the future that gave any meaning at all to my resolutions. And I made that note in my notebook: '15th April 1890. 4.30 am. My father died. L.C.' |

[*Fadeout.*]

## FOUR

ZENO's *father's bedroom.* ALFIO COSINI *is lying in bed, dozing, and* MARIA *is sitting by the bed as* ZENO *enters. The room is in semi-*

*darkness. Until* ALFIO *wakes up,* ZENO *and* MARIA *will speak in an undertone.*

MARIA  Is that you, Signor Zeno?

ZENO  Yes, Maria. Good evening. How come you're sitting in father's room? Is he all right?

MARIA  I'm not sure. He wouldn't eat his dinner. Not without you.

ZENO  No? It's nearly ten. I told him I'd be late tonight.

MARIA  He insisted he'd wait for you. Then he had a bad turn and said he'd go to bed.

ZENO  A bad turn? Isn't he well then?

MARIA  I don't think so. He was short of breath for a while. [*She rises.*] Let me take your coat.

[ZENO *hands her his topcoat.*]

ZENO  Thank you. I suppose we had better let him rest.

[MARIA *nods as she leaves the room.* ZENO *sits by his father's bedside.* ALFIO *wakes up.*]

ALFIO  [*with forced joviality*] There you are at last, Zeno ...

ZENO  Father ... Hullo. I hear you haven't had dinner.

ALFIO  No. No. Where have you been?

ZENO  Seeing an old friend. I told you I'd be late.

ALFIO  I was worried about you. I always am, of course. But particularly tonight.

ZENO  There you go again, father. Worrying over trifles. And on an empty stomach.

ALFIO  Dear me. With your mother gone, all those years ago ... just you and me left in the world ... I wanted to see you before turning in ... and have a bite to eat with you. What kept you out so late?

ZENO  Do you really want to know?

ALFIO  Yes.

ZENO  I got involved in a conversation about religion with my old friend Copler. It dragged on and on.

ALFIO  Religion? You? I didn't know you were interested in religion. Are you?

| | |
|---|---|
| ZENO | Let me put it this way: I look on religion as a ... phenomenon, to be investigated like any other. |
| ALFIO | A ph ... phenomenon? You're not poking fun at religion, I hope? |
| ZENO | No, father. I study it. Investigate it. |
| ALFIO | I know the way you study. Flitting from subject to subject like a butterfly. |
| ZENO | There you go again, father. Incidentally, it may interest you to know that I'm thinking of giving up smoking. |
| ALFIO | You and your last cigarettes! Going to make a note about it in your notebook, are you? |
| ZENO | I probably shall — the moment I find it. I've mislaid it somewhere. |
| ALFIO | You're so absent-minded, Zeno! It's a good thing I've placed you under Olivi's guardianship. Financially, I mean. Even after I'm gone ... it'll be in my will. |
| ZENO | Why remind me of it, father? It's humiliating. |
| ALFIO | Most people would give anything to be financially independent, as you are. Why, I've done you a favour. Besides, you'd be quite incapable of looking after your own affairs. |
| ZENO | I disagree. I think I'd make quite a good businessman. But you won't give me the chance. |
| | [ALFIO *groans, as if in pain.*] |
| | Are you all right, father? |
| ALFIO | Yes. Yes. [*Pause.*] Won't give you the chance, you say. You know, I was going to have a talk with you tonight, Zeno. A serious talk. That's why I was so anxious to see you. |
| ZENO | I see. |
| ALFIO | As you know, I've accumulated a great deal of experience. An intimate knowledge of life. I thought I'd pass some of that experience on to you. You don't deny I'm a man of wide experience, Zeno ... |
| ZENO | No, no ... |
| ALFIO | Yes, I know a great deal. A great many things. [*forcefully*] Surely I can't have lived all these years to no purpose! |

ZENO   Father ...

ALFIO  [*softly*] I think I've got the answer. But somehow I don't seem to be able ... just now, to get it across to you. I wish I could. I can see the inner meaning of things, do you follow? [*with a hint of sarcasm*] You could make a note of this in your little notebook ...

ZENO   I will, when I find it.

ALFIO  Naturally, the notebook isn't important in itself — it's the way you use it. [*petulantly*] What's the use of noting down hypothetical last cigarettes?

ZENO   You smoke too, father.

ALFIO  I smoke cigars, and a good cigar is as good as a tonic. [*He coughs.*] If you'd come home a little earlier I could have told you so much ... I wasn't tired earlier on. I could have made it all so clear to you ...

ZENO   You're not well, father.

ALFIO  I'm just tired. Very tired. I think I'll sleep now. And I'll think over what I wanted to tell you and put it to you in the morning. I'm sure I'll be able to convince you ...

ZENO   Very well. Goodnight, father.

ALFIO  Goodnight, my boy. Funny, at this particular moment I can't find anything to say. Absolutely nothing. Strange.

> [ALFIO *suddenly cries out and groans, then appears to faint.*]

ZENO   [*alarmed, calls out*] Maria! Maria!

MARIA  [*enters*] Yes...

ZENO   I'm afraid father's not at all well.

MARIA  Shall I get him a hot water bottle?

ZENO   No. I'll go and fetch Dr Coprosich. Stay with him till I get back.

> [ZENO *leaves.* MARIA *sits by* ALFIO'*s side. Short fadeout to denote the passage of time.*]
>
> [*An hour later.* DR COPROSICH *and* ZENO *are conversing in an undertone away from* ALFIO'*s bed, where the latter is lying asleep.*]

ZENO      Well, doctor?

DR COPROSICH   I'm sorry, Zeno. Your father is gravely ill. You must be brave.

ZENO      [*sobbing*] Oh my god!

DR COPROSICH   He'll probably recover consciousness, partially at least, in the course of the next few minutes, or hours ... who knows.

ZENO      Then there is some hope.

DR COPROSICH   None whatever. But leeches have never been known to fail in a case like this. He'll certainly regain partial consciousness, but will probably lose his reason.

ZENO      [*tearfully*] But doctor, is it fair to let him regain consciousness?

DR COPROSICH   Yes it is, my friend. Your father will never be sufficiently conscious to realise his condition. It is our duty to keep your father alive. Although medically there may be no hope, we must leave a door open for any contingency. [*pedantically*] One half-hour of life can make all the difference to the fortunes of a family. New wills, codicils ... Face reality, Zeno. I'll be back in the morning and bring a nurse with me. It's too late to get one now. Can you or the maid sit with him?

ZENO      I will, doctor.

DR COPROSICH   Good. It's important you should try to get him to lie still. A horizontal position's much better for the circulation. He may come to at any moment, as I told you. He may get a bit restless.

ZENO      Very well. You'll be back in the morning?

DR COPROSICH   Yes. And try to get some rest yourself, even if you sit with him.

> [DR COPROSICH *leaves.* ZENO *sits down on a chair by his father's bedside and crosses and uncrosses his legs. He pours himself a glass of water from his father's bedside table, and the noise wakes* ALFIO.]

ALFIO     [*breathing unevenly, until the end of the scene*] Zeno, Zeno!

ZENO      Father ... Sh ... Quiet, now. You'll be all right.

ALFIO     Give me ... give me some water.

| | |
|---|---|
| ZENO | [*handing him the glass he had poured for himself*] Here you are. But try to lie still afterwards. |
| | [ALFIO *begins to drink, then suddenly spits out the water, noisily.*] |
| | Don't you want it? |
| ALFIO | No. It doesn't taste right. It's so airless in this room. That window ... open it. |
| ZENO | The window is open, father. |
| ALFIO | My head's cold. Get me a hat. In my wardrobe. |
| | [ZENO *gets up and complies. He hands his father a wide-brimmed hat.*] |
| ZENO | This one? |
| ALFIO | It'll do. [*He puts the hat on, then looks at himself in a hand mirror he picks up from his bedside table. He attempts to laugh.*] Look at me, Zeno. I look like a Mexican. |
| ZENO | I think you'd better lie still, father. |
| ALFIO | Oh, very well. Am I seriously ill? |
| ZENO | You need rest. That's what Dr Coprosich said. And it's very important that you lie still. Now let's cover you up properly ... |
| ALFIO | Oh, do leave me alone! I want to sit up and look out of that window. At the stars. |
| ZENO | [*with some determination, though gently*] I must insist that you lie down ... |
| | [*He tries to hold him down by the shoulders.*] |
| ALFIO | [*struggling, his breathing more difficult by the second*] And I say ... that you let me ... sit up. |
| ZENO | Please, father, lie still, [*He holds him down.*] Please lie still. |
| | [*A struggle ensues, and with a supreme effort* ALFIO *slaps his son's face.*] |
| | Ouch! |
| | [*With a last gasp,* ALFIO *dies.*] |
| | He slapped my face ... He's dead ... Maria! Maria! I didn't kill him ... I didn't kill him! It was the damn doctor who wanted him to lie still. Maria! Maria! |

|  |  |
|---|---|
|  | [*Slow fadeout over this acting area as* ZENO *crosses over to* DR S's *consulting room and lies down on the couch as the consulting room is lit.*] |
| DR S | Ha ha! So your father slapped your face as he lay dying. |
| ZENO | He'd never hit me before. Not ever. And I didn't mean to kill him. I was trying to make him lie still. It must have been a reflex action on his part. |
| DR S | I wonder. |
| ZENO | But why should he have wanted to hit me? I ask you, doctor, why? |
| DR S | Ask yourself. |
| ZENO | [*meditatively*] He'd always been so gentle. No. He can't have meant to hit me. I remember every detail of the tragedy and my tremendous grief. We had never been so much together, or for so long, as when I was mourning for his death. If only I had been nicer to him in his lifetime and mourned him less later ... At his funeral I tried to recall him as he'd always been, indulgent and ... yes, weak. Somehow his memory turned into a delightful dream. I too became gentle and kind. You see ... in the dream ... we were in perfect accord. I was the weak one and he the strong. I remember that I even made a number of decisions. |
| DR S | Oh, yes. Such as giving up smoking? |
| ZENO | Yes. And to get married. |
| DR S | Indeed? How did you set about that? |
| ZENO | In a very peculiar way, I must confess. I'd nothing much to do, as Olivi was in charge of the business. So I started popping into the Trieste Stock Exchange. |
| DR S | Were you hoping to find wealth on the floor of the house? |
| ZENO | No. It wasn't quite like that. You see, my old friend Copler told me I'd be well advised to familiarise myself with the stock market, meet people, broaden my horizon, commercially and socially. It was Copler who first took me there, and that's how my matrimonial adventures began. On my first visit in fact I met my future father-in-law, a truly splendid man ... |
|  | [*Fadeout.*] |

## FIVE

*The Trieste Stock Exchange. Bustling noises: typewriters, shouts, etc.*

COPLER [*entering with* ZENO] Yes, this is where it all happens, my dear Zeno.

ZENO It's like a madhouse, Copler.

VOICE(S) [*off*] Consolidated 190. Down 3 points. Trieste Waterworks Loan 145!

COPLER It's anything but a madhouse. It's a highly organised market place. Come this way ... I want you to meet a friend of mine, who's coming our way.

[MALFENTI *enters.*]

Ah, Signor Malfenti ...

MALFENTI [*in a booming, self-assured voice*] Why, if it isn't Copler! How are you.

COPLER I'd like you to meet Zeno Cosini ...

ZENO How do you do.

MALFENTI Delighted to meet you. You must be poor Cosini's son. Sad business. Knew him well, of course. Come over here and take a pew.

ZENO My father often mentioned you. And Olivi speaks very highly of you.

MALFENTI Ah, yes, Olivi. I heard your father made him your nursemaid.

ZENO He looks after my interests, yes ... But I thought I'd start finding things out for myself, and Copler very kindly brought me along here.

MALFENTI Do you like what you see?

ZENO Frankly, it's all rather confusing.

[MALFENTI *and* COPLER *laugh.*]

| | |
|---|---|
| COPLER | Zeno is something of a novice. |
| MALFENTI | Business, my dear Zeno, isn't a science you can learn overnight, even if you've been to university. Now tell me, in your honest opinion, which do you suppose is likely to be the more instructive of the two: the stock exchange or university? |
| ZENO | The stock exchange, naturally. |
| MALFENTI | Right first time. Have a second look around. Do you see anything on the floor? |
| ZENO | Well ... yes: wastepaper baskets, paper litter. But ... nothing special. |
| MALFENTI | Nothing special, he says. Well, of course you wouldn't. I'll tell you what's on that floor, scattered all over it: money. But you need a special kind of vision to see it. A knack acquired through long experience. |
| COPLER | You're having your first lesson in high finance, Zeno. From a past master. |
| MALFENTI | Thank you, Copler. Mine is only the voice of experience. |
| ZENO | As a matter of fact, Signor Malfenti, I'd like to dispense with Olivi and run the business myself. What do you advise? |
| MALFENTI | Don't, my boy. Olivi's an excellent man. By all means come here, pick up tips ... but let Olivi run your business. He's a professional. |
| ZENO | You think so? |
| MALFENTI | Absolutely. Known him all my life. Of course, you may learn in time. Look, I'll give you the benefit of some advice. Here are three essential commandments to be followed for success in business. First — |
| ZENO | One moment, please. I'd like to note them down in my notebook. |
| MALFENTI | Splendid! Make a note of them. When your notebook's full of jottings you'll be ready to start life as a businessman. As I was saying, first: it isn't essential for you to work, but it's essential to know how to make others work for you. Second: there is only one great cause for regret — having failed to look after one's own interests. Third: theory may |

be quite useful in business, but only when the deal is already in the bag.

COPLER  You have the cunning of a fox, Malfenti.

ZENO  Is cunning an asset?

MALFENTI  What do you think?

ZENO  I wonder ... I've a feeling that people mistrust those with a reputation for cleverness. Isn't it better to appear a bit dumb? Then, when the moment comes ... What do you say, Signor Malfenti?

MALFENTI  Wrong. [*He laughs.*] And I'll tell you why you're wrong, young man. To buy or sell, one generally goes to the cleverest chap. Why? Because the chap who's not clever, even if he's honest, hasn't much to offer apart from goods he's probably paid too much for. No. It's to the clever merchant everybody goes to: they ask for information, advice, and in turn give him fresh and valuable news. [*Pause.*] They all come trooping here. To me. By Jove, boys, look at that notice board. Coal is beginning to move. It's time I got in ...

> [*Slow fadeout over this acting area as* ZENO, *as before, crosses over to* DR S*'s consulting room and lies down on the couch as the consulting room is lit.*]

DR S  An interesting man indeed. What happened next?

ZENO  He asked me to his home for the following week, to meet his family. And even before I met them I knew I'd marry one of his four daughters. Their names all began with the same initial, A. Augusta, Ada, Alberta and Anna. I dreamt about those four girls so closely linked by their names. My name being Zeno, I felt as if I were about to pick a wife from a far country.

DR S  An alphabetical meeting of opposites, you might almost say.

ZENO  Quite. According to my friend Copler, who knew them all, Augusta, the eldest, was rather plain. She had a squint, in fact. Ada was supposed to be the beauty of the family. Then came Alberta, who was about to go to university. Anna was still a child. I've always felt it's a sign of inferiority in a man not to understand women, and I certainly got off to a wrong start. On my way to the Malfentis' on the occasion of my first visit it was Ada, the beauty, that I resolved to court and marry. Yes, it was Ada who was to guide me to moral and physical health within the sacred monogamy of marriage ...

[*Fadeout.*]


SIX

*At the* MALFENTIS'.

SIGNORA MALFENTI   Come and sit down. I am sorry my husband can't be with us today, but allow me to introduce you to my daughters, Augusta ...

ZENO   How do you do.

AUGUSTA   Hullo.

SIGNORA MALFENTI   ... and Ada.

ZENO   How do you do.

ADA   Signor Cosini ...

ZENO   Please call me Zeno.

SIGNORA MALFENTI   Alberta and Anna have gone for a walk, but will be back shortly. Please sit down.

ZENO   Thank you.

SIGNORA MALFENTI   My husband tells me you're trying to acquire some business experience at the Stock Exchange.

ZENO   He's been most helpful.

ADA   He told us you couldn't quite make up your mind what to read at university.

ZENO   That's right. I drifted from one subject to the other — law, chemistry, back to law, heaven knows how many times. I should really have specialised in commerce and economics. Or gained practical experience in the business world.

SIGNORA MALFENTI   Well, you still have plenty of time. [*Giggles and young voices off.*] Here are Alberta and Anna ...

[ALBERTA *and* ANNA *enter.*]

Come in girls ... say how do you do to Zeno Cosini.

ALBERTA  How do you do.

ANNA  Hullo.

ZENO  How do you do.

SIGNORA MALFENTI  Signor Cosini used to be a bit like you, Alberta. He couldn't quite make up his mind what to study. And he regrets it now, isn't that so?

ZENO  Indeed I do. I also wasted a lot of time playing the violin, instead of getting down to my studies.

SIGNORA MALFENTI  You play the violin? That's a social grace.

ZENO  I don't play very well.

SIGNORA MALFENTI  Nevertheless you must bring your violin with you next time you call on us and make music with one of the girls.

ZENO  [*to* ADA] Do you play the piano?

ADA  No. My sister Augusta is the musician in the family.

ALBERTA  Tell me, why did you keep switching subjects?

ZENO  I used to tell myself there was no point in restricting myself to one subject when the world of knowledge was so vast.

ALBERTA  I bet you switched just before exams.

ZENO  How clever of you! Yes, I did.

ALBERTA  I doubt I'll ever get into university. School is difficult enough. And I simply can't stand Latin.

SIGNORA MALFENTI  Now, Alberta, don't start again ...

ZENO  Alberta has a point. Latin isn't really a language suitable for women. I doubt whether women ever spoke Latin, even in Roman times.

ADA  In England lots of girls know Latin perfectly.

ZENO  You've been to England?

ADA  Yes, I've been there with my father. It's an extraordinary country.

AUGUSTA  I admire the English. Enormously.

ZENO  Do you? How strange.

ADA  Have you been to England?

ZENO  Yes. I spent a few months in London studying business methods, but I can't really offer an opinion, as I hardly met anybody there.

SIGNORA MALFENTI  You didn't?

ZENO  No. On my way to England I lost all the letters of introduction which business friends of my father's had given me.

ADA  Then how did you manage to study business methods?

ZENO  I didn't. To this day English business methods are a mystery to me. It seems the English do business in secret places, cloak-and-dagger fashion. [*Laughter.*] I came to the conclusion that the English detest foreigners. I really felt I was living among enemies.

ADA  Come, come, I found them charming.

ZENO  Possibly because you're a charming, attractive young woman. No. I'm not exaggerating. Shall I tell you how my stay in London came to an end, an abrupt end at that? I went into a bookshop one day to buy a dictionary. Asleep on the counter was a magnificent cat — and I'm very fond of cats. I began to stroke it. In a fury, the cat turned on me and scratched my hand. From that moment on I could stand England no longer. The next day I was in Paris.

ADA  But ... was it the bookseller who really upset you, or the cat?

ZENO  The cat.

ADA  Are you trying to tell us that the cat somehow symbolised for you the whole of England?

ZENO  Well, an Italian cat would never have displayed such open hostility.

ADA  But it could have happened to anybody, in any country, to be scratched by a cat.

ZENO  No, no. Even the bookseller agreed. That particular cat had apparently behaved perfectly well towards others. It scratched me because I was who I was. Quite possibly because I was Italian.

ANNA  [*turning to her mother and sisters*] He's mad, isn't he? Mad as a hatter!

SIGNORA MALFENTI  Anna! Where are your manners? Apologise to our guest this instant!

ANNA  But he is mad, I tell you! He talks to cats in foreign countries! He ought to be locked up!

> [*Fadeout as* ZENO *crosses back into* DR S's *consulting room.*]

DR S  Hm ... You were saying you were going to settle for Ada, the beauty.

ZENO  Yes, I was. But it's difficult in our society to contract exactly the kind of marriage one wants. Especially in my case, as my decision to marry preceded the choice of a bride. True, when Ada and I first spoke, I was aware of a note of discord, but then discords often resolve themselves into harmony ...

DR S  Try, if you can, to avoid musical analogies and stick to the point.

ZENO  I'd plenty of opportunities to make myself at home at the Malfentis', indeed possibly far too many opportunities. I took along my violin and made music with Augusta, the only one of them who could play the piano. It was a pity Ada couldn't play; it was even worse that I played the violin so badly, and a tragedy that Augusta wasn't much of a pianist. And Ada's image haunted me all day long. She was mine already, I flattered myself. I worshipped her and endowed her with all the innumerable qualities I felt I needed and lacked in myself. Ada was to be not only my wife, but my ... second mother.

DR S  [*pointedly*] I see.

ZENO  She would forge my life into an alloy of strength, health and success. Why was I then so reluctant to say to Ada: will you be my wife?

DR S  Why indeed?

ZENO  I wonder. I walked straight from my daydreams into that house. I counted the steps up to the first floor saying to myself that if they were an odd number Ada loved me ... and of course Ada loved me every time, as I knew full well there were forty-three steps. I always approached her full of confidence, but in the end I talked of something different. I told myself that I'd wait a while before declaring my intentions. I wanted first to develop into a nobler, stronger man, worthy of this divine girl. And this could well happen at any time, from one moment to the next ...

> [*Fadeout as* ZENO *crosses into the* MALFENTIS' *living-room, as before.* AUGUSTA *is alone in the room.*]

Ada has gone to see her aunt again this afternoon?

AUGUSTA  Yes. And you haven't brought your violin again.

ZENO  No. I keep forgetting to bring it. I'm so absent-minded.

AUGUSTA  [*mischievously*] Mind that little Anna doesn't hear you say that!

ZENO  I said I was absent-minded. Not mad. I'm perfectly well balanced mentally. I've even told Ada that I had myself examined by a psychiatrist and showed my father a clean bill of mental health ...

AUGUSTA  Perhaps we could show it to little Anna ...

ZENO  I can laugh about it now, but in many ways it's a painful memory. I spoke of it to my father the night he died.

AUGUSTA  You must have suffered a great deal when your poor father died.

ZENO  It was a shattering blow, Augusta.

> [SIGNORA MALFENTI *enters.*]

SIGNORA MALFENTI  There you are, Zeno. How are you?

ZENO  Good afternoon.

SIGNORA MALFENTI  Augusta dear, little Anna could do with some help with her homework.

AUGUSTA  If you'll excuse me, Zeno ... [*She goes.*]

ZENO  Such a lovely spring we're having ...

SIGNORA MALFENTI  Yes. An endless succession of enchanting days.

ZENO  Ada is visiting her aunt, I hear.

SIGNORA MALFENTI  Yes.

ZENO  She must be very fond of this particular aunt. She is constantly calling on her. She was there yesterday, unless I'm mistaken.

SIGNORA MALFENTI   You are not mistaken, Zeno. And you have been calling on us quite regularly.

ZENO   I have. For some little time.

SIGNORA MALFENTI   Four months.

ZENO   Five, to be exact. I first called in the autumn. It's spring now, as we ...

SIGNORA MALFENTI   You're quite right. Five months. Every afternoon or nearly every afternoon. We've become old friends.

ZENO   I hope so. Sometimes I've the impression that my life revolves around this house.

SIGNORA MALFENTI   It is as a friend that I am going to speak to you, then. I hope you won't mind if I tell you, quite frankly, that you are compromising one of my daughters.

ZENO   But ... signora ...

SIGNORA MALFENTI   Yes, Zeno. You are compromising her.

ZENO   I beg you to believe that my intentions are entirely honourable.

SIGNORA MALFENTI   I don't doubt it.

ZENO   I am only sorry that you should be the one to bring up the subject, which I have long wanted to —

SIGNORA MALFENTI   [*cutting in*] One moment. Let me finish. Augusta is very young.

ZENO   Aug ... Augusta?

SIGNORA MALFENTI   It's no use pretending. A mother's eye is rarely mistaken.

ZENO   But please, believe me ... I've never considered Augusta. How could you possibly — ?

SIGNORA MALFENTI   Come, come, Zeno. What about those interminable conversations, those duets for violin and piano? I'm not blind. Or deaf.

ZENO   But ... this is a terrible misunderstanding ...

SIGNORA MALFENTI   Don't tell me you don't like Augusta.

ZENO   I respect and admire Augusta.

SIGNORA MALFENTI  Just as I thought. So you see, I wasn't far wrong when I said you were compromising the poor girl.

ZENO  Please ... I insist on clearing up the misunderstanding concerning my relationship with Augusta.

SIGNORA MALFENTI  That's just what we are trying to do.

ZENO  I should be very happy to marry one of your daughters ...

SIGNORA MALFENTI  There's no need to be quite so definite at this stage ...

ZENO  ... but as for asking for Augusta's hand ...

SIGNORA MALFENTI  One moment, Zeno. Don't be too impulsive. I have nothing to reproach you with. You're a respectable young man. You belong to our class. But a mother must know what's going on, and keep an eye on things.

ZENO  [*resigned*] Tell me what I should do in order not to upset anybody.

SIGNORA MALFENTI  Perhaps you shouldn't call on us quite so often. Come two or three times a week. Not every day.

ZENO  If you wish, I'll never set foot in this house again.

SIGNORA MALFENTI  That is not what I wish at all. All I'm asking for is discretion from you.

ZENO  And will the whole family learn that you've asked me to stay away? Even ... even your daughter Ada?

SIGNORA MALFENTI  I'm only asking you not to call quite so often. I shan't tell a soul, not even my husband. And I'll be grateful if you'll be as discreet as I intend to be. My darling Augusta is so very sensitive.

[*Fadeout.*]


## SEVEN

*A lounge next to a billiard room at* ZENO'*s club. Click of billiard balls in the background.*

ZENO  [*emerging from the billiard room with* COPLER] You beat me fairly and squarely. You're far too good at billiards for me.

|  | Let's sit down and have a drink if we can catch a steward. |
|---|---|
| COPLER | [*sitting down*] It's good to rest my leg. I've not been out of hospital long. |
| ZENO | I see you're not using your crutch though. |
| COPLER | I still do from time to time. But not at the billiard table. Incidentally, while we were playing I noticed you were limping. |
| ZENO | Me? Limping? |
| COPLER | Yes. Your left leg. Like mine. It makes us even in a way. |
| ZENO | Well, I'm not used to walking round a billiard table. Oh dear, you're worrying me now. Doctors maintain I'm a hypochondriac. |
| COPLER | And you believe doctors? |
| ZENO | I consult them often enough. |
| COPLER | I'd sooner be a truly sick man, Zeno — which I am — than you with your countless imaginary pains. At least for me there'll always be a remedy at the nearest chemist's. |
| ZENO | My pains are real enough to me. |
| COPLER | Yes, as I said just now I noticed you limp. |
| ZENO | Oh do stop it! |
| COPLER | [*undeterred*] While I was in hospital I studied the anatomy of the human leg and foot. Do you know that when a man walks at a soldierly pace, say one step per half-second, no fewer than fifty-four muscles are in motion simultaneously? |
| ZENO | [*seized with cramp, jumps up from his chair and massages his thigh vigorously before resuming his seat*] Don't! What a monstrous machine the human body is. Who'd ever have thought it possible: fifty-four muscles. Astounding. It's no wonder that I limp. I work too hard, of course; that doesn't help. |
| COPLER | You? Work too hard? You've a private income. You don't need to work. |
| ZENO | I wish that were true. |
| COPLER | Of course, appearances can be deceptive. Is business not going well? |
| ZENO | It's not so much that. It's the time it takes up. I put in at |

| | least six hours a day at my office. I've got to keep an eye on Olivi ... |
|---|---|
| COPLER | Well, I never ... |
| ZENO | ... and other matters connected with my father's estate keep me busy for at least another six hours. |
| COPLER | Twelve hours a day! That explains why you have been calling less frequently at the Malfentis'. |
| ZENO | Well, not as often as I used to. |
| COPLER | In that case you probably haven't met Guido. |
| ZENO | Who's Guido? |
| COPLER | Guido Speier. |
| ZENO | Who's he? |
| COPLER | Good-looking young fellow. Rich Argentinian father. |
| ZENO | What does he do? |
| COPLER | I gather he plays the violin. Sort of virtuoso. |
| ZENO | He plays the violin? |
| COPLER | Yes. Every night a concert at the Malfentis' these days. And guess why? |
| ZENO | Tell me. |
| COPLER | He's after one of the Malfenti girls. |
| ZENO | Really? Which one? |
| COPLER | The prettiest, of course. Ada. |
| ZENO | I see. |
| COPLER | They tell me he wants to marry her. |

[*Fadeout.*]

## EIGHT

*At the* MALFENTIS'. GUIDO SPEIER *is playing (or miming) the closing bars of Bach's* Chaconne *on the violin. Applause at the end of the piece.*

ADA [*clapping more enthusiastically than the others*] Bravo, Guido, bravo!

MALFENTI A born soloist. Paganini reincarnate.

SIGNORA MALFENTI Absolutely enchanting.

ALBERTA I never knew the violin could sound so lovely.

GUIDO You are too kind.

ZENO For an amateur ... you play extremely well.

ADA Signor Speier can only be called an amateur because he refuses to perform as a professional.

ZENO Speier. You are German?

GUIDO No. Only my surname. My family has been Italian for generations, though my father lives in South America.

ZENO Are you going to settle in Trieste?

MALFENTI Guido's already one of us. He's going to stay in Trieste and is starting a business here. A very daring thing to do in these difficult times.

SIGNORA MALFENTI Come girls ... Signor Speier, some refreshment after your exertions ...

[*She leads* GUIDO *and the girls to a table upstage.*]

ZENO Signor Malfenti ... I'd like a word with you.

MALFENTI Now?

ZENO It is rather urgent.

MALFENTI Never be in a hurry, Zeno. Sooner or later every business deal reaches its own inevitable conclusion, as has been amply proved by the fact that while the history of the world is immensely long, very few commercial transactions have been left hanging in abeyance.

ZENO This isn't a business transaction. It's something much closer to my heart.

MALFENTI All the more reason why we should wait. Come, Zeno, and have a drink ... [*He moves away.*]

[ZENO *sighs in some exasperation, and does not follow* MALFENTI.]

| | |
|---|---|
| ZENO | Right. Here goes. [*He calls out.*] Ada! Ada! |
| ADA | [*approaching him from the refreshments table*] Yes? |
| ZENO | A word with you, please. |
| ADA | What is it, Zeno? |
| ZENO | Listen carefully. I love you. I shall speak to your father presently. |
| ADA | Oh, Zeno! Is this another of your jokes? |
| ZENO | I've never been more serious in my life. I swear it. I shall expect your yes or no this evening — and treat it either as a life-giving or death sentence. |
| ADA | [*irritably*] Oh, do stop it. Augusta would be terribly upset if she heard you. |
| ZENO | Ada, you can't suspect I could possibly be interested in Augusta. |
| ADA | Oh? Do you think you're too good for her? |
| ZENO | I never said I was. |
| ADA | Quite frankly I don't think for a moment that Augusta would ever agree to marry someone like you. |
| ZENO | [*seizing her arm*] But it's not Augusta I want. It's you. |
| ADA | Let go of me! |
| ZENO | Please think about it, Ada. I'm not such a bad chap. I'm rich. I know I'm a little eccentric, but I'll put that right. No problem. I'm even prepared to give up smoking if you want me to. |
| ADA | You think about it too, Zeno. Augusta is a good girl and would suit you. Naturally, I can't speak for her, but you may stand a good chance. |
| ZENO | Don't keep mentioning Augusta to me. I shall never marry her, just as you'll never marry that fellow Guido. So he can play the fiddle — I've seen monkeys do the same! |
| ADA | How dare you! Get out of my way, you wretched man! |
| | [ADA *moves away angrily.*] |
| ALBERTA | [*approaching*] Zeno, what's the matter between you and Ada? |

| | |
|---|---|
| ZENO | Oh, nothing. [*He regards her admiringly.*] You're looking so young and pretty ... If my poor father were still alive, he'd have no hesitation in helping me choose among you girls. He'd say: take a young wife. Like you. |
| ALBERTA | Are you planning to get married? |
| ZENO | Yes. This very evening, if possible. |
| ALBERTA | At this time of night you'll never get a priest or even a rabbi to celebrate a wedding. |
| ZENO | Seriously, Alberta, wouldn't you like to get married? |
| ALBERTA | I've got to get on with my studies, Zeno. |
| ZENO | You could go on studying when you're married. |
| | [ALBERTA *laughs.*] |
| | A few minutes ago I put the same proposal to Ada, which I'm about to make to you: will you marry me? |
| ALBERTA | Do be serious, Zeno. |
| ZENO | I am being serious. Say yes and I promise you we'll be ecstatically happy. |
| ALBERTA | Don't be offended — I think the world of you, you know that. And thank you for asking me. But I'm not ready for marriage yet. You do understand, don't you ...? |
| | [*She leaves him to join the others.*] |
| ZENO | I understand only too well. The Malfenti sisters are not for me, that much is clear — at least not Ada or Alberta. All that's left now is to propose to the only one left, and I shall tell her that I proposed to her because her two sisters turned me down ... [*louder*] Ladies and gentlemen, your attention please! |
| | [*The background conversation ceases.*] |
| | I have an important proposal to make. Augusta: will you marry me? |
| | [*General reaction.*] |
| AUGUSTA | [*approaching* ZENO] If this is another of your jokes, Zeno, it's not in the best — |
| ZENO | [*interrupting her*] This is no joke, I assure you. First I proposed |

to Ada, who refused me out of hand. Then I asked Alberta to marry me and she too turned me down. I don't bear them any ill will. But I am very, very unhappy.

AUGUSTA [*close to* ZENO *and quietly*] So you want me to understand and always remember that you don't love me.

ZENO [*close and quiet also*] I can't face living alone any more.

> [*Pause.*]

SIGNORA MALFENTI Zeno has asked you a question, Augusta. It's not quite in accordance with the rules of etiquette, but we must take our dear friend as he is. I happen to know he's in earnest. I've known it for some time.

> [*Pause.*]

AUGUSTA [*loud enough for everyone to hear*] Zeno, you need a woman to help you. I want to be that woman.

> [*Voiced congratulations and some clapping from the assembled company.*]

SIGNORA MALFENTI As you see, Zeno, I guessed everything right from the start. You may kiss me.

ALBERTA Long live the happy pair!

MALFENTI I'm delighted, dear boy. I felt you were a son of mine from the moment I started to give you sound business advice.

ZENO Thank you.

MALFENTI [*taking him aside*] It is good to know I have a son at last. As perhaps you know, my health is not what it ought to be ...

ZENO [*alarmed*] Oh dear ... is there anything at all I can do ... ?

MALFENTI Thank you for your concern — and let me assure you that if I could get rid of my illness by passing it on to you I'd do so without any hesitation. I've no humanitarian scruples like you. Welcome to the family!

> [*Fadeout.*]

[INTERVAL]

## NINE

*Trieste. Exterior, night.* GUIDO *and* ZENO *are strolling.*

GUIDO  What a lovely night. Shall we walk a little more? Go home by the upper road?

ZENO  If you wish.

GUIDO  You know, I had a feeling you were keen on one of the Malfenti girls, and I kept wondering which.

ZENO  So did I, Guido, so did I.

GUIDO  I say, you're limping. I never noticed that before.

ZENO  It's nothing. I stumbled and fell.

GUIDO  You fell?

ZENO  At my club. Er ... playing billiards.

GUIDO  Did it take you long to make up your mind ...? About Augusta I mean.

ZENO  Not really. She may not be as attractive as her sisters, but she has sterling qualities. In fact — I'll tell you what — in order to celebrate this happy occasion ... [*He lights a cigarette.*] ... I shall smoke the last cigarette I'll ever smoke.

GUIDO  Two historic decisions in one evening. I have made a decision too.

ZENO  An important one?

GUIDO  I shall get married.

   [ZENO *groans.*]

Let's stop here for a while and sit on this ledge. That leg of yours seems to be troubling you. [*He sits down.*]

ZENO  It's nothing really. Still ... Mind you don't fall. That ledge is narrow and there's a drop of thirty feet on the other side ...

GUIDO  Have no fear. I've got a good sense of balance. Yes. I've decided to get married. And yet, in spite of the fact that I'm about to take the plunge I still feel, as I always have, that women are inferior beings.

| | |
|---|---|
| ZENO | Is that really what you feel? |
| GUIDO | Yes. I've no respect for them. [*more cheerfully*] But still, my dear Zeno, you and I will soon be related through marriage ... |
| ZENO | You mean you ... |
| GUIDO | Yes. I'll marry Ada just as you're going to marry Augusta. Brothers-in-law, that's what we're going to be. I've so many ideas, plans ... I feel capable of great things. And although we've only just met, Zeno, I liked you immediately. Why don't you come in with me when I set up my company? What do you say? You've got imagination, you're not like these staid Trieste merchants. We'll show them. |

[ZENO *groans.*]

What's the matter? Anything wrong?

| | |
|---|---|
| ZENO | Just my leg. |
| GUIDO | Let's go then. [*He rises.*] It's getting late. Lean against me if you like. I'll see you home. |
| ZENO | I'll be all right. |

[*They start walking again.*]

So you're going to get married.

| | |
|---|---|
| GUIDO | Yes. As soon as possible. As soon, that is, as I've got my father's blessing and the necessary funds from him to start up in business. And you will help me with that, won't you? You'll be my business partner as well as my brother-in-law! |

[*Fadeout as* ZENO *crosses over to* DR S*'s consulting room.*]

| | |
|---|---|
| ZENO | There you are, doctor: Guido got the girl I was really after. Yes. He married Ada. When he told me, sitting on that ledge with a thirty foot drop, I don't mind admitting I was tempted to give him a push. For a moment I wanted to kill him. You see, Guido was everything I was not: talented, handsome, popular and about to start his own business. [*Pause.*] But in time I got to like him. In fact I came to regard him as my closest friend. He married Ada and I married Augusta. And immediately I made a startling discovery: I really was in love with Augusta. Yes, I loved her as much as she loved me. |

|  | Our home was a haven of peace and harmony. And I was at my happiest with Augusta when Carla came into my life. |
|---|---|
| DR S | Carla? |
| ZENO | The girl who became my mistress. Mind you, I first got to know her as ... an act of charity, so to speak. |
| DR S | That's as original a definition of adultery as I've ever heard. |
| ZENO | I assure you, doctor, that it was just that — literally. To begin with, at any rate. You see, my friend Copler, ill as he was, was full of good works, and helped poor people in need. He asked me one day whether I'd contribute towards the purchase of a piano for a protégée of his, a girl who was taking singing lessons and living in straitened circumstances with her widowed mother. He took me along to meet her ... |

[*Fadeout.*]


## TEN


*At* CARLA's. *She is folding up a piece of sheet music after singing to* COPLER *and* ZENO.

| COPLER | What did I tell you, Zeno? A truly operatic voice. If only she'd work a little harder. |
|---|---|
| ZENO | [*to* CARLA] You have a lovely voice. |
| COPLER | [*to* CARLA] What do you think of the piano? It's second hand, of course, but an excellent make. You have my friend Zeno to thank for it. |
| CARLA | It's kind of you both to take care of me. |
| COPLER | He knows that I have made charitable works my main occupation. Charity is the only thing that takes my mind off my illness. |
| ZENO | You have a kind heart. And you're always trying to discover new talent. |
| CARLA | I'm most grateful ... |
| COPLER | Perseverance in your studies will be the best way of showing |

|  |  |
|---|---|
| | your gratitude. Practise every morning. Have at least one lesson a day. And only sing ballads after a hard day's scales. |
| CARLA | I promise. But I am forgetting my manners... You'll take a glass of Marsala? |
| ZENO | Thank you. |
| CARLA | [*going*] It's in the next room. I shan't be a moment. |
| COPLER | Poor girl. She and her mother have only got three rooms, and have had to sublet one of them to make ends meet. When her father died they fell on hard times. [*Pause.*] Nice-looking girl, isn't she? |
| ZENO | Mm ... yes. Are you ... interested? |
| COPLER | In Carla? |
| ZENO | Yes. Is there something between you? |
| COPLER | Ill as I am, do you think I've the time or the inclination to think about women? |
| ZENO | I know very little about the inclinations of the really sick. |
| COPLER | It's hypochondriacs like you who are more likely to be stimulated by a possible fling. |
| ZENO | You think so? |

[CARLA *returns with drinks on a tray.*]

|  |  |
|---|---|
| CARLA | [*dispensing drinks*] Gentlemen ... |
| ZENO/COPLER | Thank you. |
| CARLA | I hope you'll call on me again, Signor Zeno. If only to see how much progress I'm making. |
| COPLER | Zeno is a very busy man. I doubt whether he'll have the time. |
| ZENO | I'm not that busy ... |
| COPLER | No? You told me you worked twelve hours a day. And now you're a father you're bound to be even busier. |
| CARLA | [*to* ZENO] You are married? |
| COPLER | He is. With two children. That is, a little baby girl and another on the way. |
| CARLA | You don't wear a ring? |
| ZENO | No. A wedding ring tends to interfere with one's ... circulation. |

[*Laughter.*]

COPLER — It's nearly time for my injection. I must be going.

ZENO — You sick people are always in between pills or something.

COPLER — You'd do well to look after yourself, Zeno. You're looking a bit off colour.

CARLA — What a thing to say! I think he looks the very picture of health.

COPLER — Are we going, then?

ZENO — Very well. Goodbye.

CARLA — Goodbye. Come and see me again, won't you?

[*Fadeout as* ZENO *crosses over to* DR S's *consulting room.*]

DR S — And did you see her again?

ZENO — Yes, but I let a little time pass. You see, my desire for Carla, which was immediate, made me feel such remorse ... Although it in no way damaged my relationship with Augusta — rather the reverse: I not only spoke to her with my customary affection, but lavished on her expressions of tenderness that were welling up in my heart for the other woman. There had never been such an abundance of tenderness in my house, and Augusta was blissfully happy as a result.

DR S — Nonetheless you saw Carla again.

ZENO — Yes.

[*Fadeout as* ZENO *crosses over to* CARLA's *room.*]

CARLA — I'm so glad you've come back to see me.

ZENO — I've thought a lot about your voice. I think so highly of your singing that I'd like you to reach perfection. That's why I've brought you this singing manual. [*He hands her a musical score he will have picked up in* DR S's *consulting room.*]

CARLA — I don't think I'm a very good singer. At least not the sort of singer Signor Copler would like me to become.

ZENO — Perhaps you don't work at it hard enough.

CARLA — I work hard all right, but I don't seem to be making progress.

| | |
|---|---|
| ZENO | There's no such thing as steady progress in art, only leaps and bounds. One morning you'll wake up a great singer. |
| CARLA | That's not what your friend Copler says. We ... that is my mother and I ... are deeply indebted to him, but he is a bit difficult. He wants to be kept informed of everything that goes on in this house — he's fixed my timetable for practising and he's even threatened to check up on me at any time ... |
| ZENO | [*nervously*] Perhaps I'd better leave. |
| CARLA | Don't worry. He's already been today. |
| ZENO | Has Copler ever tried to kiss you? |
| CARLA | Never. When he's satisfied with my singing he squeezes my hand lightly and goes away. When he's angry he won't even shake hands. You can't imagine how afraid I am of him. I'd almost prefer him to kiss me. |
| ZENO | Copler isn't that sort of man. I've never known him to fool around. Besides, he's sick. To tell you the truth I myself tend to be a bit of a martinet if I take someone under my wing. Discipline is of the essence. A young and attractive girl like you can't possibly appreciate the value of time spent working. |
| CARLA | Well, I don't like the kind of singing I'm working on at the moment. I don't think I'm cut out for serious music or opera. |
| ZENO | Is that so? Would you like me to mention it to Copler? |
| CARLA | Why do you keep mentioning him? |
| ZENO | Well ... he keeps you and your mother, doesn't he? |
| CARLA | Such a tiny allowance ... |
| ZENO | What if someone else were ready to contribute? |
| CARLA | I'd send Copler packing. As well as my old singing teacher. But where could I find such a generous man? |
| ZENO | I think you've found him. |
| CARLA | But ... Signor Copler told me how much you love your wife ... |
| ZENO | What business has he to go poking his nose into my private life? It's true I admire her very much. I'm not the kind of |

|  |  |
|---|---|
|  | man on the lookout for light-hearted adventures. That's possibly what he was trying to tell you. |
| CARLA | Is your wife very pretty? |
| ZENO | That's a matter of taste. [*Pause.*] No. She's not pretty ... But I do feel a strong sense of duty towards her. She is a most ... admirable woman. |
| CARLA | How thoughtful you are towards her! I knew you were good and kind the first moment I saw you. |
| ZENO | Listen — let us send both your singing teacher and Copler packing! |
| CARLA | You really mean that? Thank you! Now there are no misunderstandings. Now I know I'll have someone who'll really care for me. [*She kisses him effusively.*] |
| ZENO | Don't let's be too hasty ... |
| CARLA | I simply wanted to thank you. Sometimes I behave like a child and people misjudge me. [*She begins to sob.*] |
| ZENO | Carla, don't be like that. Please. I ... |
| CARLA | [*sobbing*] I'm so unhappy. |
| ZENO | There, there now. Please. No — Carla ... Don't cry. There — don't. Look, we'll see what's to be done. Together. I'll come back tomorrow. No. Perhaps not tomorrow. I'll be back when I can — within the week. I'm ... I'm a very busy man. I'm at it twelve solid hours a day. Meanwhile, look, here's this envelope — just a little ... to be getting on with. |
| CARLA | No, no. Signor Copler brought us our monthly allowance yesterday. We don't need anything at the moment. I only hope you'll come to see me again soon. [*Pause.*] I'll be waiting for you. |
|  | [*Fadeout as* ZENO *crosses into* DR S's *consulting room.*] |
| ZENO | It's an old theory of mine that a really dangerous woman will never accept a small sum of money. From that day on I refused to believe in Carla's relative absence of greed. I said to myself: Zeno, be on your guard. I was right. I know it now. |
| DR S | Nevertheless you became lovers. |

| | |
|---|---|
| ZENO | Yes, although I was determined to be absolutely frank with Carla before we made love. I would tell her the whole truth about my relationship with my wife. But how do you set about seducing one woman while telling her of your love for another? |
| | [*Fadeout as* ZENO *crosses over to* CARLA's *room. He places his jacket on a chair and joins* CARLA *on a sofa, where she is reclining in a state of partial undress.*] |
| CARLA | You've been patient with me. And treated me gently. You're very sweet. You see ... you're my first lover. |
| ZENO | [*matter-of-fact*] You're my first mistress. That is, since I got married. |
| CARLA | And knowing how you feel about your wife, I know that my happiness doesn't interfere with hers. I'm so glad I've got you ... [*She embraces* ZENO.] ... Dario, my darling Dario ... |
| ZENO | Dario? My name is Zeno. |
| CARLA | I've decided to call you with a name of my very own. Dario. Dario. Dario. |
| ZENO | Call me whatever you like. |
| CARLA | Remember your promise, Dario? |
| ZENO | What promise? |
| CARLA | That we'd spend a whole night together? |
| ZENO | Out of the question. Why, my wife would be waiting up for me at the crack of dawn. |
| CARLA | You did promise. |
| ZENO | We'll talk about it some other time. I must go. |
| CARLA | So soon? |
| ZENO | It's nearly time for dinner. I must get home. |
| | [*He straightens his shirt collar, puts on his jacket and as the light fades on this area walks into* DR S's *consulting room.*] |

You see, doctor, in that very room, beside Carla, so young and desirable and after a great deal of love-making, my love for Augusta was born all over again. I had only one wish: to rush back to my one true wife, just to watch her busy as a bee about the house, putting clothes back into wardrobes in an atmosphere of dull domesticity. That night I made a note in my notebook. I wrote, L.B. and L.C. ...

DR S   Hm?

ZENO   Last betrayal and last cigarette. Neither, of course, turned out to be the last ... But then, even if I wasn't a man of unimpeachable probity, I drew consolation from the fact that I wasn't the only one. I'd just started helping Guido in his new business, as an unpaid helper and adviser ...

[*Fadeout.*]


## ELEVEN

ZENO *and* AUGUSTA *at home.*

AUGUSTA   Mama is right. The least Guido could do is pay you a proper salary.

ZENO   He will, my dear, he will. As soon as he can afford it. Just at the moment he's trying to decide exactly what business it is he wants to run.

AUGUSTA   Meantime you're slaving away for nothing. I think I know why you do it.

ZENO   [*laughing*] That old story again? Do you really believe that if I were in love with your sister Ada I'd be so fond of her husband? How could I possibly cultivate a close friendship with a rival?

AUGUSTA   [*somewhat reassured*] You have such a funny way of putting things, Zeno. But sometimes I worry that perhaps you'd prefer a different kind of life ... and maybe even a different wife.

ZENO   Don't even say it in jest. I love you — and you love me. Who'd ever have suspected that, when I limped from one Malfenti sister to the other? For a time I thought I must have been blind. Then I realised how sensibly I'd acted.

AUGUSTA   Are you really happy? What about the times you sit down and pull a face and sigh and say to yourself 'poor old Zeno!'

| | |
|---|---|
| ZENO | That's an excuse to get you to come and make a fuss of me. |
| AUGUSTA | You're sure you're not thinking of another woman? |
| ZENO | What other woman? |
| AUGUSTA | My sister Ada. Doesn't the idea of her happiness with Guido hurt you? |
| ZENO | In the first place ... how could Ada possibly be happy with an immature, selfish fellow like Guido? |
| AUGUSTA | Then you know. |
| ZENO | Know? Know what? |
| AUGUSTA | About Pina. |
| ZENO | I don't know anyone called Pina. |
| AUGUSTA | Of course you do. Ada's maid. |
| ZENO | Oh. Well? What's Pina done? |
| AUGUSTA | Ada was forced to give her notice. Over Guido. Ada caught them in each others' arms. |
| ZENO | Well well, I never! What did he say? |
| AUGUSTA | He denied everything. |
| ZENO | Naturally. He would. Guido may not think highly of women but he fancies them all the same. |
| AUGUSTA | I'm sure you'd be incapable of doing that sort of thing. You couldn't, could you? |
| ZENO | How can I tell? I'd have to take a closer look at Pina. I can't quite remember what she looks like. |
| AUGUSTA | Don't try to pass yourself off as something you're not, Zeno. Now that father's gone you're the steadiest man in the family. Ada would have been better off marrying you. |
| ZENO | But would I have been better off marrying her? Augusta, let's love each other, because life goes by in a flash ... |
| AUGUSTA | But we do love each other. We're married and we'll stay together. Always. |
| ZENO | I really admire your peace of mind. Every word you speak shows you believe in life everlasting. You don't seem to realise that when you get married, in this world, it's for such a short span of time. Short. All too short. [*Pause.*] I am frightened, Augusta. |

AUGUSTA   What of?

ZENO   Of losing you. Of handing you over to someone else. If I died.

AUGUSTA   Where would I find anyone who'd marry me?

ZENO   You would. You've no idea how often I imagine my own death. And how I picture another man coming into this room, sitting beside you ...

AUGUSTA   Are you jealous?

ZENO   All that my jealousy consists of is that I'm afraid of losing you.

AUGUSTA   Think of something else then. How peaceful our life is. How happy we are.

> [*Fadeout as* ZENO *crosses over to* DR S*'s consulting room.*]

ZENO   The hypocrisy of it all.

DR S   Your unfaithfulness to your wife?

ZENO   Not only that. I was tormented by the thought that I hadn't been sincere with Carla before making her mine. It was vital that she should know, to avoid misunderstandings, that I loved my wife.

DR S   So you told her.

ZENO   Not exactly. Carla got herself a new singing teacher, Vittorio Lali, a young, good-looking one, who steered her studies from the classical and operatic to the modern and popular. And I began to realise that the days of my relationship with her were numbered ...

> [*Fadeout.*]


## TWELVE

*At* CARLA*'s.*

CARLA   [*crossly*] Take this envelope back. You can't buy everything with money. I'm not one of those women ...

ZENO   I sometimes wish you were. It would make life so much easier.

|  | But seriously, Carla, your singing has improved enormously. |
|---|---|
| CARLA | I've got Vittorio, my teacher, to thank for it. He's very good. |
| ZENO | I don't doubt it. He'll make a name for himself, I'm sure. What's more he seems very much at home here. Ever since you engaged him we've had flowers on the piano. And I haven't been seeing you as often as before. |
| CARLA | I suppose we're going to have a jealous scene now. |
| ZENO | No. You're free to do whatever you like. |
| CARLA | Very well then. Take this envelope back. I've only kept enough for the rent. The rest's all there. Count it. |
| ZENO | But the money's yours. I left it with your mother the other day when you were too busy to see me... |
| CARLA | No, Zeno. And you may as well face it. It's all over between us. |
| ZENO | All over? |
| CARLA | You may as well know that yesterday Vittorio and I got engaged. |
| ZENO | Oh. Does he know... have you told him about us? |
| CARLA | Naturally. I told him everything. |
| ZENO | He is clearly a tolerant man. Just as well. He'll probably have to put up with a great deal in future. |
| CARLA | That was quite an uncalled for remark. |
| ZENO | But Carla ... are we to part like this, after all we've meant to each other? |
| CARLA | [*with deliberate formality*] If you wish to meet my future husband, please take a seat. He should be here in a few minutes. |
| ZENO | No. I think I'll leave. And since you seem to wish it ... goodbye. |
| CARLA | Goodbye. |

[*Fadeout as* ZENO *crosses over to* DR S*'s consulting room.*]

ZENO: I left Carla full of scorn and indignation. And yet ... I was free at last. I should have been feeling as light as air. But no. I was extremely agitated, and couldn't possibly have gone back to Augusta feeling like that. So I deliberately went for a walk in an unsavoury part of town. A prostitute accosted me, and I unhesitatingly went with her.

DR S  Hm ...

ZENO  Then I spent the whole afternoon and evening with my wife. She was busy about the house, and I followed her around. I felt as if I were being carried along by a stream of clear water: my respectable home life. Helping Guido in his office provided me with an occupation, but from the start I could see it wasn't going to work — as a profitable commercial enterprise that is. Guido had taken a splendid suite of offices in the very middle of town and installed furniture, ledgers and innumerable bits and pieces. The trouble was we were not very clear as to what we were going to do there. And Guido had some strange ideas on how to run a business.

[*Fadeout.*]


## THIRTEEN

GUIDO's *office.*

GUIDO  It's quite simple, my dear Zeno. You can't improvise a business house, set it up on the spur of the moment. You must lie low and observe. Take stock of the market and the background of business. And I have a plan. Now listen carefully, and answer this question: what's the surest road to ruin in business?

ZENO  Unwise investment?

GUIDO  Precisely. Therefore, to avoid all risk of loss, it's vital to avoid investing any money at all.

ZENO  Forgive me, but how can you do business without money?

GUIDO  Ah — there is a way, and it's called a commission agency. You deal in all kinds of goods on behalf of third parties. If you're successful you get a good percentage. If you fail, you've lost nothing. No capital outlay. See what I mean?

| | |
|---|---|
| ZENO | In that case anyone at all could set up in business. |
| GUIDO | Nothing to stop them. But you need intelligence, vision ... and these. [*He shows him a bundle of papers.*] Now look at these. |
| ZENO | What are they? |
| GUIDO | Circulars I've had printed. |
| ZENO | Who are you going to send them to? |
| GUIDO | To all the companies who might entrust us with goods on a commission basis. |
| ZENO | How many have you got there? |
| GUIDO | About a thousand. |
| ZENO | It'll cost a fortune in postage. |
| GUIDO | Ah. Yes. That's a very good point. You see, Zeno, how useful you are to the organisation? You always bring a note of cautious good sense into this office. You check and moderate my enthusiasm. Of course, a thousand circulars — quite an expense. And how many will ever reach the recipients and be effective? Six hundred ... five hundred at most? |
| ZENO | More like two hundred. |
| GUIDO | Don't let's be too pessimistic. I can see that sending the lot would be a trifle extravagant. Wait. I've got an idea. Here we go ... let's throw them all up in the air ... [*He does so.*] |
| ZENO | Guido! What are you doing? Are you out of your mind? |
| GUIDO | Now ... we pick up the circulars that fall on the side the heading is printed on. [*He kneels down and begins picking up the circulars.*] We'll only send those. What are you staring at? It's as good an idea as any other. It could even be sheer inspiration. |
| | [*Fadeout as* ZENO *crosses over to* DR S*'s consulting room.*] |
| ZENO | I tried to put him on the right path. Perhaps I would have succeeded if I had been a little less passive. |
| DR S | Business got worse? |
| ZENO | Yes. And it wasn't helped by the fact that Guido showed far |

too much interest in Carmen, our young secretary, though after a time he didn't come into the office all that often ...

> [*Fadeout as* ZENO *walks back into* GUIDO's *office.* GUIDO *enters, followed by* CARMEN.]

GUIDO   ... and I notice, Carmen, that your typing's improving. You're picking up speed, my little beauty. You're turning into a fast girl, what?

> [CARMEN *giggles as she picks up some papers and goes out.*]

Hello Zeno.

ZENO   Guido, where have you been?

GUIDO   [*sitting down*] Ah ... I'm all in, Zeno. I was up at four in the morning on Saturday, and decided to go off shooting for a couple of days. Impossible to get any sleep at home since the twins were born. The din those two make!

> [CARMEN *enters.*]

Yes?

CARMEN   [*giggling*] A lady to see you.

> [ADA *enters directly behind* CARMEN, *who leaves.* GUIDO *jumps to his feet.*]

GUIDO   What ... Ada! It's you.

ADA   Good morning, Guido. Zeno.

ZENO   Good morning.

ADA   [*to* GUIDO] You never told me there was a woman here. Who is she?

GUIDO   Well ... we needed a secretary ...

ZENO   You're looking well, Ada.

ADA   I haven't been at all well lately. I was just passing and I thought I'd try to see Guido.

GUIDO   I hope you weren't worried about me.

ADA   I haven't seen you since Saturday morning.

GUIDO   I went shooting. I told you I was going to. I brought you back some partridges. [*He begins to leave.*] I'll get them for you.

| | |
|---|---|
| ADA | Such a pity I don't like game, as I've had occasion to tell you. And the twins are a little too young to eat partridge. |
| GUIDO | I'll get them for you all the same. [*He goes.*] |
| | [ADA *bursts into tears.*] |
| ZENO | Don't, Ada. Please. Guido works very hard. You shouldn't begrudge him a little relaxation. |
| ADA | A man should be content to relax with his family. Don't you go home at a decent time every day? |
| ZENO | Well, as the owner of the firm Guido has greater responsibilities. |
| ADA | Is that why he's always off shooting and fishing? I never see him. |
| ZENO | We all have our vices. Take me, for example. I smoke. |
| ADA | And when he's not out he's busy talking to his dog. And when he's not talking to his dog he's playing that cursed fiddle. |
| ZENO | You're tired and overwrought. Try to calm yourself. |
| ADA | [*blowing her nose*] I must talk to you, Zeno. I'm worried. Really worried. About the business. Guido needs help. You'll go on helping him, won't you? I don't think he can make it on his own. |
| ZENO | Of course I will, Ada. I'll stay with him as long as he needs me. |
| ADA | I'm so glad for Augusta's sake that you turned out a better man than I thought. It makes up for my disappointment in Guido. Since father died you've been a real tower of strength in the family, and I'm sorry I once made you unhappy. Did you really suffer? |
| ZENO | Yes. |
| ADA | But now you love Augusta. Between us there can only be fraternal love. As for Guido, I'll have to be a mother to him. You will help me ... won't you? |
| | [GUIDO *comes back with a parcel.*] |
| | Do you promise? |
| GUIDO | Promise what? |
| ZENO | I was about to promise Ada I'd give up smoking. |

| | |
|---|---|
| GUIDO | Here you are, here are the partridges. Let's see you smile ... Now run along home. I'll join you presently. |
| ADA | Couldn't you come with me now? Why not just come home with me and change? |
| GUIDO | I can't just now. Zeno will tell you — we were discussing a most important deal. |
| ADA | Come as soon as you can then. |
| GUIDO | I will. Take care, now. |
| ADA | Goodbye. Goodbye, Zeno. [*She goes.*] |
| GUIDO | [*waits until she has gone*] You saw that? Checking up on me. It's always the same. Day in day out. |
| ZENO | She must have her reasons. |
| GUIDO | [*after a pause, diffidently*] I'm afraid things aren't quite right between Ada and me. |
| ZENO | She says she hasn't been very well recently. |
| GUIDO | Am I to blame for that? Her illness has made her irritable, jealous and ... unloving. I suddenly find I've got an ugly wife, Zeno. Life is so unfair. [*He looks at some papers on a desk.*] What are these? |
| ZENO | Invoices. I wanted to talk to you about them. You've listed them as petty cash. All these bills. |
| GUIDO | Yes ... what of it? |
| ZENO | This one is from a gunsmith. This one is for cartridges. More cartridges. A gun. More cartridges. Then this one for boots ... then Ada's dressmaker, cradles for the twins. This is family expenditure; it has nothing to do with the business. |
| GUIDO | No? Does it matter? |
| ZENO | I think it does. It isn't ethical towards your father for one thing — he's our backer. You shouldn't saddle him with your personal bills as if they were part of company expenditure. |
| GUIDO | What am I supposed to do? Starve? Send Ada and the twins out in rags? |
| ZENO | You should have fixed a salary for yourself. |
| GUIDO | Oh, you know what father's like. |

| | |
|---|---|
| ZENO | But — |

[CARMEN *enters waving a piece of paper excitedly.*]

| | |
|---|---|
| CARMEN | A telegram! |
| GUIDO | A telegram? Well, open it, girl, and read it out to us. |
| CARMEN | [*opens it*] It's ... it's a jumble of strange words. |
| GUIDO | Give it to me. Strange words ...? Why, it's in English. From London. Ha ha, Zeno, we're going places at last. The doors of international commerce are beginning to open. You read it out, Zeno. You understand English. |
| ZENO | Let me see. It says 'Sixty tons settled'. |
| GUIDO | I take it it means 'Please fix up sixty tons'. |
| ZENO | Not quite. Settled, past tense of the verb 'to settle', which means to determine, to fix, to arrange. |
| GUIDO | Yes, yes, yes ... This London firm in effect is telling us that they've bought sixty tons on our behalf. Good God! Sixty tons of ... what? |
| CARMEN | Could it have something to do with copper sulphate? |
| ZENO | Copper sulphate? |
| CARMEN | Yes, that business Signor Tacich put our way. |
| GUIDO | Nonsense. Tacich only comes here to chat you up, Carmen. Besides, that was weeks ago. It's true, though, that he asked us to purchase a certain quantity of copper sulphate in London. Do you remember, Zeno, your theory on copper sulphate and its cyclical fluctuations? |
| ZENO | Yes, I do. But London replied that the price was much higher than that offered by Tacich, so we decided not to take the matter any further. Besides, Tacich has since disappeared, so where could we deliver sixty tons of sulphate ... ? |
| GUIDO | Unless ... wait ... [*He riffles through some papers.*] Here, Zeno, look through these, help me find the wretched letter ... What's this? |
| ZENO | Let me see. Well, in this letter the English company tell us that they were recording our order, which would be considered valid unless cancelled. |
| GUIDO | Did we cancel it? Well, did we? We should have done. |

| | |
|---|---|
| ZENO | No, we didn't. And this means we're saddled with sixty tons of copper sulphate. |
| GUIDO | Oh, no. No! First the twins, now sixty tons of unwanted copper sulphate. I seem fated to deal in large quantities of merchandise. Who are we going to sell the damn stuff to? |
| ZENO | We'll have to look for a customer. |
| GUIDO | Right. That's what we'll do. We'll look for a customer. It's an ill wind that blows no one any good. This deal could well be the making of this firm ... |

> [*Fadeout as* ZENO *crosses over to* DR S's *consulting room.*]

| | |
|---|---|
| DR S | Not a very efficient company, by the sound of it. |
| ZENO | Alas, things went from bad to worse. Not only Guido's wife, but the whole family got wind of it. Even my dear Augusta complained. |

> [*Fadeout as* ZENO *crosses over to his own living-room, where* AUGUSTA *is sitting.*]

|  |  |
|---|---|
| | Is anything wrong, my dear? You look cross. |
| AUGUSTA | You know perfectly well what it is. |
| ZENO | I don't. |
| AUGUSTA | Mama says Ada's at the end of her tether. Guido keeps seeing that woman, his secretary. He even takes her away on trips with him. And what about the business of the copper sulphate? Mama says the firm stands to lose a lot of money. You shouldn't waste your time trying to help him. |
| ZENO | I sometimes wonder whether I'm really trying to help him. |
| AUGUSTA | And now Ada's discovered that Guido's been gambling on the stock market with the firm's money. |
| ZENO | What? |
| AUGUSTA | He's up to his eyes in debt, the irresponsible fool! He'll ruin himself. If I were you, Zeno, I'd drop Guido. Stay at home with me ... with your books and your violin and our peaceful family life. You'll never make a businessman, however hard you try. |

> [*Fadeout.*]

## FOURTEEN

GUIDO's *office.*

GUIDO     What if we tried to cut down expenditure drastically?

ZENO     It's worth a try. I've had a word with Olivi about Carmen. He'd be prepared to give her a job, but he says we were mad to pay her such a high salary. She can hardly type and doesn't know languages.

GUIDO     Surely you wouldn't want me to sack the poor girl simply because she doesn't happen to speak foreign languages?

ZENO     The figures speak for themselves. The firm has lost half its capital.

GUIDO     Are you quite sure? I'll have to check through those figures again carefully.

ZENO     According to the law, and taking into account the amount we have lost, we should go into liquidation immediately.

GUIDO     Do we have to?

ZENO     The penalty under Austrian law for fraudulent bankruptcy is imprisonment. And remember that the responsibility is yours.

GUIDO     As everything is in my name I shall of course regard myself as entirely responsible.

ZENO     Tomorrow I'll prepare a copy of the balance sheet and send it to your father.

GUIDO     Let's wait. I'll tell you when ... and how to draw up that copy.

ZENO     Please, don't even attempt to make me do anything illegal. I said you were the one responsible — well, I bear part of the responsibility as I've been keeping your books.

GUIDO     All right, all right. Nobody's asking you to forge anything.

ZENO     What about your father?

GUIDO     I'll write to him myself. But give me time.

ZENO     There is no time left, Guido. We must do something now.

|   |   |
|---|---|
|  | Get some money. Straighten out the accounts. |
| GUIDO | If only that's all there was to it. |
| ZENO | Have you lost more money on the stock market? |
|  | [GUIDO *makes no reply.*] |
|  | Oh, no! How could you? The situation is suicidal, the firm is facing bankruptcy, and you go and lose more money on the stock market ... |
| GUIDO | I don't think the position is really suicidal. And you don't, either. |
| ZENO | I don't? |
| GUIDO | No. Anna told me, who got it from Ada who heard it from her mother who was told by Alberta after a talk with Augusta: you said — 'Guido wouldn't have the guts to commit suicide'. |
| ZENO | It just shows how women can misrepresent everything. I actually said that even if you wanted to commit suicide you wouldn't succeed. I was joking, of course. In fact I added: while I have no intention of committing suicide, I know I'd succeed immediately if I tried. |
| GUIDO | Dead easy for you. You've read chemistry. You'd know at once which is more effective as a poison, pure Veronal or Veronal and sodium. |
| ZENO | That's elementary. My old chemistry professor used to say that Veronal is a vehicle which the various elements board in order to move about more rapidly. |
| GUIDO | That means that a potential suicide should take Veronal and sodium. |
| ZENO | Or pure Veronal if he wants to stay alive. Or better still nothing at all. And stop this kind of talk. You're trying to get me off the subject of the stock market. Does Ada know how serious the position really is? |
| GUIDO | Not really. |
| ZENO | We'll have to inform your father. |
| GUIDO | Leave my father alone. The sums involved are large. Who on earth is going to help me? |

| | |
|---|---|
| ZENO | What am I here for? And our mother-in-law? We'll all get together and bail you out. |
| GUIDO | Zeno ... you're a real friend. |
| ZENO | And now for once don't lie to me. Just tell me how much you've lost. |
| GUIDO | I don't know exactly. I should have the statement in my pocket ... here it is. It's all on this piece of paper. |

[GUIDO *hands* ZENO *a piece of paper.*]

| | |
|---|---|
| ZENO | Is this the lot? I feared worse. |
| GUIDO | That's not the entire loss, just the amount due on settling day, which is the fifteenth of this month. |
| ZENO | In two days' time. |
| GUIDO | Of course, I might still be able to turn the tables... |
| ZENO | [*angrily*] You're to stop gambling on the stock market immediately. You can't possibly risk adding to this already enormous loss. We'll split the liability four ways: your father, our mother-in-law, Ada and myself. |
| GUIDO | I don't think you'll get any money out of the old lady. |
| ZENO | Count on me. I'll talk to her. |
| GUIDO | Men haven't counted much in our family since old Malfenti died. Well, no point in staying here moping. I'm off to get my shotgun. |
| ZENO | [*anxiously*] Guido, don't do anything silly. |
| GUIDO | All I'm going to do is a spot of shooting. |
| ZENO | But this is hardly the time ... Besides, it's going to rain any moment. |
| GUIDO | I need to relax. Come with me if you like. On condition you don't talk shop. |
| ZENO | No. You may as well vent your spleen on poor helpless birds on your own. |
| GUIDO | You're a good friend, Zeno. But look — don't consider yourself bound to your promise ... |

[*Fadeout.*]

## FIFTEEN

*At the* MALFENTIS'.

SIGNORA MALFENTI  He didn't even go to Guido's funeral. To think he's the only one of us who didn't go.

AUGUSTA  I'm worried about him, mother. He might have had an accident.

ADA  Maybe he stayed away on purpose. Or perhaps he just forgot all about it — yes, that's much more likely.

AUGUSTA  Ada, how can you say such a thing, after all he was ready to do for Guido?

ADA  I knew it. It had to end this way. My poor Guido. Everyone in the family hated him.

SIGNORA MALFENTI  Don't distress yourself, Ada.

ADA  I have to say it, mama. I don't want to set eyes on Zeno ever again. That worm!

AUGUSTA  Ada!

ADA  He's been the cause of all our troubles. With his advice, his vagueness ...

SIGNORA MALFENTI  You don't know what you're saying ...

ADA  I can see it all quite clearly now. It was a plot against Guido. Zeno was the chief conspirator. He always envied him. Guido was by far the better man.

AUGUSTA  You're not to talk like that. Zeno spent years helping your husband, giving him good, sensible advice. He was even ready to part with some of his own money to help him out.

ADA  He'd only have done it to humiliate him. Besides, in the event he hasn't even parted with a single penny, has he?

SIGNORA MALFENTI  It was I who made that decision, my dear. I found out that a bankruptcy is not only legal, but quite convenient and honourable, provided it's all above board. And we ... all

|  | of us together told Guido he had to face up to the situation on his own. |
|---|---|
| ADA | But Zeno didn't complain, did he? |
| AUGUSTA | When Zeno offered to contribute a quarter of the money needed, you were the first to refuse, Ada. If we'd followed Zeno's advice, perhaps your husband wouldn't have been driven to taking Veronal. |
| SIGNORA MALFENTI | Stop it, Augusta. I don't want arguments and recriminations from my daughters! |
| ADA | If there's any guilt to be shared, you're all just as guilty as I am. |
| SIGNORA MALFENTI | It was nobody's fault. He was temporarily unbalanced, the poor boy ... |

[ZENO *enters, somewhat distraught.*]

Zeno ... at last!

| AUGUSTA | Where on earth have you been? |
|---|---|
| ZENO | I ... I went to the wrong funeral. |
| AUGUSTA | You did what? |
| ZENO | I went to the wrong funeral. As you know, I was busy today trying to unravel the mess left by Guido. What a job! Anyway, I left the office at three with Copler. We hailed a passing cab and when we saw a funeral procession in the distance we told the driver to follow it ... |
| AUGUSTA | Well? |
| ZENO | Somewhere along the way, where they usually come to a stop, we noticed the procession going towards the Greek cemetery. Copler asked me whether Guido was a Greek. Anyway, the hearse moved beyond the Greek cemetery and made for some other resting place, Jewish, or Serbian. Or Protestant. Perhaps Guido was a Protestant. But then I remembered he'd got married in a Catholic church. There must be some mistake, I thought. They're going to bury him in the wrong place. Then Copler burst out laughing and said: 'We're at the wrong funeral!' |
| AUGUSTA | I don't think that's at all funny. |

| | |
|---|---|
| ZENO | Nevertheless, Copler kept on laughing as we got off the cab to get our bearings and make for the right cemetery. The mourners with the funeral we'd been following were astonished. They couldn't make out why, having apparently paid our respects up till that moment, we should have decided to desert the pour soul immediately before his burial, choking with laughter for good measure. |
| AUGUSTA | It was Guido you should have paid your respects to. Why didn't you find us in the end? |
| ZENO | I did ask the caretaker, but he couldn't tell me. There had been too many funerals. Ada, my dear, I did hope you wouldn't notice my absence ... However, I've been able to do a great deal on behalf of the estate. In fact I'm delighted to tell you I've recovered three quarters of Guido's stock market losses. |
| ADA | I'm most grateful to you, especially on behalf of the children. And don't worry about not getting to the funeral. Even Guido would forgive you. [*wildly*] Besides, there was no point in your being there. You hated him. |
| ZENO | Ada! How can you say such a thing! |
| ADA | At long last I've understood. Even I never loved Guido enough. Otherwise how could I have hated his violin playing so much ... It was the highest expression of his noble soul. |
| ZENO | What's his violin playing got to do with it? |
| ADA | We none of us really loved him. |
| ZENO | What more could I have done for him? |
| ADA | You could have saved him. You and I — we could have saved him. |
| ZENO | He said he was going off shooting the other night. How could I tell he was going to commit suicide? Besides, he took pure Veronal, didn't he? |
| ADA | Yes. |
| ZENO | That's just it. Pure Veronal, not Veronal and sodium. Guido didn't really mean to commit suicide. |

| ADA | That's what you're like, always ready to cast aspersions on him and his memory. You're vile! [*She storms out.*] |
|---|---|
| SIGNORA MALFENTI | You must forgive Ada, Zeno. She's upset. You've done so much for us, hasn't he, Augusta ... ? |
| AUGUSTA | He has. You're a good, reliable man, Zeno. And a wonderful husband. |
| SIGNORA MALFENTI | We are proud of you. |

[*Fadeout.*]

## SIXTEEN

DR S*'s consulting room.*

| DR S | Good. Good, good, good. Well, my dear Zeno. You have been coming to see me for six months now. How do you feel? |
|---|---|
| ZENO | To be honest, worse than when I started. |
| DR S | You shouldn't if you are being honest. You are virtually cured. |
| ZENO | Cured? How can I be cured? What about my aches and pains? My leg ... |
| DR S | Your aches and pains are easily explained. All you are doing is seeking an illness on which you can blame your shortcomings. |
| ZENO | Of which, according to you, I have a great many. According to you I was in love with my mother as a child and wanted to murder my father. |
| DR S | Just so. However, you will eventually come to look on those desires as the most innocent longings in the world. |
| ZENO | But killing my father is a desire I never experienced! I honoured and respected him. |
| DR S | A proof that my explanation is correct is right there, in your hand. |
| ZENO | My cigarette? |

| | |
|---|---|
| DR S | You started smoking to compete with your father who smoked like a chimney. And you attributed poisonous properties to tobacco because you felt guilty. |
| ZENO | So I suppose my father was perfectly justified in slapping my face when he died? |
| DR S | [*after a pause*] When your father died you transferred your hatred to Malfenti. He became a substitute for your father. |
| ZENO | That's utter nonsense! |
| DR S | You wanted to marry one of his daughters, it did not matter which, in order to put their father in a position where you could reach him with your hatred. You did your best to dishonour the family you married into by being unfaithful to your wife and trying to seduce Ada and Alberta. |
| ZENO | There is nothing psychologically wrong with wanting to go to bed with two attractive women. |
| DR S | We come now to your dislike for Guido ... |
| ZENO | I only disliked him when I first met him. I grew to like him enormously. I even helped him run his business ... |
| DR S | ... which failed, miserably. And you even contrived to miss his funeral. I believe Ada was right when she said it was a final manifestation of your dislike for him. |
| ZENO | But I was at that very moment busy trying to save Ada's fortune. A labour of love. Why do you misconstrue everything I tell you? |
| DR S | I base my analysis on what you have told me. |
| ZENO | You attach far too much importance to my confessions. You have no idea how difficult I have found it to explain things to you. All you have had is a vague outline of my life ... mere skeletons of images. And those images change — constantly. |
| DR S | In psychoanalysis neither the same images nor the same words ever recur. You are cured, Zeno, and refuse to admit it. Examine your mind and you will find a great change in it. You will see how much good I have done you in a comparatively short time. [*Pause.*] I am going to Switzerland tomorrow for a few weeks, so we shall have to have a break in our sessions. |

ZENO   They say there's going to be war soon.

DR S   Quite likely. But keep in touch with me. Drop me a line occasionally. Here's my Swiss address ...

*[Fadeout.]*


## SEVENTEEN

*An outdoor café in Trieste.* ZENO *is writing a letter.* COPLER *is dozing on a chair at* ZENO's *table. The rumble of heavy guns can be heard in the distance.*

ZENO   Dear doctor, strange, isn't it, what they say about war being such a terrible thing. Well, war may be a terrible thing, but it has its compensations, many in my case. Take my case — yours, I should say: war has now forced you to stay on in Switzerland for the duration, which put an end to our sessions for good. It's just as well, you know. I couldn't think of anything new to tell you. I must confess to you now that I was beginning to make things up for you. And Augusta and the children were caught up on the Italian side of the border at the outbreak of war, so they'll be cut off from me till the war is over. Olivi, my manager, has also left the country. So with no guardians to harass me I can now do exactly as I like. I am in perfect health. I not only have no desire to continue with psychoanalysis, but no need to do so. My success in business has been my cure. That's it, doctor: I'm no longer a failure. It's the others who are failures: Guido, and Ada and ... yes, you yourself, doctor. I'm the survivor. I've survived, mentally and physically, and am living happily in this war-torn but surviving corner of the Austro-Hungarian empire. Yes. I spend a lot of time with my old friend Copler ... another failure. His health is still failing, incidentally, unlike mine.

[*He folds the letter and puts it in an envelope.*]

[COPLER *stirs from his nap at a louder sound of distant cannon.*]

| | |
|---|---|
| COPLER | Listen to those guns. They sound quite close. |
| ZENO | You'd think, in this year of grace 1916, they'd have found a quieter way of slaughtering people, eh, Copler? |
| COPLER | I don't like it, being cut off like this in Trieste. But you ... you seem to be doing well, Zeno. |
| ZENO | I can't complain. Business is brisk. Just think of it, thanks to the shortages due to war I've been able to sell incense as a substitute for industrial resin. |
| COPLER | You've turned into quite a businessman. |
| ZENO | A most successful one, I'm glad to say. |
| COPLER | [*yawns*] Mmm ... yes. |
| ZENO | And I've finally stopped trying to give up smoking. Yes, I now smoke a great many cigarettes, none of which is going to be the last. Are you asleep, Copler? |

[COPLER *snores gently.*]

You should really be listening to me, my dear sick friend. You see, when you're old you give up making good resolutions. You just sit and smile at life and at everything it brings. Nowadays I laugh at the things I used to tell my analyst. I'm so busy recovering from his treatment that I try to avoid unpleasant memories. Here I am, looking much like the patriarch I hated so much. Of course, now I've turned into that patriarch things are different.

[*Distant rumble of cannon.*]

Perhaps the name of the illness that gave me those mysterious aches and pains is life. [*He chuckles.*] As an illness life is quite serious, since it's always fatal in the end. Any attempt at recovery or even improvement is sheer illusion. Did you hear that, Copler?

[COPLER *goes on snoring intermittently.*]

There are times when I think we should endeavour to transform our organism, to invent modifications useful to the evolution of our organs. The mole went underground and its whole body adapted itself to its needs. The horse grew bigger and changed the shape of its foot. Man, on the other hand, only devises implements unconnected with his body — machines. Perhaps some colossal catastrophe produced by machines will lead us back to health. When the poison gases used in this war no longer suffice, a man, made of flesh and blood like the rest of us, in the quiet of his room will invent an explosive of such destructive power that all present explosives will seem harmless playthings beside it. And then another man, just like him and all the others, but weaker than them, will steal this explosive device and burrow to the centre of the earth with it, where its effect would be greatest. There will be a tremendous explosion which no one will hear, and the earth will revert to its nebulous state and go wandering through the heavens, free of parasites and disease.

THE END